MIGHTIER
than the
SWORD

FOURTH EDITION

MIGHTIER
than the
SWORD

How the News Media Have Shaped American History

Rodger Streitmatter

AMERICAN UNIVERSITY

WESTVIEW
PRESS

A MEMBER OF THE PERSEUS BOOKS GROUP

Westview Press was founded in 1975 in Boulder, Colorado, by notable publisher and intellectual Fred Praeger. Westview Press continues to publish scholarly titles and high-quality undergraduate- and graduate-level textbooks in core social science disciplines. With books developed, written, and edited with the needs of serious nonfiction readers, professors, and students in mind, Westview Press honors its long history of publishing books that matter.

Published by Westview Press,
A Member of the Perseus Books Group
2465 Central Avenue
Boulder, CO 80301
www.westviewpress.com

Westview Press books are available at special discounts for bulk purchases in the United States by corporations, institutions, and other organizations. For more information, please contact the Special Markets Department at the Perseus Books Group, 2300 Chestnut Street, Suite 200, Philadelphia, PA 19103, or call (800) 810-4145, ext. 5000, or e-mail special.markets@perseusbooks.com.

Library of Congress Cataloging-in-Publication Data

Streitmatter, Rodger.
   Mightier than the sword: how the news media have shaped American history /
Rodger Streitmatter.—Fourth edition.
     pages cm
   Includes bibliographical references and index.
   ISBN 978-0-8133-4977-0 (paperback)—ISBN 978-0-8133-4987-9 (e-book)
1. Press—United States—Influence. 2. Press and politics—United States.
3. Journalism—Political aspects—United States. I. Title.
   PN4888.I53S77 2015
   070.4'493240973—dc23
                                                      2015001786

10 9 8 7 6 5 4 3 2 1

CONTENTS

ILLUSTRATIONS

PREFACE TO FOURTH EDITION

THOSE OF US WHO WRITE ACADEMIC BOOKS TAKE PRIDE IN THE
fact that our research will add to the body of knowledge in our respective
fields, but, at the same time, we accept the fact that our words will reach a
relatively small audience. Other professors who share our area of expertise will read our books, and some of them may make a particular title
required reading for a class they teach—for a semester or two until a new
book on the topic replaces the one we wrote. Within a year or so after the
title has been released, new readers will be few and far between.

Not so with *Mightier than the Sword*.

For unlike the other books I've written, this one has continued to attract new readers, year after year, since Westview Press first released it
almost two decades ago.

People I've asked, both in academia and in the publishing world, tell
me the primary reason for the book's continued popularity is that readers enthusiastically embrace its thesis: for more than two centuries the
American news media haven't merely reported and commented on the
news, but they've also played a significant role in shaping this country's
history.

A facet of this argument is my major motivation for creating a fourth
edition of the book. Specifically, I've added a chapter to make the point
that the news media's role in influencing this nation is by no means a

phenomenon of the past but is one that's still going strong in the twenty-first century. The example I've chosen to underscore this reality focuses on journalists supporting the initiative to secure civil rights for gay men and lesbians.

A second important factor in my decision to revise *Mightier than the Sword* is that the news landscape has changed dramatically since the first edition appeared in 1997. The new chapter speaks to this transformation, as it reflects the fact that online publications and websites are an important part of today's journalistic community. That chapter includes numerous references to venues such as *Slate*, *Politico*, and the *Huffington Post*.

Although the addition of the new chapter is the most tangible difference between this edition of the book and the three earlier versions, I've also made some subtle changes in several other chapters. I've updated material on a number of topics because of new research that's been completed in recent years, and I've trimmed several chapters in an effort to keep the book at what I believe to be the optimal length for classroom use.

Rodger Streitmatter

ACKNOWLEDGMENTS

BECAUSE OF THE BREADTH OF THIS BOOK, IT WOULD BE IMPOSSIBLE for any one researcher to be a true expert on every topic covered in these pages, and I certainly won't make such a claim. Instead, I want to acknowledge that I'm deeply indebted to the many talented and dedicated scholars who have previously examined the events that are the subjects of this book. Although I've listed those individuals in the bibliography, I'd also like to speak to their contributions here.

Rather than trying to list all of these individuals, I want to highlight one representative scholar and her research. In the bibliographical listing for Chapter 3, "Slowing the Momentum for Women's Rights," readers will find an entry for Karen K. List, "The Post-Revolutionary Woman Idealized: Philadelphia Media's 'Republican Mother.'" Professor List, a member of the journalism department at the University of Massachusetts, deserves far more credit than that brief citation. It was Karen who pored over hundreds of early women's magazines to identify and analyze the messages those publications communicated to their readers, as well as to suggest the impact they had on American women writ large. In other words, Karen provided the road map that led me to the magazines that I quote from in my chapter. I went to those magazines and read the articles myself, but I readily acknowledge that my work would have been much more difficult if it hadn't been for Karen's trailblazing efforts. I gratefully appreciate her help—as well as that of numerous other scholars who preceded and guided me in researching many of the topics covered in this book.

Because much of the material contained in this book has evolved from my classroom lectures and from the materials I've written for my courses, I'm indebted to the many students who've provided me with feedback on the material. I still marvel at the fact that even though I wear the mantle of *teacher*, I learn so much from my magnificently creative students.

Some of the material in this book originated as conference papers and articles in scholarly journals. Among those persons whose contributions I want to acknowledge, therefore, are dozens of individuals I can't name because their identities are masked behind the blind review process of the American Journalism Historians Association and the Association for Education in Journalism and Mass Communication. I especially want to thank those members of the AEJMC History Division who honored my work on the 1920s newspaper crusade against the Ku Klux Klan.

Finally, I thank my husband, Tom Grooms, for continuing to enrich my life and make its activities worthwhile—whether it be writing a book or walking the dog.

Rodger Streitmatter

INTRODUCTION

SEVERAL YEARS AGO, I CREATED A COURSE TITLED HOW THE NEWS Media Shape History. The interdisciplinary course, which combined journalism and history, became part of the General Education Program at American University. After receiving positive responses from students who took the course, the director of the program urged me to teach the course not just once a year, but twice—or even more often, if I was willing. I still remember the vivid image that the director, Ann Ferren, used to persuade me. "Rodger, students are clamoring to get into this course," she said. "If you teach it only once a year, it's like putting one tiny little jelly bean in the middle of the quad and telling all 11,000 of our students to fight over who gets it."

Why have students been so eager to grab my little jelly bean of a course? They've been strongly attracted, numerous students have told me, to the concept of the news media *shaping* this country.

Today's college students, as well as the public in general, recognize that the news media are one of this country's most powerful institutions. Many students and other observers criticize the news media as being *too* powerful; others praise that power, arguing that a free press is fundamental to democracy. But the detractors and defenders both agree on one point: the news media have impact.

Those perceptions have made my course popular, and that popularity was what first impelled me to commit the material I use in the course to paper. The book's publication marked the first time that a single volume took an in-depth look at the media's influence on a broad range of events throughout our nation's history. For this fourth edition, I've revised and updated *Mightier than the Sword*, which now describes sixteen discrete episodes in American history during which the news media have played a critical role.

I've chosen the word *shaping* with considerable care. For as I try to impress upon my students at the beginning of each semester, I don't mean to imply that the Fourth Estate single-handedly *causes* events to occur. To suggest such a direct relationship between the news media and American history would be simplistic, as it would ignore the interdependence among governmental, legal, social, and economic institutions driving this nation. I'm convinced, however, that journalistic coverage can *shape*—and profoundly so—an issue. More specifically, the news media can place an issue on the public agenda . . . can move it to the front burner . . . can get people talking about the issue. And once a topic becomes the subject of public discourse, other institutions can cause concrete change to occur.

Each chapter in this book focuses on a milestone in the evolution of the United States that was significantly influenced by journalism paying attention to it. Ultimately, these sixteen separate stories coalesce to relate a single phenomenon of singular importance to understanding this country's past as well as its future: as the news media report and comment on the events of the day, they wield enormous influence on those events.

I've selected the particular episodes in this book for several reasons. They span more than two centuries—from Tom Paine's influence on the coming of the American Revolution to news organizations using their power to help reduce discrimination against gay men and lesbians. The episodes also involve a variety of media, ranging from newspapers and news magazines to radio, television, and such Internet venues as online publications and YouTube. At the same time, these particular case studies illustrate how the news media have interacted with a broad range of other forces—from foreign policy strategists to captains of industry to rabble-rousing demagogues—to have far-reaching effects on the political, economic, and social fabric of the nation.

Many of the topics will be familiar to anyone with a basic knowledge of journalism history, such as how William Randolph Hearst helped build public pressure for the Spanish-American War and how, a century later, television news played a critical role in ending the war in Southeast Asia. Other topics take communication scholarship in new directions. I show, for example, how newspapers helped defeat the Ku Klux Klan in the 1920s and how newspapers—along with radio—helped propel millions of American women into the World War II–era workforce. The topics consciously expand the definition of landmark events far beyond wars and politics to include social movements such as those that sought to secure rights for women in the nineteenth century and African Americans in the twentieth century.

Although each nexus between the news media and American history described in the following pages is important, this book doesn't provide a comprehensive history of the evolution of American journalism. No one book, by looking at such a limited number of episodes, could document the myriad incidents and trends that have marked the development of this country's news media. Indeed, I've assiduously avoided compiling any mind-numbing lists of names, dates, and newspaper titles like those that bog down standard journalism history tomes. I've also attempted to keep this book focused and concise—seeking to create a work that's not only illuminating but also engaging.

The examples I've selected include negative as well as positive assessments. As a former newspaper reporter and now a communication professor, I firmly believe that journalism is a noble pursuit that can, at its best, shine the bright beacon of truth into the darkest corners of life—and then move the human spirit to clean up those dark corners. At the same time, however, I know the news media sometimes squander the rights guaranteed to them in the First Amendment. Several chapters of *Mightier than the Sword* focus on regrettable instances when this powerful institution behaved to the detriment of the people it's supposed to serve.

This book concludes with a final chapter that focuses on *how* the news media have shaped history. Specifically, by drawing examples from the material described in the earlier chapters, I identify some of the common characteristics displayed by the news media that have helped shape this nation. I hope that contemporary newsmen and newswomen—as well as the organizations they work for—may be inspired to adopt some of these characteristics while pursuing their work today and in the future.

Mightier than the Sword: How the News Media Have Shaped American History, like my other books, builds on both my professional background in daily journalism and my PhD in US history in an effort to increase our understanding of both the American news media and the American culture.

In writing this particular book, I had two specific audiences in mind. The first is college students, those aspiring to work in the media as well as those whose lives are influenced by the media. For young news consumers, *Mightier than the Sword* provides a sense of the history, power, and responsibility inherent in the institution of journalism. The second audience is the broad one of readers who want to learn more about the intertwining of the American news media and American history—as well as what that phenomenon means in the context of the twenty-first century.

It's difficult to name, I believe, a more white-hot topic than the power of the media. The contentious debate includes such thorny questions as: Is journalism's job to *report* the news objectively, or should it also seek to *lead society*? Do news organizations represent a public trust, and therefore have a responsibility to serve the people, or are they first and foremost businesses answering to their stockholders? What are—or should be—the limits of news media influence? *Mightier than the Sword* speaks to each of these questions.

Some historians will criticize my tight focus on the news media, saying it doesn't provide sufficient context. Those critics will be on solid ground. I readily acknowledge, for example, that my chapter about the news media's role in Watergate could be expanded into a 200-page discussion of the various forces that helped expose the men responsible for that shocking episode of political corruption. Indeed, several books *have* been written on that subject. What this book provides is a synthesis of major events, such as Watergate, that have been *shaped* by the news media. This is the unique perspective *Mightier than the Sword* offers.

Other critics will find fault with several of the works I classify as *news media*. They'll argue that Tom Paine's essays are partisan rhetoric, not journalism, and that Father Charles Coughlin's anti-Semitic radio addresses were social and political commentary, not journalism. I disagree. Paine's essays were news in the 1770s because they introduced provocative new ideas into the most vital conversation of the day. The essays functioned as journalism, even though they sought not only to inform readers but also to persuade them to support a particular point of view. All colonial publications were partisan, as the concept of journalistic objectivity didn't emerge until the nineteenth century. If 1700s partisan publications weren't news media, eighteenth-century American journalism didn't exist. As for Coughlin's rants, I see little difference between them and the opinions published on the *New York Times* editorial page. Indeed, if the words of this radio commentator weren't part of the news media, then neither are *Times* editorials.

Before beginning the story of how the news media have shaped American history, I want to acknowledge the man who inspired the title for this book, Thomas Jefferson. In a letter to Paine in 1792, Jefferson lauded the essayist's critical role in propelling American colonists toward independence from Great Britain and then wrote encouragingly, "Go on then in doing with your pen what in other times was done with the sword: show that reformation is more practicable by operating on the mind of man than on the body."[1]

1

SOWING THE SEEDS
OF REVOLUTION

IN THE SUMMER OF 1776, A BAND OF POLITICAL REBELS TURNED the world upside down. They showed, for the first time in the history of the world, that the discontent of a few colonists could swell into open rebellion so potent that it could create a world power all its own. Such impudence evolving into pure might was unheard of in the eighteenth century or in any of the centuries before it. The same process would occur again—in France, Russia, Cuba, the Philippines—but the events of 1776 stand alone. For they were the first.

Such redefinition of human history doesn't erupt overnight, as forces had been working long before the fifty-six rebels signed their names to the Declaration of Independence. Among those forces were the words of determined men who possessed talent as well as intellectual insight. Passionate prose written during the era demanded freedom from an oppressive government and ultimately changed the course of human events by transforming lukewarm patriots into fiery revolutionaries.

The transformation unfolded through a series of publications produced by political dissidents. These wordsmiths created the mindset that

1

allowed for political and social revolution—as well as armed conflict. Milestones in the journalistic march toward independence included the "Journal of Occurrences" in 1768 and 1769, followed by the verbal response to the Boston Massacre of 1770. Those two publishing phenomena set the stage for Tom Paine's clarion call for independence in 1776, as his *Common Sense* impelled discontented subjects of the British crown to become insurgents fully committed both to revolution and, ultimately, to shaping American history.

Dissension Takes Root

One place to begin the political background of the American Revolution is with the 1763 British victory over the French. That military triumph meant the French were expelled from the American colonies, leaving the fur trade solely to the British. But the high cost of a decade of fighting left the British treasury nearly bankrupt.

Officials in London decided the colonists should pay the bulk of the war debts as well as the cost of defending the frontiers that had been won. The colonists were willing to help—up to a point. Colonial legislatures increased levies, but they didn't raise enough revenue to satisfy the British.

Economics wasn't the only factor in the coming revolution, as ideas were stirring people, too. This is where the press played a pivotal role. The writing of the era appeared in newspapers, magazines, and pamphlets that expressed the rebels' arguments. Revolutions don't occur because of logic. They require passion, and this emotional element was brought to the movement by a group of visionaries fully aware of the power of the press.

The earliest wave of rebels insisted that the people deserved a larger voice in their governance. Specifically, they believed the colonies should make the laws governing them, although all but the most radical of them accepted that the British crown should remain the final authority in their lives.

Sam Adams: Firebrand of the Revolution

The best known of the early writers was Sam Adams, the cousin of John Adams and the man who would, in 1773, organize the Boston Tea Party. In the 1760s, he became a prominent voice in the *Boston Gazette*, writing hundreds of essays and news articles. Because other newspapers reprinted his pieces, Adams's thoughts spread throughout the colonies.

Beginning in 1764, Adams argued that the British Parliament was imposing too many taxes on the colonists. If the House of Commons could compel New England to pay ruinous taxes on a staple such as molasses, Adams insisted, the colonists' liberty was in jeopardy. "If our Trade may be taxed," he asked rhetorically, "why not our Lands? Why not the Produce of our Lands & every thing we possess or make use of? This we apprehend annihilates our Charter Right to govern & tax ourselves." Adams's protests, in short, represented an early cry against taxation without representation.[1]

Adams and the other men who gathered around him in the *Boston Gazette* office came to believe that the only way the colonies could resolve their disputes with England was to secure home rule. This meant they'd come to the position—shocking to the vast majority of British citizens—that the colonies, not the Mother Country, should establish their own laws vis-à-vis how they'd be governed, although the crown would continue to hold veto power. This idea was considered radical—tantamount to a child determining his or her own behavior.

Although Adams was Harvard educated and from a prosperous family, he was also a backstairs politician who understood the need to arouse public opinion as a step toward gaining grassroots support for the revolutionary ideas that he and his associates espoused. He wrote, "Where there is a Spark of patriotick fire, we will enkindle it."[2]

"Journal of Occurrences" as News Service

To this end, Adams conceived of what became America's first systematic gathering and distributing of news, a precursor of today's Associated Press.

Adams named his service the "Journal of Occurrences," and it quickly evolved into a communication network that spread his anti-British rhetoric to every corner of the colonies.

Items for the journal were written by Adams and other Bostonians before being reprinted in the thirty-five weekly newspapers being published in the colonies at the time. The process began with Adams and others in Boston writing accounts of events and sending them to John Holt, who published the *New York Journal*. Upon receiving an item from Boston, Holt would print it in the next edition of his weekly paper. Holt then sent copies of the *Journal* to newspaper publishers throughout the colonies, who reprinted the items in their next issues.

Adams's impetus for establishing the news service was Britain's decision to station large numbers of troops in Boston. Officials of the crown were concerned that they were losing control of the colonies, particularly because of an increasing number of protests over tax initiatives. So the British sent four regiments of soldiers to Boston to maintain order and remind the colonists that they were, in fact, British subjects.

The "Journal of Occurrences" began in September 1768, the same month the troops arrived. It became immediately apparent that the purpose of Adams's journalistic venture was to build opposition to the troops—and therefore to the British—by creating and disseminating a record of the loathsome acts the soldiers were committing against the colonists.

The journal was organized like a personal diary. Each installment listed the dates for a particular week, and under each date were descriptions of the individual bits of news that had occurred on that particular day. The first installment ended with a note to publishers: "The above Journal you are desired to publish for the general satisfaction, it being strictly fact."[3] Adams wrote most of the items, although bylines didn't appear with any of them.[4]

The "Journal" created a startling record of misdeeds. Many items spoke of the soldiers' uncouth behavior and low morals. Some reported that the soldiers uttered "profane & abusive language," and others said the troops were constantly involved in "drunkenness," "debaucheries," and "licentious and outrageous behaviour." Still other items accused the men of committing crimes such as extorting money from colonists who were walking on the street and stealing merchandise from colonial shopkeepers.[5]

The single most frequent subject covered in the "Journal" was soldiers mistreating law-abiding citizens, with most of the victims not identified by name. Accounts told of physicians and merchants being "jostled," having bayonets thrust at them, and being knocked to the ground. Typical of the items was one relating how three soldiers surrounded a man walking on the street, "damning him, and asking why he did not answer when hail'd; immediately upon which, one of them without any provocation gave him a blow, which was seconded by another, whereby he was brought to the ground; they then stamped upon him; then they robbed him of all the money in his pocket."[6]

Most disturbing of the items were those chronicling brutalities against Boston women. One item began, "A girl at New-Boston, was lately knock'd down and abused by soldiers for not consenting to their beastly proposal." Another read, "A young woman lately passing thro' Long-Lane, was stopt and very ill treated by some soldiers, the cry of the person assaulted, brought out another woman into the street, who for daring to expostulate with the ruffians, received a stroke from one of them."[7]

Numerous items involved serious offenses. One reported that a woman had filed a complaint with a local magistrate "against a soldier, and some others for a violent attempt upon her, but a rape was prevented, by the timely appearance of a number of persons." Another described a soldier who entered the home of an "aged woman" and then "seized her, by the shoulders, threw her upon the floor, and not withstanding her years, attempted a rape upon her." The item reported that the "brutal behaviour" ended only because the woman's screams brought help from neighbors.[8]

Regardless of the circumstances, the items came wrapped in a tone of outrage, as Adams and the other correspondents made liberal use of strong phrasing. Affronts against the colonists were described as "gross" and "shocking to humanity." The soldiers were labeled "villains," "wretches," and "bloody-backed rascals."[9]

Readers found these spicy news items far more interesting than the diet of sermons and outdated weather reports that dominated the newspapers of the day. The descriptions of improper behavior by the British troops became popular reading—as the blood pressure of the colonists quickly rose.

British officials denied that the troops were the monsters Adams painted them to be. Massachusetts Colonial Governor Francis Bernard denounced the news items as "virulent & seditious lies." Thomas Hutchinson, soon to replace Bernard, wrote, "Nine tenths of what you read in the Journal of Occurrences in Boston is either absolutely false or grossly misrepresented."[10]

And yet the British officials also had to acknowledge that the accounts were having the impact Adams had hoped. As early as January 1769, Hutchinson wrote British officials that the items were turning large numbers of American colonists against the crown. Six months later, feelings toward the troops had grown so rancorous that British officials admitted that the presence of the regiments was increasing hostility rather than reducing it. Officials therefore decided to withdraw the militiamen, who left Boston in August 1769. In short, Adams and his journalistic strategy had triumphed.[11]

The "Journal of Occurrences" then ceased operation. It had produced some 300 individual entries, one for each day during the ten months that British troops had been stationed in Boston. The incidents chronicled in the "Journal"—occurring day after day, week after week, month after month—were effective in ridding Boston of the unwanted British soldiers and in gaining support for Adams and his radical notions. According to today's standards of news professionalism, however, there was a fundamental problem with most of the accounts: they weren't true.

Evidence that many of the items were either fabrications or extreme exaggerations evolves from the exact dates they appeared in the papers. The attempted rape on the elderly woman, for example, allegedly took place on April 30, but it wasn't reported in Boston newspapers until June 26. If such a violent physical attack actually had occurred, surely the Boston newsmen would have warned their fellow townspeople as quickly as possible. There's no logical reason why they would have followed the drawn-out procedure of first publishing the item in the *New York Journal* and only several weeks later publishing it in the Boston papers—resulting in a two-month delay between the attack and its being reported to local residents. If such an attack against a local woman had, in fact, occurred, and the story about it was news rather than propaganda, certainly the Boston correspondents would have reported the event in their local papers in the next weekly edition so townspeople could have taken precautions to protect themselves from the danger in their midst.[12]

The colonial editors apparently felt justified in publishing the descriptions of exaggerated and imaginary incidents because they believed fanning the flames of hatred against the British served the patriot cause.

Boston Massacre: Not to Be Forgotten

Although British officials withdrew the four regiments of militiamen from Boston in the summer of 1769, they left a handful of men in the city as guards. The colonists resented the presence of even these few soldiers. On March 5, 1770, several young colonists gathered outside the British Custom House and threw snowballs at the guards. After some time passed, one of the colonists hit a soldier with a club, knocking him to the ground. The soldier discharged his musket, possibly by accident as he fell, and the bullet struck a colonist. Action then escalated, with the colonists swinging clubs and the British firing guns. By the end of the melee, five colonists were dead and the incident became known as the Boston Massacre.

Adams shrieked with outrage when the trial of the British officer and six of his men involved in the incident led only to light punishments. Five of the men were exonerated, and the two others were ordered merely to have their hands branded. Writing angrily in the *Gazette*, Adams labeled the British soldiers "barbarous & cruel, infamously mean & base."[13]

The most incendiary material about the massacre didn't follow immediately after the trial, however, but in later years. That rhetoric appeared primarily in the form of one-page fliers that were produced more quickly than multipage pamphlets. Tacked at night on trees and the doors of neighborhood taverns, these fliers were read aloud to groups of colonists, and so their influence spread far beyond literate men and women.

Typical were the histrionic words distributed widely on the second anniversary of the 1770 event. One flier began, "AMERICANS! Bear in Remembrance the HORRID MASSACRE!" It went on to describe the five victims as "Being basely and most INHUMANLY MURDERED!" Such exclamations of rage didn't just keep the fight for liberty fresh in the minds of citizens but also fueled a public desire for retribution—challenging the colonists to avenge the murders.[14]

In the words of David Ramsay, a soldier who fought in the American Revolution, the fliers that were written about the Boston Massacre "administered fuel to the fire of liberty, and kept it burning with an incessant flame."[15]

Tom Paine: Voice of Inspiration

The final and most decisive phase of the pro-revolution media campaign began after armed hostilities had broken out in Lexington and Concord in April 1775 and was led by the most important writer of the colonial era, Tom Paine.

After an initial failure in the corset-making business in London, Paine had been hired to collect taxes on liquor and other items. When he began to agitate for higher pay for himself and his fellow workers, however, the British government discharged him. By happenstance, Paine met Benjamin Franklin, then at the height of his career as America's chief spokesman in Europe. Franklin saw so much merit in Paine that he encouraged the fiery young agitator to go to America, providing a letter of introduction for him.

When Paine arrived in Philadelphia in November 1774, the thirty-seven-year-old came with the intent of founding an academy to educate young women. But he veered from his course when his connection to Franklin led to an offer to edit *Pennsylvania Magazine*. Paine's writing in that publication gained him a reputation as an insightful commentator on the issues of the day.

Common Sense **Ignites a Nation**

In January 1776, Paine wrote the material that secured him fame as a revolutionary writer. *Common Sense* evolved after a friend urged him to write an essay on the future of the American colonies "beyond the ordinary short and cold address of newspaper publication." That he did.[16]

Others had offered political and economic arguments, but Paine advocated nothing short of social revolution. His pamphlet served as important a purpose as any piece of journalism in the history of this country. Its message has been credited with transforming thousands of mildly disillusioned colonists into defiant rebels fully prepared to fight for a utopian new world.

Before Paine published his pamphlet, most colonists had aspired only to protect their rights as English subjects. *Common Sense* argued that those men and women not only deserved, but also were obligated, as citizens of the human race, to demand much more. Paine's central message was that the issues facing the colonists weren't transitory or parochial, but timeless and universal. He wrote, "The cause of America is in a great measure the cause of all mankind . . . the concern of every man to whom nature hath given the power of feeling." He returned to the theme repeatedly in later passages, appealing to his readers' sense of destiny by writing, "The sun never shined on a cause of greater worth. 'Tis not the affair of a City, a County, a Province, or a Kingdom. 'Tis not the concern of a day, a year, or an age; posterity are virtually involved in the contest, and will be affected even to the end of time."[17]

Paine dubbed King George III "the Royal Brute of Great Britain" and the English constitution "the base remains of ancient tyrannies." He further struck out at the monarchy by boldly saying, "Of more worth is one honest man to society, and in the sight of God, than all the crowned ruffians that ever lived." Paine was the first writer in America to denounce the British monarchy and constitution so utterly.[18]

Only after dispensing with these institutions did Paine's pamphlet begin to discuss colonial independence—a concept so controversial that other patriots had counseled him to avoid using the word "independence"

COMMON SENSE;

ADDRESSED TO THE

INHABITANTS

O F

A M E R I C A,

On the following interesting

S U B J E C T S.

I. Of the Origin and Design of Government in general, with concise Remarks on the English Constitution.

II. Of Monarchy and Hereditary Succession.

III. Thoughts on the present State of American Affairs.

IV. Of the present Ability of America, with some miscellaneous Reflections.

Man knows no Master save creating HEAVEN,
Or those whom choice and common good ordain.

THOMSON.

PHILADELPHIA;

Printed, and Sold, by R. BELL, in Third-Street.

MDCCLXXVI.

After the pamphlet *Common Sense* appeared in January 1776, the concept of independence spread like wildfire through the American colonies.
Courtesy of the Library of Congress.

at all. Radicals such as Sam Adams had mentioned the concept occasionally, but most colonists still refused to consider such an extreme step. Paine, in contrast, presented separation from Britain as the only option for the colonies and then went on to sketch a breathtaking vision of what American independence could mean for all of humankind, saying, "We have it in our power to begin the world over again. The birthday of a new world is at hand."[19]

With *Common Sense,* Paine pioneered a new style of political writing aimed at extending political discussion to all classes. Authors of the eighteenth century believed that to write for a mass audience meant to sacrifice refinement for coarseness, to reject a lofty literary style in favor of a vulgar one. The American pamphleteers before Paine had come largely from the high social strata of lawyers, merchants, and ministers, but Paine had sprung from that same mass audience that he was so successful at reaching.

Paine later wrote, "As it is my design to make those that can scarcely read understand, I shall therefore avoid every literary ornament and put it in language as plain as the alphabet." He eliminated the flowery language that might have impressed highly educated readers, so the hallmarks of his writing were the same as those of journalism today—clarity, directness, force. His vocabulary and grammar were straightforward, and he carried his readers along with great care from one argument to the next. Paine's message, stated explicitly and reiterated by his tone and style, was that all citizens could grasp the nature of—and play a role in—their own governance.[20]

The response to *Common Sense* was astonishing. At a time when colonial newspapers were lucky if they sold 2,000 copies and pamphlets were printed in one or two editions of a few thousand, more than 150,000 copies of *Common Sense* were sold within three months. And by year's end the pamphlet had gone through twenty-five separate editions.

Impact wasn't measured in numbers alone, however, as Paine's words instantly affected people, reading the simple message and overnight becoming committed to independence. In a matter of weeks, his passion had infected virtually every American colonist who was either literate or was in earshot of one of the hundreds of voices who read the words aloud in coffeehouses, taverns, and town squares from Maine to Georgia.

In the most famous comment on the impact of Paine's words, General George Washington said, "By private letters, which I have lately received from Virginia, I find 'Common Sense' is working a powerful change there in the minds of many men." Others agreed. Abigail Adams thanked her husband, John, for sending her a copy and gushed about its impact in Massachusetts, writing, "'Tis highly prized here and carries conviction wherever it is read. I have spread it as much as it lay in my power, every one assents to the weighty truths it contains." Thomas Jefferson also observed, "No writer has exceeded Paine in ease and familiarity of style, in perspicuity of expression, happiness of elucidation, and in simple and unassuming language."[21]

Common Sense didn't single-handedly cause the American Revolution or propel the authors of the Declaration of Independence to craft their historic document less than six months after Paine wrote his extraordinary pamphlet. But there's no question that his words had significant impact. Paine articulated the larger meaning of the struggle with Britain to readers focused on attaining their rights—and suddenly those same citizens embraced the concept of independence that previously had been anathema to them. Paine biographer Eric Foner wrote, "The success of *Common Sense* reflected the perfect conjunction of a man and his time, a writer and his audience, and it announced the emergence of Paine as the outstanding political pamphleteer of the Age of Revolution."[22]

Crisis Essays Inspire an Army

Despite Paine's singular contribution to the revolutionary cause, his work as an inspirational writer hadn't yet ended. He joined the Continental Army in August 1776 and, like his fellow soldiers, felt the might of a well-armed and well-trained British army. As the summer wore into winter, companies began breaking up. The British cut the Americans to pieces in numerous battles, and Paine saw hundreds of his adopted countrymen die.

Making his way to Washington's headquarters, Paine saw the defeated Americans preparing to retreat across the Delaware River. Legend has it that Paine wrote his *Crisis* essays at Washington's request. The general could see that the winter cold, combined with poor food and inadequate uniforms, was taking a severe toll on his soldiers. So he called on Paine to write words that would motivate the men to continue fighting.

In December 1776, the first installment of the *Crisis* papers went into print in the *Pennsylvania Journal.* The piece was immediately reprinted as a pamphlet and distributed throughout the colonies. Washington had the essay read to his suffering and dispirited troops, and a week later they won a crucial victory at Trenton.

That first essay began with the line that was to be remembered by future generations as Paine's most famous: "These are the times that try men's souls." For more than two centuries, literature classes have admired the power of that alliterative phrasing. Paine continued, "The summer soldier and the sunshine patriot will, in this crisis, shrink from the service of their country; but he that stands it *now*, deserves the love and thanks of man and woman. Tyranny, like hell, is not easily conquered; yet we have this consolation with us, that the harder the conflict, the more glorious the triumph."[23]

Other *Crisis* papers appeared as the need demanded, with twelve being published by December 1783. Each burst with a new flurry of inspiration, including, "Let it be told to the future world, that in the depth of winter, when nothing but hope and virtue could survive, that the city and the country, alarmed at one common danger, came forth to meet it and to repulse it."[24]

After inspiring the colonists to seek independence and later fighting in both the American and French revolutions, Tom Paine died in 1809. His tombstone listed his most important accomplishment as creating *Common Sense.*

Stunning Impact

Just as the American Revolution stands as a seminal event in the history of the United States, colonial American journalism provides a salient

Historians credit essay writer Tom Paine with helping to transform lukewarm patriots into fiery revolutionaries.
Courtesy of the Library of Congress.

example of the impact the news media have had on shaping American history. For the series of publications produced in the colonies during the 1760s and 1770s helped lead the colonists toward political and social revolution. "That rebellion," one historian wrote, "would have been impossible without the spur of the press."[25]

The early phase of the campaign began in 1768 and was orchestrated by political firebrand Sam Adams. Through the "Journal of Occurrences," he and his associates artfully mobilized colonial public opinion against the crown. Their sensationalistic reports of British soldiers mistreating the people of Boston spawned strong negative reaction that, in turn, helped persuade British officials to withdraw the troops—providing the colonists with a victory that propelled them toward further action.

Colonial resentment toward the British grew even stronger during the 1770s. Patriots reported the brutality of the Boston Massacre immediately after the episode and then again used sensationalism through an incessant flow of commemorative fliers. Those retellings of the events on Boston Commons kept the massacre fresh in the colonists' minds and hearts, helping to push those men and women closer and closer to their breaking point.

Despite their importance, these early publications were mere prelude to Tom Paine's remarkable work. In the early months of 1776, *Common Sense* became the manifesto that not only helped arouse the colonists to the revolutionary concept of independence but also thrust them toward open rebellion. *Common Sense* played a singular role in transforming mildly discontented subjects of the British crown into political insurgents fully committed to social mutiny, to fighting for their freedom, and, ultimately, to changing the course of human history.

2

TURNING AMERICA AGAINST
THE SINS OF SLAVERY

IN THE FALL OF 1837, REVEREND ELIJAH LOVEJOY MADE THE
supreme sacrifice. While waging a journalistic campaign in opposition
to slavery, he gave his very life to the cause. As the editor of an abolitionist weekly, Lovejoy had endured proslavery forces destroying his first
printing press, then his second, then his third. Because he continued
to speak out against the sale of African Americans, an angry mob set
out to destroy his fourth press as well. When Lovejoy tried to stop the
destruction of his property, he was killed.

Lovejoy didn't, however, die in vain. His martyrdom propelled thousands of converts into the Abolition Movement, as his murder clearly
demonstrated that an antislavery stand endangered not only the rights of
African Americans but also the civil liberties of all Americans—white as
well as black.

Though Lovejoy's sacrifice was dramatic, his was only one of many
losses that advocacy journalists suffered from the 1820s to the 1860s as
they successfully turned the American conscience against the sins of
slavery. The most famous of the crusading editors was William Lloyd

Garrison, whose paper became synonymous with the abolitionist press. One of several dozen antislavery papers, the *Liberator* remained the focal point of the crusade because of Garrison's strident rhetoric, debates with proslavery editors, and repeated public demonstrations—including burning the Constitution. Also important were the men and women of African descent who, as early as the 1820s, began to plead their own case through the early black press.

The "Peculiar Institution" Divides a Nation

Slavery had been a controversial issue since the founding of the United States, but economic developments in the 1820s created a geographic fault line that split the country into two distinct sections on the topic. The North began to industrialize, with a burgeoning of urban-based factories, while the South remained an agrarian society, with an economy dominated by the production of cotton and tobacco, both relying on slave labor to make a profit.

But the enslavement of human beings was more than an economic issue. Slavery was the rallying cry for northern progressives who wanted massive social change, an issue that crystallized complex social and economic differences between the North and the South. And just as Tom Paine had appealed to human emotions to translate colonial opposition to the British into terms the average citizen could relate to, abolitionist editors used highly charged rhetoric to place the slavery debate on a plane that made sense to a critical mass of the American public.

In the 1830s, the Abolition Movement focused on convincing all Americans that slavery couldn't be allowed to exist. Many southerners saw slavery from a different perspective. They argued that it introduced a backward people to Christian civilization. In addition, apologists said slaves received food, clothing, shelter, and security during sickness and old age. For abolitionists, however, one fundamental fact canceled out every defense: slaves weren't free. They couldn't benefit from the fruits of their own labor, weren't guaranteed the right to participate in the domestic relations of marriage and parenthood, and couldn't regulate their conduct to prepare the immortal soul for eternity. Slaves were, in short, denied their rights as children of God.

To spread this message, abolitionists created their own newspapers—such as the *Instigator* in Providence and the *African Observer* in Philadelphia. The motivation behind these publications was a determination to spread the antislavery ideology to a larger audience throughout the nation as a step toward ending the "peculiar institution."

Reverend Elijah Lovejoy: Journalistic Martyr

Elijah Lovejoy was born in Maine in 1802, the son of a Congregational minister. After graduating from Waterville College in his home state, Lovejoy earned a divinity degree from Princeton Theological Seminary. Powered by a desire to reform society, he established a Presbyterian newspaper in the far western state of Missouri in 1834.

Slavery soon emerged as his *St. Louis Observer's* most controversial topic, particularly because Missouri continued to condone slavery. Lovejoy wrote, "Slavery is a *sin*—now, heretofore, hereafter, and forever, a sin."[1]

The establishment press in St. Louis mobilized opposition to the *Observer*. Lovejoy's paper should be silenced, the *Missouri Republican* argued, because commercial operations in the South would refuse to do business with Missouri if the state allowed Lovejoy to continue preaching against slavery. Virtually demanding violence against Lovejoy, the *Republican* said of Missouri citizens, "Every consideration for their own and their neighbor's prosperity requires them to stop the course of the *Observer*."[2]

Fearing for the safety of his wife and toddler son, Lovejoy relocated to Illinois, a free state. But during the move, slavery advocates pushed his printing press into the Mississippi River. He then bought a second press and proceeded to publish his paper. In the first issue of the *Alton Observer*, he wrote, "American negro Slavery is an awful evil and sin, and it is the duty of us all to effect the speedy and entire emancipation of our fellow-men in bondage."[3]

The idealistic editor soon learned that Illinois wasn't as accepting of his abolitionist stance as he'd hoped. One day when Lovejoy was in his home, a mob went to the *Observer* office and destroyed his second press. Antislavery leaders then sent him money to buy a third press, which pro-slavery forces promptly destroyed. Despite the continuing setbacks, the editor remained steadfast.[4]

Lovejoy borrowed the money to purchase a fourth press. When it arrived on November 7, 1837, he stored it in a warehouse near the river. That night, a crowd of 200 men gathered outside the building and directed Lovejoy to leave. When he refused, events escalated into a riot. Several men placed a ladder against an exterior wall of the warehouse, and one carried a torch to the top and set the roof on fire. As the building began to blaze, Lovejoy ran outside and aimed his pistol at the man on the ladder. Shots rang out from the crowd, and Lovejoy fell to the ground.

The violent death of a well-educated, thirty-five-year-old clergyman—compounded with the failure of law enforcement officials to arrest anyone for his murder—sent shock waves through the nation. It also transformed the Abolition Movement, as the issue mushroomed from the relatively narrow one of denying rights to members of a disenfranchised minority group to the much broader one of threatening the civil liberties of all Americans.

In an editorial outlined in a heavy black border, William Lloyd Garrison used the murder of "a representative of Justice, Liberty and Christianity" to condemn the United States. Garrison wrote, "In destroying his press, the enemies of freedom have compelled a thousand to speak out in its stead. In murdering a loyal and patriotic citizen, they have stirred up a national commotion which causes the foundations of the republic to tremble."[5]

Such statements ignited a tide of resentment and rage that spread like wildfire. Hundreds of ministers preached sermons eulogizing Lovejoy, and thousands of activists organized public protests supporting free expression. The American Anti-Slavery Society capitalized on the groundswell of protest, undertaking a campaign to keep the murder fresh in the memories of the American people. The society adopted the slain editor as a martyr, printed 40,000 copies of a publication that described the Alton riot, and issued stationery embossed with the slogan,

"LOVEJOY the first MARTYR to American LIBERTY. MURDERED for asserting the FREEDOM of the PRESS."[6]

As thousands of men and women previously indifferent to the issue of slavery came to believe that their own civil liberties were in jeopardy, local antislavery societies burst into existence and new members flocked into the national network, which was infused with new life and energy.

In addition to swelling the antislavery ranks, Lovejoy's martyrdom also propelled the Abolition Movement into a new phase. Before this time, abolitionists had believed that once slave owners realized they were committing a sin, they'd voluntarily free their slaves. Lovejoy's murder demonstrated, however, that this strategy would fail. The Alton riot showed antislavery forces that their crusade wouldn't succeed unless they took direct action. If men and women committed to the cause hoped to end slavery, they'd have to enter the rough-and-tumble of politics.

William Lloyd Garrison: Radical Abolitionist Editor

William Lloyd Garrison founded and emerged as chief prophet of the American abolitionist crusade during the early nineteenth century. The primary vehicle he used to spread his gospel was the *Liberator*, the Boston weekly he edited for thirty-five years.

Garrison was born in Massachusetts in 1805. Poverty forced him to leave school at the age of ten, when he became an apprentice printer. While helping edit *Genius of Universal Emancipation* during the 1820s, Garrison grew increasingly vehement in his attacks on American slave traders.

In 1829, he set his sights on Francis Todd, who took slaves from Africa to Louisiana sugar plantations on his ship, the *Francis*. In an item labeled "Black List," Garrison accused Todd of mistreating his slaves, stating, "Any man can gather up riches, if he does not care by what means they are obtained. The *Francis* carried off seventy-five slaves, chained in a narrow place between decks."[7]

Todd filed a libel suit, saying the slaves hadn't been chained but had been free to move below deck. The jury agreed with Todd, finding the

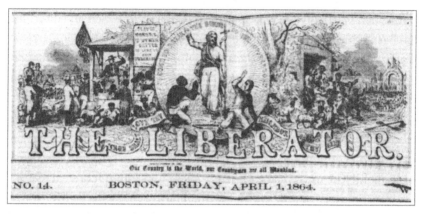

Each week the *Liberator*'s nameplate provided readers with
a graphic reminder that African-American men, women, and
children were sold on the auction block just like horses and cattle.
Reprinted from the Abraham Lincoln Papers at the Library of Congress.

accused guilty. Garrison could have avoided jail if he'd been contrite, but
he refused and spent the next forty-nine days behind bars.

Garrison then moved to Boston and began publishing, in 1831, what
emerged as the archetype of advocacy journalism in American history,
the *Liberator*.

The strident editor was a man of courage and conviction. Most abolitionists were willing to compromise by supporting a gradual reduc-
tion in slavery over a period of years, but Garrison demanded immediate
emancipation of all slaves. He wrote, "I will be as harsh as truth, and as
uncompromising as justice. On this subject, I do not wish to think, or
speak, or write, with moderation. No! No! Urge me not to use moderation
in a cause like the present. I am in earnest—I will not equivocate—I will
not excuse—I will not retreat a single inch—AND I WILL BE HEARD."[8]

Garrison was soon known throughout the country because of his success as a provocateur. His ingenious system began with the simple act of
exchanging his paper for those of some 100 other editors, most of them
proslavery. The editors Garrison sent his paper to were so offended by his
invectives that they quoted his words—accompanied by their own words

of outrage—to show readers the extreme nature of the abolitionist ideology. When Garrison received his copy of a paper in which an editor had lambasted him, he didn't shudder with pain: he celebrated. For Garrison would then reprint the editorial attack, along with his own vehement response, thereby giving his readers far more compelling content than his original editorial had.

For instance, after the editor of Connecticut's *Middletown Gazette* read Garrison's first editorial against slavery, the proslavery editor retorted with contempt, "Mr. Garrison can do no good, either to the cause of humanity or to the slaves, by his violent and intemperate attacks on the slaveholders. That mawkish sentimentality which weeps over imaginary suffering, is proper to be indulged by boarding school misses and antiquated spinsters; but men, grown up men, ought to be ashamed of it." Garrison not only reprinted the *Gazette*'s attack but also used typographical flourishes to ridicule the paper's suggestion that slavery didn't cause pain, repeating the phrase in disbelief, "*IMAGINARY suffering!!*" Garrison then attacked the *Gazette* for betraying the progressive nature of the region of the country that it and the *Liberator* shared, writing, "Such sentiments, emanating at the south, would excite no surprise; but being those of New-England men, they fill us with disgust."[9]

Although the explosive combination of Garrison's extreme positions and his ability to set off editorial chain reactions raised his national profile, they didn't make him popular. One letter to the editor read, "Your paper cannot much longer be tolerated. Shame on the freemen of Boston for permitting such a vehicle of outrage and rebellion to spring into existence among them!" Another screamed, "O! you pitiful scoundrel! you toad eater! you d—d son of a—! hell is gaping for you! the devil is feasting in anticipation! you are not worth—!"[10]

Evidence of Garrison's growing influence on the nation's conscience came in the form of the numerous governmental bodies that tried to silence him. The Georgia legislature offered a $5,000 bounty for Garrison, and a group of men in Mississippi later upped the ante to $20,000. On the federal level, US Postmaster General Amos Kendall condoned southern vigilante groups that rifled mail sacks in an effort to destroy copies of the *Liberator*.

Boston took its own action. In 1835, a mob of men assembled outside a hall where Garrison was speaking. Fearing for his safety, the editor slipped out a back window and sought refuge in a carpenter shop, where he climbed into the loft and hid behind a pile of lumber. The mob tracked him down, screaming, "Lynch him!" Several men then dragged Garrison to the window of the loft, stripped him, and coiled a rope around his neck. Just as the mob was poised to hurl Garrison out the window, supporters rescued him.

Such acts of intimidation didn't cause Garrison to reduce his radicalism, but to increase it. In 1844, he proclaimed that Americans could no longer pledge their allegiance to a slaveholding and racist government and that all non-slaveholders should secede from the union. Garrison wrote, "The existing national compact should be instantly dissolved. Secession from the government is a religious and political duty. The motto inscribed on the banner of Freedom should be, NO UNION WITH SLAVEHOLDERS."[11]

Despite the *Liberator*'s status as the most widely known voice for abolition, the paper didn't build a large circulation. Paid subscribers never exceeded 2,500, most of them powerless African Americans. Garrison paid his printing costs through the fees he charged for speaking engagements, even though his words were almost always accompanied by jeering and heckling—and often stones and rotten eggs—from proslavery demonstrators.

The most notorious example of how far Garrison would go to arouse the American people to his cause came during an 1854 Fourth of July celebration in Framingham, Massachusetts. An article about the event in the *Liberator* described Garrison's dramatic gesture: "Holding up the U.S. Constitution, he branded it as the source and parent of all the other atrocities—'a covenant with death, and an agreement with hell.'" Garrison then set fire to the document. As the Constitution burst into flames, he declared, "So perish all compromises with tyranny! And let all the people say, Amen!" A few hisses and protests were drowned out by a tremendous shout from the crowd: "Amen!"[12]

By the 1850s, Garrison was by no means a lone voice against slavery, as mainstream newspapers also had joined the crusade. The *New York*

William Lloyd Garrison, founder of the *Liberator*, was credited with raising the consciousness of the nation on the issue of slavery.
Courtesy of the Library of Congress.

Tribune had a circulation of 200,000 and was widely acknowledged as the leading opponent of slavery among mainstream papers. Publisher Horace Greeley became an ardent abolitionist and helped organize the Republican Party that brought Abraham Lincoln to the White House in 1860. In the West, Joseph Medill built the *Chicago Tribune* into an abolition advocate as well.

Between 1861 and 1865, more than 600,000 Americans died in the Civil War. And then, finally, in December 1865, the Thirteenth Amendment to the Constitution abolished slavery.

With Garrison's goal achieved, he ceased publishing the *Liberator*. Other journalistic voices then praised him for transforming public sentiment on the most controversial issue of the era. The *Nation* wrote of Garrison's commitment to the Abolition Movement, "It is, perhaps, the most remarkable instance on record of single-hearted devotion to a cause." The magazine went on to say of the *Liberator*, "It has dropped its water upon the nation's marble heart. Its effect on the moral sentiment of the country was exceedingly great. It went straight to the conscience, and it did more than any one thing beside to create that power of moral conviction which was so indomitable."[13]

In recognition of the central role Garrison had played in abolishing slavery, he was invited to Charleston for a great jubilee. The climax of the day came when liberated slaves hoisted the editor onto their shoulders and carried him to a platform, surrounded by thousands of African-American men and women who understood what he'd done for them. Black orator and activist Frederick Douglass spoke for the multitude, calling Garrison "the man to whom more than any other in this Republic we are indebted for the triumph we are celebrating today."[14]

Men at the highest level of government joined in lionizing Garrison. US Senators Charles Sumner and Henry Wilson accompanied Garrison onto the Senate floor. And in the ultimate statement of honor, President Abraham Lincoln received Garrison at the White House for a session in which the men talked privately; it was a historic meeting that brought together the two men who'd done more to end slavery than any others.

African-American Journalists Find Their Voices

Although African Americans had begun, by the late 1820s, to publish their own newspapers, the abolition of slavery didn't dominate the early black press to the degree that it dominated Garrison's *Liberator*. In a country that remained largely hostile to people of African descent, it was remarkable for newspapers owned by blacks to speak at all. For such voices to speak loudly was impossible.

The first black newspaper was *Freedom's Journal*, founded in New York City in 1827. The premier issue contained the eloquent purpose that would continue to sustain the genre for generations to come, saying, "We wish to plead our own cause. Too long have others spoken for us." That "we" referred to Reverend Samuel Cornish, who had founded a Presbyterian church in Manhattan, and John B. Russwurm, who had graduated from Bowdoin College the previous year. The two young men focused their weekly on promoting education, convinced that it was the key to the advancement of their race. Not until halfway through their inaugural editorial did the editors so much as mention slavery. Even then, the reference was a vague one. "We would not be unmindful of our brethren who are still in the iron fetters of bondage," the editorial stated. "They are our kindred by all the ties of nature; and though but little can be effected by us, still let our sympathies be poured forth, and our prayers in their behalf, ascend to Him who is able to succour them."[15]

Freedom's Journal faced severe financial difficulties. Advertising was impossible to secure because very few businesses targeted black consumers, whose economic strength was minimal. The first black newspaper ceased publication in late 1829, never having approached the decibel level of the *Liberator*.

It's not surprising, then, that the first defiant African-American journalist spoke from the pages of the *Liberator* rather than those of the black press. What *is* surprising is that the voice came from a woman. For during the early nineteenth century, society relegated women—black or white—to the home, reserving the realms of business, economics, and politics exclusively to men.

Maria Stewart, however, refused to accept that limited definition of a woman's place. Born free in Connecticut in 1803, Stewart was orphaned at the age of five and widowed while still in her twenties. Propelled by the zeal of religious conviction, she began writing for the *Liberator* in 1831. Garrison showcased Stewart's essays by creating a "Ladies' Department," complete with a woodcut of a black woman in chains.

Much of Stewart's passion was aimed at the abolition of slavery. She urged her fellow African Americans to look up from their labor and see the reality surrounding them, "Cast your eyes about, look as far as you can see; all, all is owned by the *lordly* white." Stewart went on to call the United States a civilization defined by sin, saying: "America has become like the great city of Babylon, for she has boasted in her heart—'I sit a queen and am no widow, and shall see no sorrow!' She is indeed a seller of slaves and the souls of men; she has made the Africans drunk with the wine of her fornication." Using terms such as "*lordly* white" and "fornication" while accusing white America of practicing "fraud" and committing the sins of Babylon clearly placed Stewart in the camp of militant abolitionists, far closer to the radicalism of Garrison than the caution of Cornish and Russwurm.[16]

Boston's African-American community denounced Stewart's fiery discourse, saying it was unseemly for a woman to speak so boldly. In a graphic expression of their disapproval, local black men pelted Stewart with rotten tomatoes. In 1833, Stewart shifted her energies from journalism to education, eventually founding her own school for African-American children.

The country's first strident black abolitionist newspapers were the publishing enterprises of Frederick Douglass. Born into slavery in about 1817, Douglass ran away from his Maryland plantation in 1838. With the support of abolitionists, he became a riveting public speaker who described from firsthand experience the most heinous dimensions of chattel slavery. His intellect and gift as an orator made him the most important African-American leader of the nineteenth century.

Douglass's most influential journalistic product was the *North Star*, which he founded in Rochester, New York, in 1847. Douglass stated, "The object of the *North Star* will be to attack Slavery in all its forms and aspects; Advocate Universal Emancipation; and hasten the day of FREEDOM to the Three Millions of our Enslaved Fellow Countrymen."[17]

Douglass modeled his paper after the *Liberator*, with his editorial tone and content mirroring Garrison's—differing only in that the black editor's writing had a grace the white editor's didn't. Douglass's prose was often informed by memories of his early life in bondage. An 1848 article read, "He is no other than a thief who calls *me* or *you* his own property, and if one sinner is such above all others, it is he who would inflict stripes upon a human being, and quote scripture in justification, as did a master of mine, when brutally flogging a female slave—'They who know their master's will and do it not, shall be beaten with many stripes.' The slaveholder is a depraved man."[18]

The *North Star* was read not only in the United States but also in Europe and the West Indies. Its international distribution during an era when two-thirds of northern blacks and virtually all southern blacks were illiterate served to boost circulation considerably. With five white subscribers for every African-American one, the *North Star* soon surpassed the *Liberator* in circulation, reaching a subscriber list of 3,000.

Like Garrison, Douglass aroused the wrath of proslavery forces. The *New York Herald* demanded that Douglass be banished to Canada, and the *Albany Sunday Dispatch* called him a "saucy nigger." The *Dispatch* encouraged readers to take action against Douglass, advising, "As a moderate sum of money would, doubtless, induce Douglass to go to Toronto or Kingston, in Canada, where he will be much more at home, the Rochester people will do well to buy him off."[19]

By mortgaging his home and soliciting financial support from England, Douglass continued publishing his paper for thirteen years.

And so, by 1850 a sustained African-American press had emerged. It had become an important source of racial pride and identity as well as a powerful instrument in the abolitionist struggle. This advocacy press served several purposes. By providing firsthand descriptions of the brutality that defined slave life, the writing by Douglass and other former slaves destroyed the myth that southern masters were kind. In addition, the eloquence and high literary qualities of the work of women and men such as Stewart and Douglass undermined charges that black people were intellectually inferior. On a broader scale, creation of black abolitionist papers was a crucial step in establishing that the Abolition Movement wouldn't be a phenomenon resting entirely on white shoulders.

Moving Abolition onto the National Agenda

Even though Americans historically have prided themselves on being a freedom-loving people, two of the landmark events in the history of this nation's first century were armed conflicts. The Revolutionary War was the most important event of the 1700s, and the Civil War was the most important event of the 1800s. Both conflicts were fueled partly by economic factors—the American Revolution by the colonists refusing to pay high taxes to the British and the Civil War by the incompatibility of the agrarian South with the industrializing North. In neither case, however, did economics alone propel citizens into open warfare, as emotional forces also played an essential role in igniting the conflicts. And, likewise, in both cases those emotional elements were articulated to the American people in the form of journalistic publications.

In the decades leading up to the war between the North and the South, the emotionalism was focused on the issue of slavery, and the journalistic force that placed that debate on the national agenda was the abolitionist press. Beginning in the 1830s, antislavery newspapers such as Elijah Lovejoy's *St. Louis Observer* and William Lloyd Garrison's *Liberator* raised the consciousness of the nation to a sinful abomination in fundamental conflict with the ideals of democracy. Garrison strategically positioned the *Liberator* at the center of the storm. The epitome of the activist editor, he calculated a formula by which his strident discourse, angry rhetorical conflicts with proslavery editors, and dramatic acts of public defiance ensured that neither he nor his crusade was ignored.

Between 1830 and 1850, the abolitionist press—black as well as white—succeeded in articulating and disseminating throughout the nation the moral indictment of slavery that precipitated the Civil War and ultimately forced the "peculiar institution" into a dark corner of American history.

3

SLOWING THE MOMENTUM
FOR WOMEN'S RIGHTS

IN JULY 1848, A GROUP OF PROGRESSIVE-MINDED AMERICANS announced a concept that some people considered every bit as revolutionary as colonists demanding their independence or slaves seeking their freedom. The women and men who gathered in upper New York state said, simply and forthrightly, that liberty wasn't the province of men alone but was—or should be—the birthright of women as well. The tangible product of their first historic meeting in Seneca Falls was a paraphrase of the Declaration of Independence, reading, "We hold these truths to be self-evident: that all men *and women* are created equal." Despite the impressive commitment, sound logic, and noble purpose of this stalwart band of activists, more than seven decades would pass before the crusaders were finally able to secure the right of American women to vote.[1]

One of the most serious impediments to the march toward gender equality was the same force that already had built a record as a highly influential institution in American history: the news media. For by the mid-nineteenth century, it had been firmly established that the Fourth Estate was a body overwhelmingly peopled by—and largely committed to serving—

men. Threatened by the possibility that women might be rising from their second-class citizenship to command a share of the male power base, the men who dominated the institution of journalism either ignored the Women's Rights Movement or wrote about it in a tone of mockery and disdain.

American journalism's oppressive treatment of women didn't begin in Seneca Falls. From the beginning of the republic, the media had worked to limit women's role in society, with publications of the late eighteenth century systematically restricting half the population to a narrow existence that had become known as the women's sphere—essentially, the home. That strategy intensified with coverage of the Seneca Falls Women's Rights Convention in 1848 and remained firmly in place throughout the nineteenth century. Eventually, women's rights leaders decided they'd need to follow the example of the abolitionists and create an entirely alternative publishing network—the suffrage press—in hopes of counteracting the male journalistic opposition that blocked their progress. But the feminists found that the male dictatorship was so pervasive that even this separate communication system did little to weaken it.

Confining the American Woman to Her Place

American women had begun making major contributions to society by colonial times, succeeding in such diverse fields as education, medicine, literature, law, and printing. Indeed, in 1777, Mary Katherine Goddard was such a respected printer that the founders of the country sought her out to print the first official copy of the Declaration of Independence. Despite the many accomplishments of colonial women, however, it became apparent after the American Revolution that women wouldn't have the rights promised in the Constitution.

The Founding Fathers didn't specifically state that women would be denied rights. Instead, those men simply ignored female citizens, failing to explore the possibility of defining women as part of "the people." Western political thought provided no context for women being included as part of the body politic, and this was one political convention the male architects of democracy opted not to tamper with.

The average eighteenth-century woman assumed her place in society based on her husband's identity. She was considered, by nature, to be incapable of serious thought or important decision-making. In addition to not being allowed to vote, a woman couldn't retain property in marriage, even if she'd owned that property before her wedding day. So in case of divorce, she retained neither the ownership of land nor the custody of children. She typically married at sixteen and gave birth to a child every two years through her forties. A third of those children died early, and she lost her own health—as well as her looks—by her mid-twenties.

Women's limited role in society was reinforced by the editorial content in the publications of the era. Fundamental was the message that the men's sphere encompassed all of business and politics, with the women's sphere being restricted to the four walls of the home. This distinct division of roles had to be faithfully adhered to for the well-being of the country, according to the American media of the late 1700s and early 1800s, because women lacked the ability to succeed in the public world, as they were intellectually as well as physically inferior to men.

The primary publishing venue for disseminating these messages was the handful of women's magazines that emerged in the late eighteenth century. *Ladies Magazine*, founded in 1792, became the first American publication aimed exclusively toward women, although it was owned and published by a man. Other magazines, some exclusively for women and others for men as well as women, soon joined the Philadelphia monthly to create the first generation of periodicals that shaped the lives of the country's women—but didn't advance their progress.

Women's limited abilities were a consistent theme in the magazines, through both their content and their paternalistic tone. Typical was an article in *Ladies Magazine* that bluntly stated, "The number of women who have solid judgment is very small." *American Museum*, another magazine of the era, made the intellectual inferiority of women clear when it stated, "The author of nature has placed the balance of power on the side of the male, by giving him not only a body more large and robust, but also a mind endowed with greater resolution, and a more extensive reach."[2]

The message was that domesticity dominated women's very being because they weren't capable of acting autonomously, and therefore only one path was appropriate for them: marrying a man. Once wed, a woman was to focus all her energy on pleasing her husband above all other goals. *Ladies Magazine* announced, "To make her husband happy and contented will ever be her wish, not to say her greatest pleasure."[3]

While idealizing the docile woman, the magazines criticized the woman who allowed temptations to interfere with her wifely duties. *Ladies Magazine* warned women that their natures dictated that they had to struggle constantly to resist their "almost irresistible inclination to pleasure" through such follies as shopping and gossiping. "The female nature constantly shows a greater proclivity to the gay and the amusive, than to the sober and useful scenes of life." And *Weekly Magazine* provided women with a checklist of some of the most common errors they committed when speaking, with those mistakes ranging from women not "acknowledging his [a husband's] superior judgment" to women voicing their own opinions.[4]

Discrediting the Women's Rights Movement

The historic meeting in the summer of 1848 was very much in conflict with the paternalistic tone that dominated late eighteenth- and early nineteenth-century magazines. And so, as women made their first dramatic assault on men's political and economic stranglehold on American society, the Fourth Estate responded by replacing paternalism with unrestrained hostility.

The event that marked the beginning of the Women's Rights Movement in the United States unfolded in Seneca Falls, New York, because that community was the home of Elizabeth Cady Stanton. The woman who ultimately became the movement's leading theorist, writer, and orator was born in Johnstown, New York, in 1815 and married lawyer and abolitionist Henry B. Stanton. Her marriage was happy, but her husband's work often took him away from home, leaving her with their seven children and the boredom of homemaking in an isolated setting. Stanton initiated the

Seneca Falls convention by placing a public notice in the *Seneca County Courier*.[5]

Some 300 people heeded Stanton's call. They included a large number of women, such as Lucretia Mott and Amelia Bloomer, whose confidence and organizational skills had been developed through their work within the Abolition and Temperance Movements. At the end of the two-day meeting, sixty-eight women and thirty-two men signed their names to a Declaration of Sentiments.

The signers directly challenged the concept of sex-segregated spheres. Their declaration read, "The history of mankind is a history of repeated injuries and usurpations on the part of man toward woman, having in direct object the establishment of an absolute tyranny over her." The twelve resolutions encouraged women to enter the professions and demanded that women be granted property and child custody rights.[6]

The most controversial resolution demanded women's suffrage, stating, "Resolved, That it is the duty of the women of this country to secure to themselves their sacred right to the elective franchise." Only after an eloquent appeal by African-American leader Frederick Douglass did the resolution pass.[7]

One of the less prominent statements in the Declaration of Sentiments was that women's rights proponents would try to enlist the press on behalf of their cause, while acknowledging that, "In entering upon the great work before us, we anticipate no small amount of misconception, misrepresentation, and ridicule." How right they were.[8]

The *New York Herald*, one of the most influential newspapers in the country, called the Seneca Falls meeting a "Woman's Wrong Convention," adding that it proved the country's political and social fabric was "crumbling to pieces," and the *Worcester Telegraph* in Massachusetts mocked the women at the meeting as "Amazons" who were "bolting with a vengeance." The *Philadelphia Ledger and Daily Transcript* summarized its position on women's rights perhaps more succinctly than any other journalistic voice of the era, saying, "A woman is nobody. A wife is everything."[9]

The Seneca Falls convention was the first of many events designed to build momentum for the Women's Rights Movement. By the early 1850s,

Susan B. Anthony had emerged as an important complement to Stanton. Born in Adams, Massachusetts, in 1820, Anthony taught school for fifteen years before committing her life to reform efforts, beginning with temperance and abolition but eventually focusing on women's rights. Unmarried and willing to devote her abundant talents to the effort, Anthony brought to the movement, in particular, strengths as an intellect and organizer.

Stanton and Anthony combined their abilities to create a dynamic partnership at the head of the movement. Hundreds of women's rights meetings, petition drives, and public lectures erupted all over the country during the 1850s, with many of them attracting thousands of supporters. The two women also organized a national convention almost every year from 1850 until the beginning of the Civil War in 1861. And after the war ended and the Fourteenth Amendment gave former male slaves the vote, the women intensified the campaign for their own enfranchisement.

Regardless of what the particular event was, a flurry of hostile newspaper articles followed in its wake. The *Syracuse Star* derided an 1852 meeting in that city as the "Tomfoolery Convention," calling the three days of speeches and discussions a "mass of corruption, heresies, ridiculous nonsense, and reeking vulgarities which these bad women have vomited forth." After women attempted to take their campaign to the New York state legislature, the *Albany Daily State Register* wrote that women's rights advocates initially were amusing, like "clowns in the circus" or "gentlemen with blackened faces." The newspaper then cast aside all sense of amusement, saying, "The joke is becoming stale. The ludicrous is wearing away, and disgust is taking the place of pleasurable sensations, arising from this hypocrisy and infidel fanaticisms."[10]

In addition to trivializing the movement, the newspapers attacked feminists on the ground that they were abandoning their responsibilities in the home. Typical was a vitriolic article in the *Mechanic's Advocate* in Albany that criticized women for attending women's rights activities "at the expense of their more appropriate duties." Because increased rights would destroy the traditional division between women's and men's spheres, the *Advocate* insisted, such a shift would "demoralize and degrade from their high sphere and noble destiny women of all respectable and useful classes, and prove a monstrous injury to all mankind." James Gordon Bennett was a leader on this theme, thundering from the *New York Herald*'s editorial page that feminists were belying woman's true nature. He asked rhetorically, "How did woman first become subject to man, as she now is all over the world? By her nature, her sex, just as the negro is and always will be, to the end of time, inferior to the white race and, therefore, doomed to subjection."[11]

Newspapers carried this accusation of violating the laws of nature to the point that they equated supporting women's rights with committing a sin against God. The *Herald* screamed, "These ladies are, at least, trenching on immorality, and are in dangerous contiguity to, and companionship with, the most detestable of vices."[12]

In an effort to discredit prominent leaders of the movement, papers attacked their unmarried status. Ignoring the fact that a nineteenth-century wife had to devote such enormous effort to household chores that little time remained for activism, the papers characterized the single leaders, especially Anthony, as sexual freaks. The *New York Sun* wrote, "The quiet duties of daughter, wife or mother are not congenial to those hermaphrodite spirits who thirst to win the title of champion of one sex and victor over the other." The *Herald* added, "These women are entirely devoid of personal attractions. They are generally thin maiden ladies, having found it utterly impossible to induce any young or old man into the matrimonial noose."[13]

Newspapers routinely referred to women in the movement by such degrading terms as "poor creatures," "unfortunate women," "old maids," and "unsexed women," while calling men involved in the movement "Aunt Nancys," suggesting, by innuendo, that men who supported women's rights were either homosexual or totally dominated by their wives.[14]

Despite the scornful tone in mainstream newspapers, Stanton believed all publicity was good publicity because it ultimately would help move women's rights onto the national agenda. Assessing the widespread coverage of the Seneca Falls convention, Stanton wrote in her personal correspondence, "There is no danger of the Woman Question dying for want of notice. Every paper you take up has something to say about it." Opting for the point of view that it was better to be deplored than ignored, Stanton

Many American newspapers published denigrating
comments about women's rights leaders Elizabeth Cady
Stanton, seated at left, and Susan B. Anthony, right.
Courtesy of the Library of Congress.

continued, "Imagine the publicity given to our idea by thus appearing in a
widely circulated sheet like the *Herald*. It will start women thinking, and
men too; and when men and women think about a new question, the first
step in progress is taken."[15]

Other women's rights advocates expressed similar sentiments. Lucretia
Mott acknowledged in 1855 that the newspapers "ridiculed and slandered
us" but was convinced, based on her work in the Abolition Movement, that
the press went "through three stages in regard to reforms; they first ridicule

them, then report them without comment, and at last openly advocate them. We seem to be still in the first stage on this question [of women's rights]."[16]

Creating a Voice of Their Own

Visionary leaders such as Stanton and Anthony realized that if the Women's Rights Movement were to succeed, the leaders would need to follow the example of the Abolition Movement and create their own alternative medium of communication. In January 1868, Stanton and Anthony founded the *Revolution*. Based in New York City, the newspaper carried the masthead "Men, Their Rights and Nothing More; Women, Their Rights and Nothing Less." As radical in content as in its name, the *Revolution* insisted that securing suffrage was merely the first step in the women's rights campaign. The paper argued, "The ballot is not even half the loaf; it is only a crust—a crumb." With Stanton as its driving editorial force, the *Revolution* expressed liberal views on a wide range of social issues such as prostitution and divorce. Such controversial content alienated many potential readers and even more prospective advertisers. The *Revolution*'s circulation never exceeded 3,000, and the paper ceased publication in 1870, surviving only two years and leaving $10,000 in unpaid bills.[17]

Not all feminists agreed on the breadth of the women's rights agenda, creating a major split in the movement. After Stanton and Anthony founded the National Woman Suffrage Association in 1869, Lucy Stone and her husband, Henry Blackwell, formed the considerably less strident American Woman Suffrage Association in 1870.

Stone then founded *Woman's Journal*, a more moderate journalistic voice than the *Revolution*. The Boston-based *Journal* focused on suffrage and its importance to such middle-class efforts as establishing women's clubs and encouraging women to obtain higher educations. The *Journal* adopted the conventional journalistic writing style of an establishment paper, reporting on suffrage activities and legislative campaigns around the country and printing transcripts of women's suffrage speeches and conventions. The newspaper's stands appealed to many Americans, giving *Woman's Journal* the support it needed to publish without interruption from 1870 through 1933, building a circulation of 6,000. What's more, the *Journal* was a real business, financed through a stock company, that achieved financial solvency.

The *Revolution* and *Woman's Journal* weren't the only members of the suffrage press, as several dozen publications were created to spread the women's suffrage ideology. Most of them served local communities and were short-lived, as they struggled both for circulation and financial support during an era when most women had little independent income. The various journals also tended to be driven by an individual editor and aimed at an audience of middle- and upper-class white women. One exception was *Woman's Era*, a monthly paper that was distributed nationally by Josephine St. Pierre Ruffin, a member of Boston's African-American elite, from 1890 to 1897. "The stumbling block in the way of even the most cultured colored woman is the narrowness of her environment," Ruffin wrote. "It is to help strengthen this class and a better understanding between all classes that this little venture is sent out on its mission." A large number of the journals were published in western states where many of the earliest advancements in women's suffrage were made.[18]

It would be misleading, however, to suggest that the suffrage press was a major force in transforming American society's views on women's rights. Few of the publications were able to build their circulation figures beyond a few hundred, and the majority of their readers were already committed to the Women's Rights Movement. And unlike William Lloyd Garrison, editors focusing on women's suffrage didn't attract national attention by orchestrating spectacular public events—such as burning the Constitution during a Fourth of July celebration—or by provoking editorial screaming matches with mainstream editors who disagreed with them.

The most significant impact of the suffrage press was on the movement itself. The publications bridged the gaps of time and space, providing an important tie that bound together women from different locations to create a grassroots social movement. During an era when mass transportation didn't exist, a women's rights convention or lecture generally couldn't draw more than a few dozen people, but a journal could reach several hundred, including people living in rural areas. Once a publication arrived at a woman's home, it informed her of activities nationwide, articulated the ideology of feminist theorists, offered her arguments to use in her own community, and reinforced her sense of purpose. In fact, the very existence of a journal provided a tangible product that was vital to sustaining a long public campaign.

Intensifying the Attack

Even after many decades of women's rights activism, most members of the mainstream press continued to express scorn toward the reform efforts. Indeed, many of the male-dominated papers responded to the increasing power of women leaders by increasing the intensity and viciousness of their attacks.

During the final decades of the nineteenth century, mainstream newspapers focused much of their unrelenting assault on the personal characteristics of the most high-profile women. Typical was an article in the *New York Tribune*, the most widely read and respected paper in the country, that attacked the leaders, saying, "Our heart warms with pity towards these unfortunate creatures. We fancy that we can see them, deserted of men, and bereft of those rich enjoyments and exalted privileges which belong to women, languishing their unhappy lives away in a mournful singleness." That same year, the *New York World* sank to an equally low level of hate-filled rhetoric. One tirade insulted everyone in the Women's Rights Movement by describing the women as "mummified and fossilated females, void of domestic duties, habits and natural affections," and the men as "crack-brained, rheumatic, dyspeptic, henpecked men."[19]

The most mean-spirited comments were written about Anthony. Newspapers ignored the substance of Anthony's discourse and focused instead on her appearance and status as a "spinster." In 1866, even though Anthony was by that time a figure of international stature, the *New York World* demeaned her by referring to her by her first name, saying, "Susan is lean, cadaverous; with the proportions of a file." In 1870, the *Utica Herald* described Anthony in equally insulting language, asking, "Who does not feel sympathy for Susan Anthony? She has striven long and earnestly

THE NEW NAVY.

A drawing from *Life* magazine depicted Elizabeth Cady Stanton as smug and grossly overweight, while portraying bespectacled Susan B. Anthony as grim and rail thin.
Reprinted from Life *magazine.*

to become a man. She is sweet in the eyes of her own mirror, but her advanced age and maiden name deny that she has been so in the eyes of others." And in 1879, the *Richmond Herald* wrote, "Miss Anthony is uncomely in person, has rather coarse, rugged features and masculine manners."[20]

By the final decades of the nineteenth century, technical advances in paper and printing production had ushered many inexpensive magazines into the journalistic mix. They attracted huge numbers of middle- and working-class readers by appealing to popular topics, including the various controversies involving women's rights. Articles with titles such as "Manly Women" and "Is Marriage a Failure?" fueled the negative attitude toward the changing role of women.[21]

Magazines also exploited the emotional impact of images to lambaste women's rights advocates. Particularly adept at this technique was *Life*, a forerunner of the photo magazine of the same name that would capture the American public's imagination in the 1930s. The nineteenth-century version of *Life* used line drawings to place the modern generation of liberated women in uncomplimentary poses. One showed a female minister preaching to an empty church, and another depicted women smoking, drinking alcohol, and cavorting in a modern-day club for women. A two-page image in an 1896 issue was particularly memorable, depicting an obese Stanton and a resolutely grim Anthony dressed in the uniforms of male naval officers in front of an all-woman navy. The caption read, "The New Navy."[22]

Victory Despite the Fourth Estate

After twenty years of separation, the two wings of the Women's Rights Movement united in 1890 to create the National American Woman Suffrage Association. The activists still, however, stood far from victory. Between 1870 and 1910, feminists waged some 500 campaigns in cities and states nationwide to place initiatives before the voters, with only seventeen of those efforts even succeeding in bringing their issues to a vote.

Success didn't begin in earnest until the early years of the twentieth century when the Progressive Movement pushed reform and liberal social thought into the national spotlight. This era of rapid change meant that the Women's Rights Movement's demands no longer seemed so radical compared to those of the men and women determined to remake American government and industry. The emphasis on efficiency and productivity that was key to the Progressive Movement manifested itself in a new generation of youthful leaders brimming with pragmatic strategies centering on public agitation, direct confrontation, and political tactics. These hard-driving, resourceful women focused much of their energy on women's suffrage.

The rise of the adept new generation was dramatically demonstrated in 1907 when Harriot Stanton Blatch, Elizabeth Cady Stanton's daughter, created the Women's Political Union. Blatch broadened the movement to appeal to working-class women and to organize the first suffrage parades, which immediately became a popular and productive device. Alice Paul, another young activist, mobilized public demonstrations to push hard for a constitutional amendment and, in 1913, formed what later became the National Woman's Party. When Paul's militant tactics led to women being harassed and even imprisoned, the American public finally began paying attention and giving support to the issue of women's suffrage. In the last phase of activism, Carrie Chapman Catt incorporated effective organization and political strategy into the movement. Catt's "winning plan," which she began in 1916, was a tactical and organizational masterpiece that pressured the House of Representatives into passing the Nineteenth Amendment in 1918. Two years later, after hard-fought battles in the Senate and then in the individual states, women's suffrage became the law of the land in August 1920—seventy-two years after the call had gone out at Seneca Falls.

Suffering from the Power of the Press

It wasn't until 1919 that mainstream American journalism finally began to treat the Women's Rights Movement as a major social and political initiative. The majority of the press supported women's suffrage only after the Nineteenth Amendment had cleared the Senate and ratification by the states appeared inevitable. Until that time, establishment newspapers and magazines chose to portray the American woman as they had throughout the late eighteenth and early nineteenth centuries—as a physical and intellectual cripple who had to be cared for and protected. Even though such highly capable women as Elizabeth Cady Stanton, Susan B. Anthony, and Lucy Stone were leading the potentially far-reaching movement by the mid-nineteenth century, the American institution charged with informing the public opted to treat this particular social movement with ridicule and hostility.

The role that American newspapers of the nineteenth century played in slowing the momentum for women's rights is an example of the press abusing the mighty power it wields. Had the Fourth Estate mobilized that power as a positive force in support of the Women's Rights Movement, there's no question that half the American citizenry would have been granted its rightful voice in the democratic process far earlier than ultimately was the case. Nor would the nineteenth century provide the only example of the American news media slowing women's march toward equality. Many observers have noted that journalistic attitudes toward women's rights didn't change until the few women involved in the field advanced to positions as editors and other policy makers. Anthony created a vivid image supporting this point of view in 1893 when she told the *Chicago Tribune*, "If the men own the paper—that is, if the men control the management of the paper—then the women who write for these papers must echo the sentiment of these men. And if they do not do that, their heads are cut off."[23]

4

ATTACKING MUNICIPAL CORRUPTION

THE TWEED RING RULED NEW YORK CITY IN THE 1860S AND EARLY 1870s like no political machine before or since. Payoffs, kickbacks, padded contracts, extortion, election fraud—they were all part of what came to personify corruption by errant public "servants." William Marcy Tweed and the band of political henchmen who did his bidding ultimately stuffed their pockets with some $200 million taken from city taxpayers.

This crime against democracy was finally exposed by an unlikely antagonist: cartoons. Thomas Nast's illustrations in *Harper's Weekly* attacked municipal corruption with a vengeance. By defying "Boss" Tweed, Nast provided a dramatic example of the power that journalistic images can wield.

A year after Nast began attacking Tweed in *Harper's*, the *New York Times* joined the crusade, putting into words the accusations that Nast was communicating through pictures. When the *Times* published secret documents laying bare the extent of the ring's illegal activities, the series hastened the end of the corruption.

Nast deserves the most credit. The passion and impact of his unrelenting visual attacks stand alone in the annals of American editorial cartooning. Even Tweed himself ultimately came to acknowledge that Nast had destroyed him, saying, "I didn't care a straw for the newspaper articles—my constituents didn't know how to read. But they couldn't help but see them damned pictures." This crusade by a journalistic David against a political Goliath stands as a stunning example of how the news media have shaped history.[1]

Heyday of Corruption

After the Civil War, the United States underwent fundamental changes at a dizzying pace. Many of the changes had their roots in the confluence of three phenomena of immense dimension—urbanization, industrialization, and immigration. These powerful forces opened the door to wholesale corruption in politics as well as business, and an army of opportunists took advantage of the fluid situation for their personal gain.

William Marcy Tweed was born in New York City in 1823. After working briefly as a city fireman, Tweed entered politics and a career in the public realm. His rise up New York's political hierarchy between 1864 and 1869 was boosted by his membership in Tammany Hall, a powerful political organization. The Society of Saint Tammany had been founded soon after the American Revolution as a social and patriotic club that vowed to oppose New York's moneyed interests. By 1850, however, Tammany Hall had created its own Democratic Party power base and had mushroomed into a potent force in city politics that skillfully manipulated the electorate.

Tweed, at the height of his control, from 1869 to 1871, wielded enormous influence because of his many political connections. He was simultaneously the highest official of Tammany Hall, chairman of the New York Democratic Party Central Committee, a member of both the New York County Board of Supervisors and the New York State Senate, director of New York City's Department of Public Works, and construction supervisor for the New York County Court House. Also, in a blatant example of conflict of interests, Tweed was one of the city's largest property owners and real estate developers.

Boss Tweed's actions were supported by his cronies led by New York Mayor A. Oakey "Elegant Oakey" Hall, City Controller Richard B. "Slippery Dick" Connolly, and City Parks Director Peter B. "Brains" Sweeny. These four men were involved in every facet of New York government, using their political muscle to make the city treasury their own.

Tweed maintained his position by handing out payoffs that came from the city treasury. Hundreds of thousands of dollars went to lobby the state legislature to ensure the laws it approved were those that the Tweed Ring wanted, and lesser sums bought votes at the ballot box and "judicial" decisions in the courtroom. Most of the payoffs for his constituents, who were overwhelmingly from the city's immigrant poor, came in the form of city jobs. The number of patronage positions Tweed doled out to keep the city's political machine well lubricated ultimately totaled some 60,000.

Tweed also developed an intricate kickback system to support this political organization and amass an obscene quantity of wealth for himself and his associates. The unwritten procurement policy was that the ring received 65 percent of all city contracts. The contractors learned to take this policy into account when bidding for city projects.

Though Tweed's abuse of the city coffers was an open secret in political circles, no one had the power and courage to stop it. His control over the newspapers as part of his success in averting public clamor was insidious as well. In 1862, New York aldermen passed a resolution to pay individual reporters $200 a year for "services" to the city. And, in the expansive manner of Tammany Hall, this figure increased tenfold. Even more fundamental to the administration's ability to influence the editorial content of the papers was the city advertising budget. Tweed subsidized the largest dailies in New York City—the *World*, *Herald*, and *Post*—by annually placing some $80,000 worth of city advertising in each. During the ring's reign of corruption, the city funneled $7 million to the papers in exchange for their silence.[2]

Pictures Confront Politics

Thomas Nast was born in Germany in 1840, and his family immigrated to America in 1846, drawn by the dual appeals of personal freedom and economic opportunity.

Young Nast showed an early talent for drawing and joined the staff at *Harper's Weekly* in 1862. The New York–based magazine aimed its content at common laborers, following the motto, "Never shoot over the heads of the people." This philosophy lifted circulation to 100,000, making it the largest publication in the country. As a social and political cartoonist for *Harper's*, Nast soon proved himself to be an artist whose social commentary could move vast audiences. In 1864, the most important American art critic of the day, James Jackson Jarves, wrote, "Nast is an artist of uncommon abilities. His works evince originality of conception, freedom of manner, lofty appreciation of national ideas and action, and a large artistic instinct."[3]

During a *Harper's Weekly* career spanning more than two decades, Nast crafted some 3,000 drawings. Perhaps the most legendary symbols to emerge from his pencil were the Republican elephant and the Democratic donkey. Another image he created was the classic Santa Claus with his rosy cheeks and jolly demeanor.

In the early 1860s, Nast focused on capturing the tragedy of the Civil War. After the fighting had ended and Ulysses S. Grant was asked to name the person most responsible for saving the country, the general responded, "Thomas Nast. He did as much as any one man to preserve the Union and bring the war to an end." President Lincoln praised Nast as well, saying, "His cartoons have never failed to arouse enthusiasm and patriotism, and have always seemed to come just when those articles were getting scarce."[4]

By the late 1860s, Nast was well positioned to begin an assault on the most corrupt city administration in American history. He launched his crusade in September 1869, with his initial caricatures aimed at Tammany Hall. One depicted New York Governor John Hoffman, a stalwart Tammany Democrat, above the slogan "'Peter the Great' Chief of the Tammany Tribe." The cartoon suggested that Tammany leaders were taking on the

Thomas Nast was one of the most influential political cartoonists in the history of American journalism.
Courtesy of the Library of Congress.

tyrannical bearing of Russian czars. Tweed remained in the background of those early cartoons. In a scene showing self-righteous Catholic bishops giving the Pope huge trunks labeled "Tax Payers' and Tenants' Hard Cash," Tweed was depicted only as one of the many bishops—albeit one of the most overweight.[5]

As Nast's campaign evolved, however, Tweed's profile rose. In partic-ular, Nast used Tweed's ostentatious symbols of power to redefine the corrupt politician's public image. Nast took the very marks of respect-ability and success that Tweed cherished, such as a $15,000 diamond stickpin, and made them emblems of greed and vulgarity. The cartoonist also sometimes dressed Tweed in suits with broad horizontal stripes, out-fits reminiscent of prison uniforms. He consistently mocked Tweed as bloated and gluttonous—a man who feasted on the richest of foods while the city's poor went hungry.

Through the relentless strokes of Nast's pencil, the dignity and spoils of political office were rendered liabilities. Nast made it first possible and then popular for the citizens of New York to laugh at the man whose iron grip controlled every element of their lives. Through the journalistic art-work that appeared week after week in *Harper's*, the public began to see Tweed as a rapacious scoundrel.

The *New York Times* Joins the Crusade

The fall of 1870 marked a turning point in the journalistic campaign against the Tweed Ring. Until that time, James B. Taylor had been a member of the board of directors at the *New York Times*. Because Taylor's New York Printing Company received hefty advertising contracts from city hall, Taylor kept the *Times* editorial staff from speaking out against Tweed. Instead, the *Times* joined other New York papers in reaping the financial profits of a cozy relationship with the ring. Late in the summer of 1870, however, Taylor died. A month later, the *Times* ran its first anti-Tweed editorial.

That piece began with the request, "We should like to have a treatise from Mr. Tweed on the art of growing rich." It then shifted to a personal narrative style that readers could relate to, "Most of us have to work very hard for a subsistence, and think ourselves lucky if, in the far vista of years, there is a reasonable prospect of comfort and independence. But under the blessed institution of Tammany, the laws which govern ordinary human affairs are powerless. You begin with nothing, and in five or six years you can boast of your ten millions." The editorial ended with a sweeping indictment: "There is foul play somewhere."[6]

Meanwhile, *Harper's* kept up its barrage. Nast created one of his most inspired cartoons by translating into a compelling image the rumors that Tweed had bought his influence in the Democratic Party—using money from city taxpayers, of course. The caption read, "The 'Brains,'" and the car-toon showed Tweed's rotund body with his head replaced by a bag of money marked with a huge dollar sign where his facial features should have been.[7]

The harsh depictions angered Tweed. He was particularly unhappy with how Nast's cartoons were affecting the working class that represented his political base. Tweed told his cronies, "The people get used to seeing

THE "BRAINS"

One of Nast's most famous cartoons depicted "Boss"
Tweed with a rotund physique, a diamond stickpin,
and a bag of money instead of a face.

Reprinted from Harper's Weekly.

me in stripes, and by and by they grow to think I ought to be in prison."
Tweed knew that for his despotic methods to continue, Nast had to be
persuaded to end his crusade. He ordered his hired thugs to "stop them
damned pictures."[8]

First, Tweed sent a banker to tell Nast that local art benefactors so
admired his work that they were offering him $100,000—twice his annual
salary at *Harper's*—to travel to Europe and study art. Recognizing the offer as a bribe to get him out of New York, Nast declined. The banker then
upped the offer to $500,000. At this point, Nast ended the discussions,
vowing to put Tweed in jail. Before departing, the banker warned Nast,
"Dead artists don't draw." Not long after hearing that statement, Nast no-
ticed strangers loitering near his Manhattan home. So, for safety's sake, he
moved his family to suburban New Jersey.[9]

After the *New York Times* joined *Harper's* in the crusade, Tweed also tried to silence that publication. When *Times* publisher Henry J. Raymond died, his estate put a third of the company's shares on the market. In 1871, Tweed representatives tried to buy the shares, hoping to quiet the opposition. The new publisher, George Jones, rejected the offer and found another buyer. When the *Times* turned up the heat even further, the ring went to Jones and offered $1 million in exchange for the paper's silence. Jones refused, telling his readers, "The public may feel assured that the *Times* will not swerve from the policy which it has long pursued, but that it will hereafter be more persistent than ever in its efforts to bring about those political reforms which the people require and expect."[10]

Help from an Insider

The *Times* made good on that promise in July 1871 when it entered into a secret arrangement with James O'Brien, a former supporter of the Tweed Ring who'd served as city sheriff but held a grudge against the ring for not treating him as he thought he deserved. The vengeful defector obtained copies of hundreds of documents and gave them to the *Times*, which used the material in a blockbuster series that exposed a variety of criminal acts.

The first articles showed that the city was paying exorbitant rents for two dozen buildings purportedly used as National Guard armories. The *Times* reported not only that the city was paying $190,000 a year to rent buildings that went unused but also that the properties had a fair-market rental value of only $46,000. The *Times* reproduced documents that showed the profits were being funneled to James Ingersoll, Tweed's brother-in-law.[11]

Later and even more explosive stories focused on Tweed's fraudulent activities related to constructing the new county court house. In 1854, an architect estimated the building would cost $250,000. Anyone involved in construction expects cost overruns, but no one foresaw that by 1872 the price tag would have skyrocketed to an incredible $12.5 million—a startling fifty times the original estimate.

Every day for a month, the *Times* exposed one misappropriation after another. Ingersoll's bill to the city for three tables and forty chairs: $180,000. A month's work by a single carpenter: $360,000. Carpeting: $566,000. Light fixtures: $1.2 million. Cabinets: $2.8 million. Furniture: $5.7 million.[12]

The *Times* pulled no punches in either the terms it used to describe the greedy lawbreakers or the headlines it placed above the stories. The paper called the men "thieves of the ring," "swindlers," and the "city's plunderers." Headlines ranged from "Proofs of Theft" and "More Ring Villainy" to "The Betrayal of Public Liberties" and "How the Public Money Is Embezzled by the Tammany Rulers."[13]

Such hard-hitting news didn't remain a local story for long. Within days of the first revelation, the nation's newspapers began reprinting the stories, many of them adding words of praise for the *Times*. The *Philadelphia Press* said, "The wholesale robbery practiced by the Democratic government of New York city is being clearly shown us by the *Times*." The *Daily Advertiser* in Boston began its summary of the disclosures with approval, saying, "The *New York Times* is doing New York and the whole country excellent service by its bold warfare on Tammany." The *Providence Daily Journal* also weighed in on the positive side by commenting, "The exposure of the *Times* will have a wholesome effect upon State and Nation."[14]

New York newspapers that received substantial advertising revenue from the city responded to the *Times* investigation very differently. The *New York Herald* published little about the exposé except to criticize the *Times* as being "sensationalistic" and "over-excited." The *Herald* went on to accuse the *Times*, which generally supported the Republican Party, of being driven by the political harm the scandal would cause Democrats, saying, "We are led to the opinion that its case is vastly exaggerated." The *New York Tribune* questioned whether the *Times* had acted with professional integrity in publishing financial accounts that it had secured "surreptitiously."[15]

The strongest defense of Tweed and his allies came from the Democratic *New York World*, which reprinted none of the accusations. In fact, two days after the *Times* began its bruising exposé, the *World* thanked Tammany Hall for bringing "energy" and "order" to the city. The *World* also chastised *Times* editors for being "slanderers" who were overstating the negative aspects of the city's Democratic administration in an effort to divert attention away from the "monstrous corruption" being carried out by President Ulysses S. Grant and other Republicans in Washington.[16]

The *Times* responded to the rival papers by accusing them of being bought off by Tweed. It wrote, "We voluntarily rejected the City advertising when we found that it could only be had at the cost of gagging the paper. We demand to see a list of the amounts the city has paid to all newspapers during the last three years." To questions regarding the veracity of the material it reported, the *Times* challenged city officials to sue for libel if the information was incorrect. When no suit materialized, the *Times* argued that Tweed and his cronies had, thereby, admitted their guilt. "The Tweed Ring admits the truth of our charges and the accuracy of our figures," the newspaper said. "Let the public judge between us."[17]

Reaching the Masses

The only regret the august *Times* expressed was that it wasn't reaching the New York laboring class. So the paper took a big step toward speaking to that group when it printed 200,000 copies of a news supplement summarizing the charges against city officials. The extraordinary aspect of the special section was that, in hopes of reaching the city's huge immigrant population, it was written both in English and in German, marking the only time in the paper's history that it was produced in a foreign language.[18]

That *Times* special supplement notwithstanding, Thomas Nast's work in *Harper's Weekly* was more successful at reaching a broad readership. Although the *Times*'s work was unparalleled in its detail and documentation, articles weren't easily accessible to New Yorkers of lower educational levels. Indeed, the mind-numbing lists straight from account ledgers were difficult even for the most learned readers to comprehend. For many people, Nast's images, therefore, were much more effective because the cartoons translated the *Times's* complicated accounting and numerical evidence into indictments that appealed to a citizen's basic sense of right and wrong. Because he relied on images rather than huge blocks of words, Nast also was able to overcome the language difference and high illiteracy rate—and even people who didn't buy *Harper's* saw Nast's images being hawked by newsboys on street corners throughout the city.

Nast picked up the major themes in the *Times* charges and brought them to life in a way that only images could. An August 1871 *Times* editorial said, "What the public wants to know is *who stole the money?*" Nast's next cartoon showed Tweed and his chums standing in a circle, each pointing to the man to his right. The caption read, "'Who Stole the People's Money?'—Do tell *N.Y. Times.*"[19]

Triumph of the Press

As state and municipal elections approached in the fall of 1871, *Harper's* and the *Times* combined forces in an all-out campaign to remove the Tweed Ring from office. One Nast cartoon showed a crowd of laborers looking into a safe labeled "N.Y. Treasury" but finding only pieces of paper marked "debts," while behind the safe Tweed and his cohorts toasted each other with glasses of champagne. The caption asked, "What are you going to do about it?"[20]

Meanwhile, the journalistic crusade had aroused the New York citizenry to organize against the ring. When a public meeting was called to discuss the accusations that *Harper's* and the *Times* had made, 3,000 men and women packed the hall. A committee evolved from the meeting, charged with investigating city officials. The group's first act was to petition one of New York's few honest judges for a court order to prevent officials from spending any more public funds. Based on the cartoons and articles, the judge granted the request.

The journalists maintained their pressure. On the eve of the 1871 city election, Nast co-opted Tammany Hall's signature emblem to his

This dramatic cartoon distributed throughout the city of New York
on the eve of the 1871 city election depicted Tammany Hall as
a savage tiger and helped turn the public against the Tweed Ring.
Reprinted from Harper's Weekly.

purposes. For years, corrupt politicos had used a ferocious tiger as a
symbol of the Democratic administration's power. But now Nast transformed the mascot, the "Tammany Tiger," into a symbol of the Tweed
Ring raging out of control. In a double-page drawing distributed two
days before the election, Nast drew the tiger—with eyes glaring and
jaws distended—in the Roman Coliseum. The arena was strewn with
the mangled bodies that were labeled "the law," "the republic," and "the
ballot." While the savage tiger ripped the bodies apart, Tweed and his
comrades in crime, dressed in togas reminiscent of the final days of the
Roman Empire, looked on from their thrones high above the fray. The
caption asked New York voters, "The Tammany Tiger Loose—'What are
you going to do about it?'" The image was one of Nast's most influential.
Tweed's opponents reprinted it and distributed it broadly on election

day, taking particular care that the image was widely seen in the city's poorest neighborhoods.[21]

Harper's reinforced the message in a dramatic editorial printed next to the drawing. It began, "The contest in New York is that of the whole country. It involves a great deal more than the punishment of individual swindlers and the recovery of more or less money. The question is whether free institutions can rescue themselves from corruption." The editorial ended, "Forward, then, and God speed the right!"[22]

When the votes were counted, the ring had been swept from office. Tweed was the only Tammany candidate who won reelection, thanks to massive ballot fraud. Regardless of what illegal means Tweed had used, the victory was a hollow one because he was left without a single ally. Nast's next cartoon showed Tweed as a naked Roman soldier surrounded by crumbling columns—the empire had fallen.[23]

Late in 1871, Tweed was indicted on fraud-related charges and named conspirator in a multimillion-dollar civil suit filed by the citizens of New York. In 1873, he was sentenced to twelve years in prison. Several of his political accomplices were tried as well, although most of them fled to foreign countries.

Tweed's final years unfolded with a series of bizarre twists. In 1876, he bribed his way out of jail and escaped to Spain. His plan was foiled, however, because of his long-standing nemesis—Thomas Nast. American law enforcement officials, in hopes of locating Tweed, circulated an image of the fugitive to law-enforcement officials in countries around the world. The particular image they chose was one from *Harper's* that showed Tweed, dressed in horizontal stripes, grabbing two young boys and shaking the pennies from their pockets. Spanish officials didn't read English, but arrested Tweed based on Nast's image, assuming the fat man in prison stripes was a kidnapper.[24]

Spanish officials deported Tweed to New York, where he was returned to jail. The powerful kingpin didn't fare well behind bars. Because Tweed had grown grossly overweight from indulging in too much alcohol and rich food, his health went the way of his power. He died in 1878, at the age of fifty-five.

Based on this Thomas Nast cartoon, Spanish law enforcement officials captured and deported "Boss" Tweed.

Reprinted from Harper's Weekly.

The Journalistic Legacy

Harper's Weekly and the *New York Times* both received praise for the leading role they played—by combining compelling visual images with relentless verbal attacks—in destroying William Marcy Tweed and his band of disreputable rogues. Ministers across the country showered the publications with flowery blessings from the pulpit, and rising star Theodore Roosevelt was among the many elected officials who sought to enhance his political fortunes by claiming close allegiance to the press heroes.

For *Harper's*, one of the most eloquent commendations came from its closest competitor, the *Nation* magazine. The progressive publication wrote, "To Mr. Nast it is hardly possible to award too much praise. He has carried political illustrations to a pitch of excellence never before attained in this country." In particular, the magazine praised the power of the images to reach the masses, saying that Nast "brought the rascalities of the Ring home to hundreds of thousands who never would have looked at the figures and printed denunciations."[25]

Readers also expressed exuberant appreciation for the heroic feat the publications had accomplished on their behalf. During the two years that *Harper's* pummeled Tweed, its circulation tripled, rising from 100,000 to 300,000. In that same period, not only did the *Times* circulation increase 40 percent and the value of a share of its stock soar from $6,000 to $11,000, but the paper was set firmly on its course to becoming the country's most highly respected newspaper.

Far more important than what the destruction of the Tweed Ring meant for the individual publications, however, was what the victory said about American journalism. In a *Harper's Weekly* editorial praising not itself but the *Times*, the magazine wrote, "The significance of the political victory in New York can scarcely be exaggerated. The result is the triumph of a free and fearless press."[26]

The crushing defeat of the Tweed Ring showed the world that democracy could—when kindled by a free press—cleanse itself of an evil so pervasive that it infected all three official branches of government. History recorded an unequivocal example of the Fourth Estate fulfilling its role as watchdog, as well as a stunning example of the news media helping to shape history.

5

PUSHING AMERICA TOWARD AN INTERNATIONAL WAR

AT THE END OF THE NINETEENTH CENTURY, AMERICAN IMPERIALISM and journalistic dynamism came together to create one of the darkest moments in the history of the country's news media. The United States raced onto the global stage as a world power, eager to flex its muscles and expand its geographic and economic boundaries. Journalism bounded forward as well, driven by a desire to grab a larger slice of the growing population.

The changing news business attracted entrepreneurs who saw journalism as an exciting frontier worthy of their creative talents. Two publishing visionaries in particular dominated the era and ultimately changed the craft. After Joseph Pulitzer and William Randolph Hearst revolutionized journalism, their bitter rivalry gave birth to a brand of sensationalism known as yellow journalism. Its toxic formula—one part news to one part hype—fueled an infamous circulation war.

Yellow journalism took on a life of its own after Hearst began championing, mainly to boost circulation, the cause of Cuban rebels seeking to break the Spanish shackles that bound them to colonial status. As Hearst's campaign intensified and Pulitzer joined in, the Cuban crusade led to irresponsible behavior. The two men's newspapers engaged in a variety of unethical practices, from distortion of events to the dissemination of misinformation and the systematic manufacturing of news. The sensationalism that Hearst and Pulitzer practiced, especially their coverage of the 1898 explosion of the battleship USS *Maine*, created a high-pitched and bumptious jingoism that led to a national hunger for war. That public frenzy ultimately helped push the president of the United States to abandon his antiwar policy and thrust America into an international conflict with Spain that, in a less hysterical climate, could have been avoided.

The *New York Evening Post* was among the papers that, on the eve of the Spanish-American War, denounced the yellow journals as "public evils" and "a national disgrace." The *Post* wrote caustically, "Every one who knows anything about 'yellow journals' knows that everything they do and say is intended to promote sales. No one—absolutely no one— supposes a yellow journal cares five cents about the Cubans, the *Maine* victims, or anyone else."[1]

Joseph Pulitzer Pioneers a New Journalism

Born in Hungary in 1847, Joseph Pulitzer came to the United States as a mercenary who fought in the Civil War. While still in his teens, he drifted west and wrote for a paper in St. Louis. By working ferociously, the reporter—taunted by his competitors as "Joey the Jew"—was able to buy one bankrupt paper and merge it with another to create the *St. Louis Post-Dispatch*.

Beginning in 1878, Pulitzer pioneered a new style of newspapering that targeted the masses of Americans who'd previously been ignored by the staid sheets of the old order. According to Pulitzer, papers should be cheap, should be written clearly and concisely, and should crusade in the community interest. The facts Pulitzer highlighted on page one were to be gathered and written with an emphasis on accuracy unknown to his journalistic predecessors. He vowed, "Accuracy is to a newspaper what virtue is to a woman."[2]

Pulitzer led St. Louis in such reform initiatives as exposing fraud at the polls, cleansing the city of brothels, and putting an end to high profits and poor service by gas and streetcar monopolies. Pulitzer built the *Post-Dispatch* into a financial success that pushed the once-penniless immigrant's annual income to $200,000.

In 1883, Pulitzer broke into the biggest market in the country, targeting his *New York World* at the urban laboring class. The legendary "people's paper" was committed to being readable and serving the masses by exposing fraud and fighting public evils.

Pulitzer's innovative enterprise was controversial, as many erudite New Yorkers denounced the *World* as vulgar. They accused Pulitzer of introducing multi-column illustrations and dramatic headlines—such as "Baptized in Blood" and "A Brutal Negro Whips His Nephew to Death"—merely to shock readers. Pulitzer defended the techniques as essential to attracting people to his paper so they'd read his progressive editorials.[3]

Critics be damned, Pulitzer catapulted the *World* into the largest paper in the country. Its circulation soared from 15,000 when he bought it to 250,000 four years later. This growth was aided by innovative techniques. After Jules Verne's novel *Around the World in 80 Days* created a national stir, for example, Pulitzer sent "stunt girl" Nellie Bly on a global adventure to circle the world in seventy-two days. The pretty twenty-four-year-old's stunt was a legendary triumph.

Pulitzer also expanded the definition of news into the world of sports and revolutionized the American newspaper by introducing women's pages brimming with articles on social etiquette, home decorating, and romantic advice aimed at female readers—the target buyers for the department stores that became major advertisers in the *World*.

William Randolph Hearst Stupefies the World

Born in California in 1863, William Randolph Hearst began life very differently from Pulitzer. Hearst was the only son of an engineer who struck it rich in the silver mines of the Comstock Lode. George Hearst used his wealth to buy a seat in the US Senate, along with his son's admission into

Harvard. But young Hearst was an indifferent student who drank too much and spent more time playing with his pet alligator than studying. After sending his professors personalized chamber pots with each man's likeness drawn on the bottom, he was expelled.

Willie Hearst, who idolized Pulitzer, worked briefly on the *World* and then persuaded his father to let him edit the financially failing *San Francisco Examiner*. The young Hearst took to journalism like Babe Ruth took to baseball. With his father's deep pockets at his disposal, he hired the best staff money could buy and undertook ambitious and progressive crusades, including a campaign to lower city water rates.

Hearst, like Pulitzer, appealed to the masses, telling his reporters, "There's a gripman on the Powell Street line—he takes his car out at three o'clock in the morning, and while he's waiting for the signals he opens the morning paper. Think of him when you're writing a story. Don't write a single line he can't understand and wouldn't read." Hearst also was innovative, pushing sports and theater news to page one while hiring reporters exclusively to cover society and financial news.[4]

The publisher was a showman who set out to entertain and startle his readers. And when the actual news of the day was too dull, he *created* stupefying events. He paid a young couple to be married in a hot-air balloon and hired hunters to go into the mountains to trap a grizzly bear and bring it to San Francisco—while writing exclusive stories for the *Examiner*. Readers became so eager to see what Hearst would come up with next that the publisher kept the city at a carnival pitch.[5]

After eight years in Hearst's creative hands, the *Examiner* had become a popular and profitable business. Circulation had jumped from 12,000 to 200,000.

The War of the Newspapers

Willie Hearst was a privileged young man who, in 1895, at the age of thirty-two, realized his life's dream of competing with Joseph Pulitzer. Hearst's vehicle was the *New York Journal*, a scandal sheet that had been nicknamed "the chambermaid's delight." Pouring his father's money into

The *New York World*'s mindless and impudent cartoon
character Yellow Kid has remained a symbol of
sensationalistic journalism for more than a century.
Reprinted from the New York World.

the paper, Hearst dropped the price from two cents to one, introduced
color printing, and lured advertisers away from the *World*.

Within a year, the *Journal* ranked as New York's second largest paper, trailing only the *World*. Hearst and Pulitzer then became engaged in
the most notorious newspaper war in history. Editors filled their pages
with emotion-packed stories that set out not merely to inform but also to
entertain and shock.

The term "yellow journalism" evolved from a battle between the publishing titans. *World* artist Richard Outcault created a cartoon featuring tenement dwellers who lampooned such upper-class fads as golf matches and dog shows. The central character in each drawing was a grinning, snaggle-toothed boy who wore a bright yellow nightshirt that earned him the nickname Yellow Kid. Hearst wooed Outcault away from the *Journal*, but Pulitzer had another artist continue to draw the popular cartoon. So when the newspaper war heated up, both publishers hired boys to plaster lampposts with posters featuring the cartoon character. The mascot—impudent, mindless, and with a manic gleam in his eye—came to represent the sensationalism that defined the era, and the concept of yellow journalism was born.

Among Hearst's innovations was hiring Annie Laurie as the first "sob sister" who stressed the tragic and emotional side of stories. Sent to investigate the city hospital, the young woman dressed in shabby clothes and intentionally collapsed on the street. Taken to the hospital, she was pawed by lustful interns who gave her nothing but hot water and mustard. Laurie's front-page exposé shook up the hospital and led to the head physician being fired. In later stories, Laurie moved to Utah and lived with the Mormons to describe polygamy and interviewed prostitutes to offer readers a window into the underbelly of urban life.

By 1897, Hearst had pushed the *Journal*'s daily circulation to 500,000, within striking distance of the *World*'s 600,000. It was in this atmosphere of scrambling for the hottest scoop of the day that the two papers focused on the events that helped thrust the nation full tilt into international warfare.

The Battleground Shifts to Cuba

As the Industrial Revolution evolved, the United States grew eager to expand its boundaries and enlarge its economic markets. Many imperialistic eyes turned south. By 1895, Cuban rebels had grown tired of their colonial status and were striking out at Spanish economic interests by wrecking trains and burning sugar plantations.

When Hearst heard about the ragged rebels, the *Journal* heralded them as—*voilà!*—courageous freedom fighters struggling against Spanish oppressors. Hearst's praise conflicted with the US State Department's assessment, which regarded the insurgents as insignificant because they didn't control even one city of any size. But Hearst, who liked to reduce complex phenomena to simple terms, cast the Cuban rebels as patriotic heroes thirsting for liberty. He told readers, "Their proceedings have been animated by the same fearless spirit that inspired the patriot fathers who sat in Philadelphia on the 4th of July, 1776."[6]

To champion the Cuban cause, Hearst painted a portrait of Spanish brutality. One article said, "The Spaniards stab to death all Cubans who come under their power." Another described Spanish soldiers dragging people from a hospital and bayoneting them to death. *Journal* readers found the accounts compelling, though the stories weren't based on the firsthand observations of correspondents but on statements from partisan Cubans who'd recently fled to the United States.[7]

Pulitzer initially opposed American involvement in Cuba, but he soon shifted to supporting it. Years later he admitted that the motivation for his change of heart had been to increase his paper's circulation.[8]

In 1896, Hearst sent reporter Richard Harding Davis and artist Frederic Remington to Cuba. Remington initially said the activities taking place there didn't deserve the coverage Hearst wanted to give them. According to legend, the artist sent Hearst a telegram reading, "Everything is quiet. There is no trouble here. There will be no war. I wish to return." The publisher is said to have replied, "You furnish the pictures and I'll furnish the war." Although historians question whether this verbal exchange ever took place, it accurately captures Hearst's style during the era.[9]

The reporter and artist soon produced the kind of journalism their boss demanded. Davis wrote that Spanish officers had boarded an American ship anchored off the Cuban coast and forced three pretty young Cuban women to submit to strip searches. Spread across five columns was a Remington drawing that showed Spanish officers leering at a young woman's naked body as she stood helpless on deck. The story set off a political firestorm. Members of Congress introduced resolu-

Frederic Remington's drawing of Spanish officers
forcing young women to submit to strip searches helped
propel the United States toward war with Spain.
Reprinted from the New York Journal.

tions denouncing the brutish Spanish officers and praising the *Journal*
for bringing the incident to light. Disgruntled at being scooped, the
World tracked down the women and quoted them as saying they'd been
searched by a female officer in the privacy of a cabin—not by male officers on the deck of the ship.[10]

Although the *World* didn't manufacture stories with the abandon the
Journal did, Pulitzer also sent correspondents to Cuba and published
sensational reports. One announced, "Old men and little boys were cut
down and their bodies fed to the dogs," and another said, "The Spanish
soldiers habitually cut off the ears of the Cuban dead and retain them as
trophies."[11]

The lurid coverage reaped the benefits the dueling papers had hoped for. By 1897, Pulitzer's circulation had climbed to 800,000 and Hearst's to 700,000. What's more, the *World's* and *Journal's* circulation figures and resources far surpassed those of any other paper in the country, so hundreds of small papers reprinted their stories—hyperbole and all.

Coverage of the era ranks as a disgraceful example of journalistic distortion. Cuban officials kept reporters away from the action because they wanted to control how the world perceived the situation. Reporters cooperated because they preferred to trade the primitive conditions of the jungle for Havana's palatial Inglaterra Hotel, complete with sterling silver serving trays and exotic Spanish delicacies. So each day, reporters gathered around a rebel spokesman who fed them "eyewitness reports."

The accounts aroused so much public attention that members of the US Congress quoted from the *Journal* and *World* in floor debates concerning the Cuban insurrection. These hawkish legislators knew the grisly details would win support in Washington, just as they were selling papers on street corners.[12]

"Remember the *Maine!*"

News coverage of the Cuban rebels from 1895 to 1898 primed the weapons for war, and coverage of the USS *Maine* disaster pulled the trigger. Officials had anchored the battleship in Havana Harbor as a reminder that the United States was watching the Cuban conflict because of American business interests there. On February 15, 1898, the *Maine* exploded, killing 260 US sailors.

The *Journal* and *World* exploited the American public's horror and anger to create warmongering coverage that still stands today as the epitome of the news media at their most truthless. Screaming headlines, misleading drawings, and shrill editorials blamed the Spanish government and demanded that the United States declare war.

In reality, it was preposterous to suggest that Spain had destroyed the *Maine*. Spanish officials had desperately avoided bringing the United States into their conflict with Cuba because they knew the American Navy

Although William Randolph Hearst immediately proclaimed
the 1898 destruction of the USS *Maine* "The Work of an Enemy,"
most experts attribute the tragedy to an explosion aboard the ship.

Reprinted from the New York Journal.

would crush theirs. The *Maine* disaster was, in fact, the worst setback Spain could have suffered.

The cause of the explosion has never been definitively determined, but the most logical explanation is that the ship blew up accidentally. The *Maine* was part of the first generation of coal-powered warships with their coal bunkers located near the ship's magazines. Heat generated in the bunkers could have ignited the magazines and caused the ship to explode. During the previous year, a dozen such incidents had been reported on American ships.

Regardless of who or what was responsible for the *Maine* tragedy, Hearst pulled out all the stops. The most memorable of the *Journal's* front pages remains a textbook example of distortion. The banner headline read "Destruction of the War Ship *Maine* Was the Work of an Enemy." Below the incendiary headline, Hearst ran a drawing of a ship with cables leading from a submerged mine to a Spanish fortress on shore—a flight of fancy that many readers undoubtedly accepted as fact. Six headlines on page one carried an eye-popping "$50,000!" as the reward the *Journal* offered for evidence related to "the crime."[13]

The shrieking headlines for the next week testify that truth was the 261st casualty of the explosion—"The War Ship *Maine* Was Split in Two by an Enemy's Secret Infernal Machine," "War! Sure! *Maine* Destroyed by Spanish," "The Whole Country Thrills with War Fever."[14]

Hearst didn't confine his warmongering to the headlines. He introduced a "War with Spain" card game, with the object being to sink Spanish ships, and he ordered his reporters in Havana to skulk about the city at night plastering walls with posters that read "Remember the *Maine!*"[15]

Hearst's sensational coverage paid off. Three days after the explosion, the *Journal* became the first paper in American history to surpass the 1 million circulation mark—and the *World*.[16]

Although Pulitzer wasn't as willing as Hearst was to sacrifice truth for circulation growth, he also pushed hard for war. Immediately after the *Maine* explosion, the *World* expressed skepticism that foul play had destroyed the ship by placing a question mark at the end of its first headline: "*Maine* Explosion Caused by Bomb or Torpedo?" The paper highlighted President William McKinley's belief that the explosion had been the result of the ship's magazines catching fire. But the *World* didn't remain skeptical for long. Four days after the disaster, with his rival at the *Journal* insisting that the Spanish had killed the American sailors, Pulitzer announced the findings of his own investigators. Indeed, Pulitzer went even further than Hearst, not only announcing that the Spanish had destroyed the *Maine* but also crediting that discovery to his own paper. A page-one headline boasted "*World*'s News of the Evidence of a Mine Under the *Maine* Changes the Feeling Throughout the Country." Pulitzer adopted a tough stance on the editorial page as well, stating, "Two hundred and sixty of our brave sailors have been hurled to sudden and awful death. What more is needed? Is there no limit to our patience?"[17]

Overpowering the President

The most significant impact of the campaign wasn't on readers but on the country's commander in chief. The *Journal* and *World* whipped public fury to such a fever pitch that the words initially uttered by voices of reason were drowned out by the din of screaming headlines.

Both papers ridiculed McKinley's measured statement that the *Maine* explosion had been an accident. Hearst called the president's peace stance "cowardly" and dictated by Wall Street financiers who feared that war might upset the stock market. The *World* also pushed McKinley, writing, "The army is ready. The navy is ready. The people are ready. And now the President says 'Wait!'—Wait for what?"[18]

McKinley judiciously refused to act until navy investigators studied the remains of the ship. Hearst, in contrast, had no intention of being judicious. Three weeks before the report was released, he quoted anonymous sources as stating definitively, "The disaster in Havana harbor was due to the explosion of a submarine mine. This mine was planted by officials of the Spanish Government."[19]

When the navy report was released in early April, it concluded that a mine had destroyed the *Maine*. The findings were inconclusive, however, because investigators weren't able to determine who'd placed the mine in the harbor. Unstated was the fact that navy officials hadn't even considered the possibility that the ship's design had been at fault. For navy officers, admitting that they might have ignored a design flaw that had caused a battleship to blow up would have made this the most embarrassing incident in the history of the US Navy.

When McKinley, not a dynamic leader, continued to call for "deliberate consideration," the *Journal* and *World* turned up the heat. Hearst gave prominent placement to stories about McKinley's effigy being hanged and burned. Hearst also sent reporters to interview the mothers of the dead sailors, quoting one as saying, "How would President McKinley have felt, I wonder, if he had had a son on the *Maine* murdered as was my little boy?" Pulitzer was less emotional but no less insistent, telling McKinley, "Stop deliberating and proceed to action."[20]

Amid such statements from a war-hungry press, it became increasingly difficult to continue diplomatic efforts. McKinley's popularity waned as public sentiment mounted for war. McKinley felt relentless pressure as the press frenzy swept across the nation. The entire country seemed to be seething under the daily onslaught of misinformation and sensationalism. The president clearly lacked the personal charisma to sway public opinion in such a high-pitched environment.

Spanish officials made a determined bid for peace, giving indications that they were willing to compromise in the hope of reaching an amicable settlement. When the United States demanded that Spain abandon its controversial policy of separating noncombatants from the rebels, for example, Spain agreed. But it was too late for concessions. War fever had become so pervasive that rational thinking no longer played a role.

To survive politically and stabilize the nation, McKinley finally caved in to the pressure and adopted a prowar stance. The might of the Fourth Estate had forced the president of the United States to capitulate on a matter of grave importance. On April 19, the US Senate passed a war resolution by a vote of forty-two to thirty-five.[21]

On the Battlefront

After war was declared, Hearst and Pulitzer continued to maintain a hysterical pitch. Symbolic of Hearst's attitude was the question he began posing to his readers on the upper corners of page one: "How do you like the *Journal's* war?"[22]

Hearst assembled a journalistic armada by chartering ten ships to shuttle news stories from Havana to the nearest telegraph station in Key West, then selling as many as forty editions a day on the streets of New York during the height of hostilities. Unable to contain his zeal, Hearst hired a luxury steamer for himself and sailed for the war zone with a lightweight printing press that let him publish a newspaper on Cuban soil. He claimed the *Journal-Examiner* was for the benefit of American soldiers fighting in the field, but the real purpose of the Cuban edition was to reap favorable publicity back home.[23]

The master showman received additional positive press when he set up a trap to catch Pulitzer at blatant plagiarism. That is, Hearst published a totally fallacious item that stated, "Colonel Reflipe W. Thenuz, an Austrian artillerist of European renown, who, with Colonel Ordonez, was defending the land batteries of Aguadores was so badly wounded that he has since died." The *World* took the bait and the next day published a slightly rewritten version of the item, saying, "Col. R.W. Thenuz, an Austrian artillerist, well known throughout Europe, who, with Col. Ordonez, was defending the land batteries of Aguadores, was so badly wounded in the bombardment of Monday that he has since died. He performed many acts of conspicuous gallantry."[24]

The *Journal* pounced on the *World*, announcing that Colonel Thenuz had never existed and then gloating about how it had caught the *World* in an embarrassing journalistic faux pas. Thrilled with the success of his trickery, Hearst ran letters from editors condemning the *World* for plagiarism and published a tongue-in-cheek "In Memoriam" poem honoring the fictitious colonel. Refusing to allow the prank to die, Hearst proposed building a monument to the colonel. Meanwhile, the humiliated *World* had no choice but to maintain a painful silence.[25]

Hearst had even more fun when he strapped on a pistol and covered the war firsthand—often on horseback. In one incident, the publisher and reporter James Creelman were double-teaming the same battle when a bullet struck Creelman in the arm. The reporter later recalled waking up in a hospital to see Hearst, "his face radiant with enthusiasm," as he clutched his notebook. "'I'm sorry you're hurt,' said Hearst. 'But wasn't it a splendid fight? We beat every paper in the world.'" The story about the battle carried only Hearst's byline.[26]

American soldiers and sailors weren't having nearly as much fun. US military forces suffered badly from lack of experience and poor planning. Although the one-sided war lasted only four months, the toll in American lives surpassed 5,000. At war's end, Spain granted Cuba its independence and ceded the Philippines, Guam, and Puerto Rico to the United States.

From Hearst's point of view, the war was a glorious success. Not only did the United States thrash Spain, but Hearst also achieved the massive circulation he'd dreamed of. By August 1898, when the fighting ended, the *Journal* and *World* both were claiming figures of 1.25 million.

Legacy of Shame

The Spanish-American War probably could have been avoided, as the Spanish gave clear signals they were eager to negotiate. But the decision to go to war wasn't made entirely by politicians. For it was, more than any American conflict before or since, a war fueled by the news media. If Hearst, with his tawdry flair for publicity and agitation, hadn't filled his pages with sensational and misleading stories—making the explosion of the *Maine* a symbol of Spanish treachery, pushing McKinley to abandon his antiwar stance, and whipping the public into such a war frenzy that senators no longer acted on the basis of reason but for political survival—there may have been no war.

Hearst later yearned to become president of the United States. Though he failed in that effort, he served in the US Congress and built a huge publishing empire. When he died in 1951, Hearst left assets of $160 million and a legacy of accomplishment overshadowed by shame.

Numerous participants in and scholars of the Spanish-American War have attributed much of the blame for the conflict to Hearst. Spanish Commander Valeriano Weyler insisted the catalyst was neither Spanish oppression nor Cuban rebellion, saying, "The American newspapers are responsible." Spanish Prime Minister Canovas del Castillo agreed, telling an American reporter, "The newspapers of your country seem to be more powerful than the government." John Winkler was among the many historians who have blamed Hearst for the war, saying, "The Spanish-American War came as close to being a 'one-man war' as any conflict in our history." Joseph Wisan, who wrote a book about the press during the Cuban crisis, concluded, "The Spanish-American War would not have occurred had not the appearance of Hearst in New York journalism precipitated a bitter battle for newspaper circulation." Wisan continued, "The *Journal* and *World* used Cuba to achieve their prime purpose—an increase in circulation."[27]

Statements regarding Hearst provoking the war also came from the egotist himself. His editorial-page editor wrote in his memoirs, "Hearst was accustomed to referring to the war, in company with the staff, as 'our war.'" The publisher summarized his own reflections on the war—and the mighty power of the news media more generally—in an editorial published in the *Journal* a month after the war ended. Hearst boasted,

> The newspaper is the greatest force in civilization.
>
> Under republican government, newspapers form and express public opinion.
>
> They suggest and control legislation.
>
> They declare wars . . . The newspapers control the nation.[28]

6

ACHIEVING REFORM
BY MUCKRAKING

DURING THE SECOND HALF OF THE NINETEENTH CENTURY, THE American economy experienced an unprecedented orgy of expansion. Propelled by new inventions that made American offices and factories the most efficient operations in the history of the world, business and industry raced into the future at breakneck speed. Production figures doubled and redoubled, foreign exports soared, and the number of factories boggled the mind. America, fueled by unbridled genius and energy, established itself as the nation of the future.

In politics, the Republican Party charged mightily onward to use the country's abundant resources, human as well as material, to transform the United States into an industrial giant, while protecting American business from foreign interference. Prosperity lay in adopting laissez-faire policies—which often meant adopting no policies whatsoever—while building more railroads, digging more mines, and increasing factory production by finding a new man who worked faster than the previous one.

At the same time, however, the country had evolved into one that the Founding Fathers wouldn't have claimed. For the world's democratic stronghold had been "let go," turned into a nation *of* the corporation, *by* the corporation, and *for* the corporation. Though industrialists and investors made enormous profits, the economic boom largely bypassed the common man. In particular, the throngs of new immigrants, drawn by the radiance of America's promise, were crowded into dark factories and foul slums. The nation founded on the bedrock concept of equality had deteriorated into a society dominated by a few gluttonously rich robber barons who feasted on life's pleasures while the teeming masses struggled to stave off starvation. The pungent odor of corruption had spread into politics as well; in government at all levels, the wholesale flouting of laws and the sprawling spoils systems rivaled those of the infamous Boss Tweed in New York some thirty years earlier.

But then, at the moment of greatest need, the Fourth Estate stepped into the fray. Armed with literary talent and investigative skill, reform-minded journalists boldly accused the nation of auctioning off its birthright for private gain. These progressive warriors exposed a stunning variety of crimes against democracy. They reported the rampant misdeeds of greedy industrialists and grafting politicians—from the local level all the way to the US Senate—to show how the scofflaws had climbed to success by being ruthless and lawless. Other reporters revealed the vast differences between the fraudulent claims of patent medicines and the actual contents of the products, and still others exposed the unsanitary techniques used in preparing foods.

To the delight of their readers, the reporters provoked political, industrial, and social change by describing the sordid details to create a new style of magazine writing that was gripping—office clerks and shop girls never knew business and politics could be so *interesting*. Fortunately for those relatively low-paid workers, technological advances in printing and paper production allowed magazines to lower their prices to an affordable level. Also contributing to the rise of the magazine as America's first truly national medium were the country's rapid growth—the population doubled between 1880 and 1900—and the advent of advertising as an institution standing on the shoulders of the plethora of new products and new competition. Responding to these forces, popular magazines vied for attention with vivid and compelling exposés. In the early years of the new century, a dozen national publications boasted a combined monthly circulation of 3 million.[1]

The term that ultimately came to define this journalistic phenomenon was coined by President Theodore Roosevelt, who led the larger reform movement that the journalists helped to spark. During the Progressive Era, government attempted to reassert its control of business through myriad new agencies and regulations. The youthful and buoyant Roosevelt supported journalistic reform, but, in one volatile moment, he lashed out at the crusaders for finding nothing good about society but looking constantly at the negative elements—as if *raking muck*. The epithet took hold, and the golden age of reform journalism became known as *muckraking*.[2]

The contributions that progressive journalists made to this country in the early twentieth century established a high-water mark that remains unsurpassed—in both breadth and intensity—in the epic drama of how the news media have shaped American history.

Attacking Municipal Corruption

Lincoln Steffens, an intellectual who wore spectacles and a string tie, is widely acknowledged as the first muckraker. After studying at the finest universities in the United States and Europe, Steffens joined the *New York Evening Post*, covering Wall Street and city police. Ten years later, in 1902, he switched to *McClure's*, the greatest of the muckraking journals.

Steffens then undertook the project that would make him a journalistic icon—investigating the state of municipal government in the United States. For three years, he visited the country's largest cities to conduct detailed studies, first digging through public documents and then interviewing city officials.

He designed his first article, "Tweed Days in St. Louis," as a wake-up call to alert the American public to the immorality driving city officials throughout the country. Steffens's exposé of St. Louis politics and government reported that city aldermen had crafted a system of governance based on bribery and corruption. In the October 1902 article, Steffens said of St. Louis, "Taking but slight and always selfish interest in the public councils, the big men misused politics." He went on to describe how the wrongdoing spread, writing, "The riff-raff, catching the smell of corruption, rushed into the Municipal Assembly, drove out the remaining respectable men, and sold the city—its streets, its wharves, its markets, and all that it had—to the now greedy business men and bribers." Steffens ended with a bitter tone, "When the leading men began to devour their own city, the herd rushed into the trough and fed also."[3]

Steffens did more than expose. As a result of his blockbuster article, St. Louis District Attorney Joseph Folk gained the public support he needed to prosecute dozens of city officials for a variety of offenses, from stuffing the ballot box to padding contracts. Folk was so successful, in fact, that in 1904 he was elected governor of Missouri. And all the time he continued to credit Steffens for building the popular support that allowed him to reform the city and then the state government.[4]

After publishing the St. Louis article, Steffens moved on to other cities, creating blockbuster articles that exposed wrongdoing in Minneapolis, Pittsburgh, Philadelphia, Chicago, and New York. Steffens then moved on to state governments, reporting the illegal practices among government officials in Missouri, Illinois, Rhode Island, and New Jersey.[5]

Contemporary newspapers lauded Steffens's series. The *St. Paul Pioneer Press* in Minnesota praised the reporter's "keen deductions," and the *Emporia Gazette* in Kansas wrote, "Mr. Steffens has made an important step in the scientific study of government in America. This work should be in every social and economic library, for it is a work of real scientific importance."[6]

The most tangible legacy of Steffens's journalistic work, published as a book titled *The Shame of the Cities*, was that it helped usher in the city-manager form of government. After Steffens revealed the corruption that inevitably occurred when elected politicians ran local government, cities such as Toledo, Cleveland, and Detroit opted to hire professional administrators who had training and experience in operating large organizations. And these men, in turn, reduced the political spoils system by requiring that job applicants possess formal credentials and pass standardized tests.[7]

After her blockbuster exposé of Standard Oil, Ida Minerva Tarbell was proclaimed the Terror of the Trusts, "a modern-day Joan of Arc," and the Queen of the Muckrakers. *Courtesy of the Library of Congress.*

Busting the Trusts

S. S. McClure, the Irish immigrant who founded the leading muckraking magazine, decided to tackle the enormous power of corporations by focusing on a single trust and tracing its history, leaders, and inner workings. For his example, McClure chose Standard Oil, which was supplying an astounding 90 percent of the oil to light American homes and power American factories. For the reporter, he selected a serious-minded woman who looked like a schoolmistress.

Born in the oil region of northwestern Pennsylvania, Ida Tarbell grew up surrounded by derricks, tanks, and pipelines, and her father and brother earned their livelihoods in refining. After receiving her bachelor's and master's degrees, Tarbell wrote for *Chautauquan* magazine on such progressive subjects as education and public health. She later specialized in biographies, writing a book about a female leader of the French Revolution and articles on Napoleon Bonaparte and Abraham Lincoln.

In the first installment of her monumental series "History of the Standard Oil Company," which began in the November 1902 issue of *McClure's*, Tarbell described how the trust had achieved its position through

John D. Rockefeller's shrewd and ruthless approach to competition. She revealed that he'd created a system of secret—and illegal—agreements with selected railroads to give him preferential rates. Under the contracts, Rockefeller transported his oil exclusively via those railroads in exchange for rates equal to half what his competitors paid. The discount made it impossible for other companies to compete with Standard Oil, driving the smaller operations out of business.[8]

Though the articles were packed with financial information, Tarbell's abundant anecdotes made compelling reading. She told, for example, of a Cleveland refinery owner whose bereaved widow went to Rockefeller and begged him for financial advice so she could feed her three children. Rockefeller said he'd help her and then paid her $79,000 for a refinery worth $200,000. In another article, Tarbell described how Standard Oil officials paid the chief mechanic at a competing refinery to stoke the fire in a tank to such a high temperature that the safety valve blew off and thousands of barrels of oil were lost. She also told how Rockefeller's henchmen had paid the most valued employee of a competing East Coast refinery to move to California, forcing the company out of business.[9]

Publications throughout the country lauded Tarbell's work. The *Chicago Inter Ocean* called her series "absorbing," and the *Louisville Courier-Journal* wrote, "This series of impartial narration has attracted wide attention, not only for the subject-matter, but for the vividness with which the light is thrown upon one of the most corroding ulcers of modern times."[10]

Enthusiasm among readers was so great that the series, initially scheduled for three articles, was expanded to eighteen. By the time the stories ended in October 1904, Tarbell was being hailed as one of the most courageous women in American history—"a modern-day Joan of Arc," the Terror of the Trusts, and the Queen of the Muckrakers.

Tarbell's series, which was credited with boosting *McClure's* circulation from 350,000 to 500,000, had profound impact on public policy. The first tangible result came in 1906 when Congress passed the Hepburn Act, making the penalties for preferential arrangements by railroads so severe that the practice quickly ceased. Then, after federal grand juries indicted Standard Oil on fraud charges, the US Supreme Court ruled in 1911 that Standard Oil was violating the Sherman Anti-Trust Act. The High Court then forced the mammoth monopoly to dissolve to form thirty-eight smaller companies.[11]

Although Rockefeller avoided going to jail, the series damaged his image so severely that he hired the country's first publicity man, Ivy Lee, to improve his tarnished reputation. When the most renowned of the robber barons began making huge contributions to charities, the public again credited Tarbell, thanking her for opening the Rockefeller purse to the common good.

Most important, the series fulfilled McClure's goal of showing the public not only that many big businesses were corrupt but also that the Fourth Estate could force them to abide by the law. Tarbell's journalistic triumph encouraged other muckrakers to investigate other monopolies. *McClure's* and *The Arena* exposed the railroads, and *Cosmopolitan* tackled the telephone and telegraph companies. *Hampton's* focused on the mining and sugar trusts, *Collier's* on liquor interests, *Everybody's* on the beef trust.[12]

Awakening the Public to Dangerous Foods and Drugs

Another issue that attracted the attention of muckraking journalists was the poor quality of the food and medicine America was consuming. Because refrigerated railroad cars were now speeding perishable products hundreds of miles, the public was consuming, for the first time, food preservatives with such strange names as "borax" and "benzoate." Drugs were of concern as well. The health field was overrun with quacks who were selling patent medicines to the American public to the tune of $100 million a year. Some products promised to cure cancer, others to curb addiction to tobacco, and still others to enlarge female breasts. Most users had no idea that many soothing syrups contained alcohol or were laced with morphine. In reality, the widely used products were destroying the nation's health while transforming unsuspecting men, women, and children into drug addicts.

The most spectacular assault on the food industry began after the newspaper *Appeal to Reason* made a tantalizing offer to an idealistic young writer named Upton Sinclair. The paper would pay him $500 to live among Chicago stockyard workers while writing a series of articles describing the conditions he found there. Sinclair accepted the Socialist weekly's offer and spent seven weeks talking with meatpacking workers and their families, while also interviewing plant managers, doctors, lawyers, and social workers.

After the first installment appeared in February 1905, it was clear that the food industry would never be the same. For Sinclair wrote his series, "The Jungle," with the fire of a man who'd witnessed human suffering at its most base level. In one shocking revelation, Sinclair reported that exhausted workers sometimes fell into the huge vats where meat was being canned—which meant that consumers were unknowingly eating human flesh. Sinclair wrote, "For the men who worked in tankrooms full of steam, their peculiar trouble was that they fell into the vats; and when they were fished out, there was never enough of them left to be worth exhibiting. Sometimes they would be overlooked for days, till all but the bones of them had gone out to the world."[13]

Some critics argued that Sinclair's series wasn't muckraking because it was written as fiction, but the author defended his work as journalism because it was based on intensive reporting. Sinclair said, "'The Jungle' will stand the severest test—it is as authoritative as if it were a statistical compilation." Readers agreed with Sinclair rather than his critics, as have the generations of students who've read the series in book form. In one history of the muckrakers, Louis Filler wrote, "'The Jungle,' from the moment it began to appear in the *Appeal*, was recognizably the literary sensation of the time."[14]

One reader was President Roosevelt. After completing the series, he sent his own agents to Chicago to confirm what Sinclair had written. And confirm they did. The agents' words weren't as graceful as Sinclair's, but they told a strikingly similar story.[15]

The leader of the muckraking campaign against drugs was *Ladies' Home Journal*. Editor Edward Bok fired the first salvo in 1904 by urging

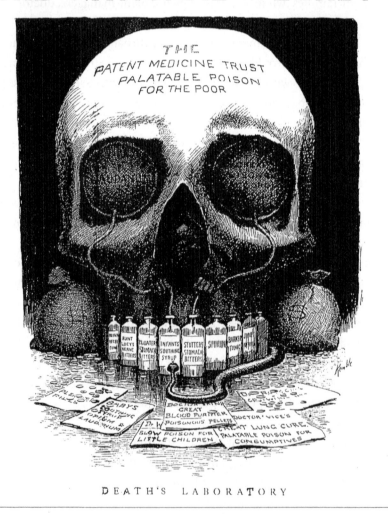

A ghoulish drawing from *Collier's* magazine came to symbolize
the deadly patent medicine fraud at the turn of the century.

readers to boycott patent medicines. "A mother who would hold up her hands in holy horror at the thought of her child drinking a glass of beer, which contains from two to five per cent alcohol, gives to that child with her own hands a patent medicine that contains from seventeen to forty-four per cent alcohol—to say nothing of opium and cocaine!"[16]

Among the other magazines joining the crusade was *Collier's*, which boldly announced it would no longer accept ads from patent medicine companies. This was a daring step for any magazine to take, as publications of the era bulged with page after page of ads promoting these products and providing them with a major source of revenue. Nevertheless, the list of magazines that ultimately were willing to make the sacrifice included not only *Collier's* and *Ladies' Home Journal* but also *McClure's*, *Good Housekeeping*, the *Saturday Evening Post*, and *Everybody's*. The decision had serious financial consequences. A year after *Collier's* purged patent medicine ads from its pages, the magazine announced, "We spoke out about patent medicines, and dropped $80,000 in a year."[17]

Like *Harper's Weekly* during its campaign against Boss Tweed, *Collier's* recognized the power of images. The magazine printed a full-page cartoon titled "Death's Laboratory" that became a symbol of the hollow promises and deadly results of drug fraud. Dominating the drawing was a skull branded with the words "The Patent Medicine Trust—Palatable Poison for the Poor." The skull's teeth were bottles of patent medicine, and its cheeks were bags of money. Papers strewn in front of the skull read "Slow Poison for Little Children" and "Baby's Soothing Syrup—Opium and Laudanum."[18]

By 1906, *Ladies' Home Journal* believed the muckrakers had raised public awareness to the point that it could take proactive measures. Bok printed "An Act to Regulate the Manufacture and Sale of 'Patent' Medicines," urging readers to clip out the simulated bill and send it to their congressmen in Washington. The editor who'd initiated the crusade two years earlier now insisted, "This and other magazines have done their parts: the remedy of the fearful evil they have laid bare is in the hands of the people: in *your* hands. The question is: Will *you*, now, do your part?"[19]

Readers flooded Washington with thousands of copies of the sample bill along with letters demanding that the government protect consumers from unsafe drugs. In his annual message to Congress, President Roosevelt advocated a law regulating food as well as drugs. Senators then introduced such legislation, along with a bill requiring inspection of meat. Propelled by public indignation, Congress passed the Pure Food and Drug Act, requiring medicines to be analyzed and approved by the Department of Agriculture, and the Meat Inspection Act, requiring meat to be examined before it was sold. Respected publications such as the *New York Times* joined prominent historians in calling the laws direct products of muckraking.[20]

Exposing "Treason" in the US Senate

In the early years of the twentieth century, the upper house of Congress was widely known as the most reactionary body in America. Elected by state legislatures rather than directly by the people, senators were political puppets who were bought and paid for by Standard Oil and other corporations driving the national economy.

As muckraking rose to its zenith, the conservative nature of the Senate—widely known as the "millionaire's club"—stood in stark contrast to the reform movement sweeping the country. The senators opposed each and every initiative the muckrakers championed. Only when public sentiment grew to leviathan proportions—as when the muckrakers agitated for regulation of patent medicines—did progressive measures break through the sturdy walls of the Senate.[21]

The man who ultimately challenged this institution was no minion himself. William Randolph Hearst, the bad boy of American journalism, bought *Cosmopolitan* magazine in 1906 and poured money into it. To conduct his most important exposé, Hearst chose a writer named David Graham Phillips.

The series debuted in March 1906, beginning, "The treason of the Senate! Treason is a strong word, but not too strong, rather too weak, to characterize the situation in which the Senate is the eager, resourceful, indefatigable agent of interests as hostile to the American people as any invading army could be, and vastly more dangerous."[22]

That first article focused on New York's senators. Chauncey M. Depew was described as the "archetype of the sleek, self-satisfied American opportunist in politics" and accused of receiving $50,000 a year from dozens of corporations in return for political favors. Of Thomas Collier Platt, the story said he had a "long and unbroken record of treachery to the people in legislation of privilege and plunder."[23]

The charges reverberated throughout the country, and the series was a runaway success. "Glory Hallelujah!" cried one letter praising *Cosmopolitan*'s courage and service to the public. The writer continued, "You have found a David who is able and willing to attack this Goliath of a Senate."[24]

In later installments, Phillips documented how senator after senator—Arthur Pue Gorman of Maryland, Joseph Weldon Bailey of Texas, Stephen Benton Elkins of West Virginia—played leading roles in an enormous conspiracy to circumvent the needs of the people. Phillips eventually documented that corporations controlled seventy-five of the ninety senators.[25]

The series provoked vehement protests and denunciations from the accused. Hearst and Phillips both received hundreds of threatening letters and were repeatedly castigated on the Senate floor. But "The Treason of the Senate" continued, as did public interest. In June, *Cosmopolitan* boasted that its circulation had more than doubled since the series had begun three months earlier, jumping from 200,000 to 450,000.[26]

Phillips wasn't satisfied, though, simply to create a sensation or ensure the defeat of individual men, as he argued that the larger problem was senators being selected by their state legislatures. And then, in the last of his nine articles, he proposed a solution: the voters of each state should elect senators directly.[27]

"The Treason of the Senate" demolished the walls that previously had seemed impossible to penetrate. A dozen senators were defeated in 1906, more in 1908 and 1910. By 1912, all seventy-five of the senators Phillips had exposed were gone. The final triumph in the crusade came in 1913 when a constitutional amendment transferred the election of senators from state legislatures to the American people. Political observers cited Phillips's stunning series as the catalyst for that extraordinary reform.[28]

Muckraking: An Unparalleled Legacy

In synthesizing the era of reform concentrated in the first dozen years of the twentieth century, historian Arthur Schlesinger wrote, "Aggressive and sensational measures were required to awaken the nation from its lethargy and to rejuvenate the old spirit of American democracy. To this mission a new generation of Americans dedicated themselves. The protest first found expression through the popular magazines."[29]

Schlesinger is one of many scholars of the Progressive Era to praise the muckrakers for their leading role in helping the nation recover from a dark period in its history. As these scholars have pointed out, the journalists spearheaded the campaign of investigation and agitation that ultimately set the nation on a more admirable course as it marched boldly into the twentieth century. Some historians have focused on documenting the governmental reforms rightly credited to the crusading journalists; Arthur and Lila Weinberg wrote, "Muckraking was directly responsible for such initiatives as the Pure Food and Drug Act, direct election of senators, and city and state reform." Others have lauded the seminal impact that Ida Tarbell and her fellow trustbusters had on American business; C. C. Regier wrote, "The whole tone of business in the United States was raised because of the persistent exposures of corruption and injustice." Still others have made more sweeping observations about the muckraking phenomenon; Vernon Parrington described the muckraking era as "a time of brisk housecleaning that searched out old cobwebs and disturbed the dust that lay thick on the antiquated furniture."[30]

The muckrakers' reform impulse ultimately triggered a list of specific activities that was both long and broad. In city after city, corrupt municipal officials were replaced with men and women with professional training and experience. John D. Rockefeller's vice grip on the oil industry was broken, and then other trusts dominating the railroad, mining, liquor, sugar, and beef industries were busted. The public was made aware of the fraudulent claims and harmful ingredients of food and patent medicines, prompting federal legislation to protect consumers. Likewise, the unscrupulous profiteering in the US Senate was revealed, and a constitutional amendment was enacted to reform that body.

Despite this formidable list of achievements, a truly comprehensive roll call of reform-oriented journalism would be longer still. It would include *Everybody's* exposés of the inner workings of the stock market and fraud among life insurance companies, *Collier's* assault on the autocratic leaders of the House of Representatives, and *American Magazine*'s denunciation of society's shameful treatment of African Americans.[31]

For a final appraisal of this splendid chapter in the evolution of the news media's relationship to American history, it may be best to return to Schlesinger's concluding comments about muckraking. The historian said the journalistic phenomenon played a profoundly important role in saving democracy from the clutches of the robber barons and returning it to the common people who rightly governed America. "The most beneficial effect of the literature of protest was the moral awakening of the masses," Schlesinger said. "In growing numbers they gave their support to a new group of political leaders who fought to restore government to the people."[32]

7

DEFYING THE KU KLUX KLAN

In the fall of 1915, a strange spectacle unfolded near Atlanta when William Joseph Simmons led a dozen men up a rocky trail on the imposing granite crest of Stone Mountain. As the night wind whipped the American flag that the men carried, Simmons ignited a pine cross that lit up the Georgia sky. Against this theatrical backdrop and with Bibles in hand, the men then vowed their allegiance to the Knights of the Ku Klux Klan.

That dramatic ceremony expanded, during the next decade, into a nationwide organization that inflamed America's social and political landscape, providing a mooring to the thousands of frightened Americans who'd been uprooted by the rapid changes that were erupting during the 1920s. The KKK offered them a sense of fraternity, a commitment to self-defined traditional American values, and a list of people to blame for the social upheaval—Catholics, Jews, blacks, and recent immigrants.

The Invisible Empire became a force to be reckoned with. Texas Klansmen elected one of their own to the US Senate. In Oregon, the KKK captured the governorship and enough of the legislature to ban parochial schools. The Klan also elected both senators in Colorado as well as both senators and the governor in Indiana. In 1925, the KKK invaded the nation's capital when 40,000 robed figures paraded down Pennsylvania Avenue.

Then the tide turned.

By the end of the decade, the Klan's power had faded into history—at least for the time being. The Invisible Empire's decline can be attributed partly to its failure to produce the results its followers had been promised. But as during other chapters of American history, another key element was the Fourth Estate. For while much of the press either supported the Ku Klux Klan or remained silent, a handful of newspapers crusaded against the powerful organization.

Three valiant journalistic voices, in particular, waged successful campaigns against the most powerful nativist organization in American history. The seminal anti-Klan campaign began in 1921 with a blockbuster exposé in the *New York World*. The series documented the KKK's immorality and violence in riveting detail. Another assault evolved two years later when the *Commercial Appeal* in Memphis combined compelling front-page cartoons with relentless reporting in a courageous effort to defy the Klan in that Tennessee city. Even deeper in the South, Alabama's *Montgomery Advertiser* concentrated its blistering attack on the editorial page. These three papers' anti-Klan efforts earned them national acclaim as well as Pulitzer Prizes, American journalism's highest honor.

US Representative Peter Tague, speaking to a congressional hearing called to investigate the Klan, said, "It has only been through the searching investigation of the great newspapers of the country that the evidence has been brought to the surface." Ku Klux Klan scholar Kenneth T. Jackson expressed a similar sentiment, saying, "Opposition from the newspapers severely damaged the Klan."[1]

Sweeping the Nation

Confederate veterans had organized the original Ku Klux Klan in 1866 in hopes of preventing former slaves from exercising their recently acquired rights. Within three years, they felt they'd completed their work, and the KKK ceased to exist.

After Simmons revived the Klan in 1915, his followers remained minuscule until 1920, when two enterprising promoters recognized that the Klan was a financial gold mine. Edward Young Clarke and Elizabeth Tyler persuaded Simmons to pay them one-fourth of the $10 each member paid, an arrangement that yielded the recruiters the handsome sum of $30,000 a week. Propelled by Clarke's ambition and Tyler's creativity, Klan membership soared to 4 million by 1924. In addition, the Invisible Empire mushroomed into a national phenomenon, exploding in numbers and influence throughout the West, Midwest, and Northeast while continuing to grow in the South.

Clarke and Tyler urged recruiters to fill their rhetoric with such loaded phrases as "100 percent Americans" and "the tenets of the Christian religion"—crafted to communicate that the country was being overrun by enemies from within. KKK recruiters promised to provide better schools, improve law enforcement, and hold fast to the traditional values being threatened by the socially permissive Roaring Twenties.

Klan growth was aided by the prevailing mood among many Americans. President Woodrow Wilson's pledge that World War I would make the world safe for democracy had produced a palpable idealism among the American people, but the armistice had failed to deliver. When the US Senate repudiated the League of Nations and Europe was again reduced to a gaggle of squabbling nations, Americans became disillusioned. In addition, the all-out war effort wasn't easily put aside, as wartime hatred for the Germans was transformed into a peacetime suspicion of everything foreign—which the KKK eagerly capitalized on.

For the most part, American journalism didn't stand in the way, as most newspapers feared the Klan's burgeoning power. Unwilling to challenge the organization's network of support, many editors covered the public events and official announcements of the KKK as they did those of any group. Others maintained a stoic silence regarding this secret society that was growing larger and more powerful each day.

The *New York World* Hurls a Hand Grenade

The first and most comprehensive journalistic crusade in defiance of the Klan was a no-holds-barred exposé in the paper that Joseph Pulitzer had built. The *New York World* promoted its September 1921 blockbuster with full-page ads that screamed, in three-inch letters "Ku Klux Klan Exposed!"[2]

What the ads promised, the series delivered. The opening article characterized the Klan's growth as a financial scam that had bilked members out of $40 million in initiation fees and charges for Klan regalia. "The Knights of the Ku Klux Klan, Inc.," the story read, "has become a vast enterprise, doing a thriving business in the systematic sale of race hatred, religious bigotry, and '100 percent' *anti*-Americanism."[3]

The series continued full throttle day after day for three weeks, boldly and relentlessly answering tantalizing questions about the mysterious organization, much as Ida Tarbell had told the public about Standard Oil two decades earlier—but with considerably more flash.

Although the exposé was written in a sensational style, the *World* was as committed to destroying the Klan as it was to building its own circulation. To ensure the series had maximum impact, the paper syndicated it to eighteen dailies around the country. With such major voices as the *Boston Globe* and *Pittsburgh Sun* in the East, the *St. Louis Post-Dispatch* and *Cleveland Plain-Dealer* in the Midwest, the *Seattle Times* and Oklahoma City *Oklahoman* in the West, and the *New Orleans Times-Picayune* and *Dallas Morning News* in the South reprinting the articles, the series held more than 2 million readers spellbound each day.

The series missed nothing. One article reported the Klan advocated a return to chattel slavery, and another quoted lawyers saying the organization was illegal because it required members to obey the Imperial Wizard even when his orders conflicted with the Constitution. Still another story meticulously recorded the names and addresses of 214 recruiters—from E. Y. Clarke, Imperial Kleagle, Suite 501 Flatiron Building, Atlanta, to W. S. Coburn, Grand Goblin, 519 Haas Building, Los Angeles—much as a paper might report the names on an FBI most-wanted list.[4]

To guarantee that the series held the public's attention, editors packaged each installment with compelling artwork. Accompanying one article was a facsimile of the application that each member completed—with questions reading "Were your parents born in the United States?" and "Are you a Jew?" Other images were created by reproducing some of the letters the *World* received from anonymous Klansmen. One hand-scrawled letter reprinted on the front page read, "You will seal your death warrant. Watch out—you nigger lovers."[5]

One of the most explosive articles revealed the immorality of the organization's two master recruiters. The *World* reported that during a 1919 raid on a house of prostitution, Atlanta police had identified the drunken occupants of one bed as Tyler, who was widowed, and Clarke, who was married—but not to Tyler.[6]

The *World* also went beyond reporting. In one proactive effort, the paper contacted New York public officials and forced them to go on the record as either opposing or supporting the Klan. Because their comments would become part of the *World*'s exposé, the officials had little choice but to criticize the Klan, thereby providing the paper with public statements it could revive if the Invisible Empire tried to make inroads into New York City. In response to the paper's inquiry, the president of the borough of Brooklyn said, "The Ku Klux Klan is an un-American movement," and New York City's police commissioner railed, "There is no room in America for an organization of religious and racial bigots."[7]

The *World* climaxed its campaign with a withering summary of KKK violence. The article began with impassioned rhetoric, saying of the Klan, "For the forces of the law it substitutes terrorism, replacing trial and punishment of offenders with anonymous threats and masked infliction of vengeance." Next to the dramatic prose ran a tabulated list of outrages attributed to the Invisible Empire—including 4 murders, 27 tar and featherings, 41 floggings—that totaled 152 violent acts.[8]

Despite the *World*'s extraordinary efforts, a surprise development followed on the heels of the final installment of the series. In one of the more ironic twists in the history of American journalism, the *World* soon discovered that its bold campaign had backfired. The New York editors gradually came to learn the painful lesson that legions of news people of every generation have been forced to accept: editors often are out of touch with their readers.

In this instance, the *World* editors eventually had to acknowledge that their sensational crusade ultimately hadn't destroyed the Klan but—quite the opposite—had given it a tremendous boost. For by reporting the KKK's acts of bigotry and violence, the series described in great detail the exact elements of the Klan that potential members found so appealing. The widely printed series, in fact, gave the Klan its first national publicity—free of charge. Before these masses of frustrated Americans read the series, many of them had never heard of this secret society that offered members a way to fight change while hiding under the anonymity of hoods. By the end of the series, KKK recruiters were finding thousands of worried citizens who weren't outraged by what they'd read but instead were eager to join the Klan. Hundreds of zealots even clipped the application form straight from the *World*, filled it in, and mailed it to Atlanta with their membership fee. Historians have stated that while the series increased the *World*'s circulation by 100,000, it also boosted Klan membership by thousands of new admirers.[9]

So as the *World* basked in the glory of winning the 1922 Pulitzer Prize for its series, the paper couldn't ignore the fact that its reporting had spurred the growth of the organization. The Invisible Empire clearly was a formidable force that wouldn't be defeated merely by one series of articles.[10]

The *Commercial Appeal* in Hand-to-Hand Combat

The next major battlefield in the press war against the Klan unfolded in 1923 in Memphis. The city's major paper, the *Commercial Appeal*, criticized the KKK by characterizing it as a profit-making scam. The editorial page also condemned the Klan's use of vigilante violence as a means of terrorizing the city's African Americans, Catholics, and Jews. "The law is the soul of the nation," the paper stated. "No aggregation of individuals has a right to take unto themselves the duties of judges and juries."[11]

This editorial cartoon by J. P. Alley took a light approach
to depicting the ugliness of religious and racial bigotry.
Reprinted courtesy of the Memphis Commercial Appeal.

Even more effective than the editorials were the front-page cartoons
that portrayed Klansmen as cowardly fiends hiding under bedsheets as
they preyed on the powerless. The first frame of one cartoon showed a
hooded Klan member being ordered to unmask, with the second frame
revealing the face to be grotesquely ugly; the caption read "No wonder he
puts a sack over that mug!" Another memorable drawing juxtaposed a man

"I'M UNWORTHY—MY RELIGION AIN'T RIGHT!"

The biting *Commercial Appeal* cartoon captured
the absurdity of the KKK hating all Catholics—
even disabled World War I veterans.
Reprinted courtesy of the Memphis Commercial Appeal.

draped in a white bedsheet and wearing the label "100% American" against
a uniformed World War I veteran whose military duty had cost him one
of his legs; the soldier smirked, angled his thumb toward the robed figure,
and said sarcastically, "I'm unworthy—my religion ain't right!"[12]

The war between the Klan and the *Commercial Appeal* intensified when
the Invisible Empire became the key issue in the 1923 city election. After Mayor Rowlett Paine rejected invitations to join the Klan, the hooded
society nominated W. Joe Wood for mayor and four other Klansmen for

the Memphis City Commission. In a blatant act of intimidation, the Klan placed its campaign headquarters directly across the street from the Commercial Appeal Building.

The KKK, with nightly meetings, raised the campaign to a fever pitch. At these events, Wood and his fellow candidates stood on either side of a white floral cross, while 2,000 Klansmen crowded together to hear speakers decry the pope and international Jewish bankers. During the rowdy meetings, every mention of the Klan brought applause, but any reference to Mayor Paine or the *Commercial Appeal* drew boos and curses.

As the election neared and tension built, national Klan leaders descended on the city. Intimidation tactics then mounted, with the Klan's *Tri-State American* newspaper warning voters, "If you fail to fulfill the duty you owe to your family, the Ku Klux Klan will banish you and report your negligence to the duly constituted authorities."[13]

The *Commercial Appeal* stated somberly, "The eyes of the nation are on Memphis," and then gave prominent play to negative stories about the KKK. When Louisiana law officials investigated Klan involvement in the deaths of two men in that state, the accusations covered page one. And when the Invisible Empire's top publicity agent shot the organization's chief counsel, the *Commercial Appeal* made the incident its lead story three days in a row.[14]

On election day, a powerful cartoon appeared on the front page. The eloquently simple drawing showed a man's hand covered in a white glove, rendered so the thumb and each finger looked like a Klansman wearing a pointed white hood: the middle finger was labeled "Mayor" and each of the other four was marked "Commissioner." On the shirtsleeve were written the words "Imperial Wizard of Atlanta." The cartoon's message was clear: if local Klan candidates were elected, they'd be mere puppets of the KKK's campaign to make hatred America's driving value. The caption read "The Sinister Hand. 'HALT, MEMPHIS!'"[15]

Despite the rousing political rallies and intimidating tactics, the Klan was soundly defeated and Paine and his commissioners were reelected. When the mayor led his followers in a jubilant victory parade, he stopped

THE SINISTER HAND.
"HALT, MEMPHIS!"

Appearing on the day of the crucial 1923 city election,
this searing J. P. Alley cartoon helped to defeat the KKK in
Memphis by suggesting that if Klansmen were elected, the
city would be run from the KKK headquarters in Atlanta.

Reprinted courtesy of the Memphis Commercial Appeal.

in front of the Commercial Appeal Building and directed the band to serenade the newspaper in honor of its decisive role in the election.[16]

In fact, when the results were announced, the entire nation seemed to breathe a sigh of relief. The *New York Times* hailed the election as "the biggest black eye the klan has yet received" and showered the credit on the *Commercial Appeal*. The most substantial praise, though, came from another New York institution when the School of Journalism at Columbia University awarded the Memphis paper the 1923 Pulitzer Prize for public service. The citation lauded the paper's "courageous attitude in the publication of cartoons and the handling of news in reference to the Ku Klux Klan."[17]

The *Montgomery Advertiser* Wages War

Though the anti-Klan crusades of the *World* and *Commercial Appeal* were courageous, a third paper deserves even more praise. For this journalistic voice waged its battles in what, during the 1920s when the KKK was at its peak, can be described as the belly of the beast: the Deep South.

The most sinister sign of the Klan in this region was in secluded spots on country roads. In response to what Alabama Klansmen perceived as the moral decay of the 1920s, they imposed a self-defined code of personal behavior that they enforced through acts of physical violence. Specifically, Klansmen meted out their vigilante justice through floggings. Exactly how many men and women were kidnapped and lashed with bullwhips isn't known, but the figure was in the thousands. Many victims were beaten because the Klan objected to their gambling or drinking habits, with others suffering because of their color or religion.

In 1927, the lone journalistic voice raised in opposition to flogging was that of Grover Cleveland Hall, editor of the *Montgomery Advertiser*. His editorials recounted the appalling details of specific incidents, such as a mob of masked Klansmen descending on Arthur Hitt, a respected African-American farmer, and "beating him unmercifully" until he sold them his farm for $80, though the land was worth ten times that amount. Hall wrote, "It is perfectly outrageous that a negro or any other person should be bullied and frightened into sacrificing the fruits of a lifetime of toil in order to save his life."[18]

The violence could be stopped, Hall argued, if a state law were passed to prohibit people from wearing masks or bedsheets. "The flogging evil cannot be effectively grappled with until it is made unlawful in Alabama to wear disguises in public places, and made a felony for men thus disguised to attack citizens of this state."[19]

Hall didn't, however, speak for all of Alabama journalism. Many papers supported flogging, commending the Klan for taking the moral leadership that, the papers argued, public officials were failing to provide. The *Alabama Christian Advocate*, for example, argued that flogging victims deserved the treatment they received, saying, "They are menaces to their communities." Papers that refused to criticize flogging didn't hesitate to attack the *Advertiser*. Calling Hall's editorial crusade a "hysterical paroxysm," the *Monroe Journal* wrote, "Just what good purpose the *Advertiser* imagines might be served by unrestrained denunciation of this particular form of criminality we fail to fathom." The *Evergreen Courant* made the same point, asking, "Why raise such a howl?"[20]

Instead of backing off, Hall adopted the additional tactic of reprinting the statements of outrage that began to appear in the northern press as word of the floggings spread. An item that initially appeared in the *New York Herald Tribune* screamed, "When a mob of masked men invades a citizen's home at night, renders him helpless and then takes his wife out of bed, ties her to a barrel in the front yard and flogs her, is there any punishment within the law too drastic for the crime? We doubt it." One that first appeared in the *Milwaukee Journal* asked of Alabama, "Aren't there enough men down there to say that there must be an end to this bigotry and intolerance and brutality? Isn't there someone strong enough to lead a successful movement to blot out this new monstrosity?" Hall reproduced each negative characterization of Alabama along with his own comments about how the Klan was damaging the state's reputation.[21]

Hall succeeded in stirring public sentiment to the point that the state legislature could no longer ignore the KKK's violence. And so, progressive representatives introduced tough anti-mask bills calling for exactly what

Hall advocated: to outlaw masks and robes such as those worn by KKKers. Hall threw his editorial weight behind the proposals, saying, "The bills are an honest effort to go to the heart of the evils that have grown out of the use of hood and robe. They are designed to end terrorism in Alabama."[22]

Klansmen in the legislature, however, responded to the proposals by mounting a formidable defense. When the governor, who was a member of the Klan, sided with the pro-mask legislators, the fate of the anti-mask proposals was sealed. They were soundly defeated.

But Hall's battle with the Klan had only just begun. In hopes of silencing the editor, Klansmen in the statehouse proposed what became known as the "muzzling" bills. The sponsors said they would protect the state's national reputation, which the men argued had been severely damaged by the unfavorable publicity that Hall's crusade had promoted throughout the country. As evidence, the legislators cited the various editorials from papers such as the *Milwaukee Journal* that Hall had reprinted.

To quiet the *Advertiser*, the legislators proposed broadening state libel laws to an unprecedented degree. According to the bills, any paper that published information that was deemed to be false and damaging to the state would be fined $25,000. The diabolical element of the legislation concerned who would do the deeming. Specifically, a widely distributed paper such as the *Advertiser* could be sued in every county where it circulated. That meant the decision about whether a particular statement was libelous could be decided by a jury of Klansmen in any remote county in the state. In addition, the bills stipulated that no higher court could alter the verdict of the original jury. And, finally, the law would be retroactive, meaning the *Advertiser* could be fined for all the negative statements it had made about the KKK during the anti-mask campaign.

Hall's criticism of the proposed legislation was ferocious. "These bills are designed to kill freedom of the press in Alabama," he wrote. "They are a malicious, tyrannical, outrageous scheme to bulldoze and punish a free press."[23]

Despite Hall's attacks, the governor lobbied hard for the muzzling bills, and national Klan leaders swarmed to Montgomery to lobby for the legislation. The bills moved onto the House floor, prompting what the *Advertiser* labeled "a four-hour battle which transcended in heat and passion legislative battles for a score of years." The final vote couldn't have been closer. But with forty-eight in favor and forty-eight opposed, the bills failed.[24]

Hall was recognized for his courage in defying the Klan when he was awarded the Pulitzer Prize in 1928. The citation read, "Grover Cleveland Hall, *Montgomery Advertiser*, for his editorials against gangsterism, floggings, and racial and religious intolerance."[25]

Turning Back the Ku Klux Klan

Receiving the Pulitzer Prize is journalism's highest honor, but papers truly dedicated to fulfilling their role in a democratic society find even greater reward in having positive influence on their communities. The *New York World*, Memphis *Commercial Appeal*, and *Montgomery Advertiser* all found themselves in that position, as each journalistic voice ultimately had the satisfaction of knowing that it had delivered a body blow of no small impact.

Although observers have acknowledged that the *World's* blockbuster series boosted the Klan's growth, they have applauded the positive impact it had on New York City. The paper's proactive effort in getting city officials on the record as opposing the Klan played a pivotal role in stopping the organization from gaining a foothold in America's largest urban center. The KKK built strong chapters in Albany, Buffalo, Schenectady, Syracuse, and Utica, but recruiters failed utterly in their efforts to attract New York City residents into their membership. The *Commercial Appeal* enjoyed similar success, as the Klan's defeat in the 1923 Memphis elections became a model of how a city could halt the Klan—if it was blessed with a courageous newspaper. Likewise, the *Advertiser* earned praise for its role in slowing the Klan's rise to power in the state capital; Alabama's largest city, Birmingham, became a KKK stronghold, but the Invisible Empire failed in its efforts to become a power in Montgomery, the state's second largest city.[26]

Scholars who have studied the Ku Klux Klan also have praised the Fourth Estate more broadly, lauding its vital role in keeping the Klan in check. David M. Chalmers wrote in his book, *Hooded Americanism*, that the papers had more impact on the Klan than any other force, and Kenneth T. Jackson wrote in *The Ku Klux Klan in the City* that the beginning of the country's resistance to the 1920s Klan can be dated precisely to the newspaper campaigns.[27]

American journalism historians have echoed these commendations. John Hohenberg wrote in *The Pulitzer Prize Story* that the anti-Klan coverage "shows what digging and documenting can do to a seemingly powerful organization." One of the most effusive tributes to journalism's offensive against the Klan came in the 1930s, in the immediate wake of the Klan's decline, when Silas Bent wrote in *Newspaper Crusaders: A Neglected Story*, "That the klan is widely discredited, and in most places is an object of ridicule, is due to the drubbing administered it by the newspapers."[28]

8

SPREADING ANTI-SEMITISM VIA THE RADIO

DURING THE 1930S AND 1940S, A VIRULENT ANTI-SEMITISM pervaded American society. Jews were unacceptable to many employers and unwelcome at many universities and social clubs. Oceanside beaches posted signs stating, "No Dogs or Jews Allowed." More than 100 civic organizations around the country publicly blamed Jews for the nation's economic problems. In 1939, a Roper opinion poll found that 53 percent of Americans believed restrictions against Jews were fully justified, and, three years later, in the midst of World War II, respondents to another opinion poll said the three groups representing the greatest threat to the American way of life were Germans, Japanese, and Jews.[1]

Such flagrant hostility toward a segment of society didn't emerge of its own accord. The American news media helped fuel anti-Semitism, with many newspapers openly supporting the various forms of discrimination. Anti-Semitic papers such as the *American Gentile*, *National American*, and *American-Ranger* spewed bigotry on American street corners with headlines such as "Communism Is Jewish" and "Jews Defile Our Christmas!"[2]

The single most influential anti-Semitic spokesman in the country was a Roman Catholic priest who took to the radio airwaves and spread a hateful venom across America. Father Charles Coughlin had a voice like honey, but his message was pure poison. Between 1926 and 1940, his weekly Sunday afternoon radio broadcast routinely reached 15 million listeners and sometimes attracted an extraordinary 45 million—more than a third of the country's population. *Social Justice*, the magazine Coughlin published, boasted a weekly circulation of 1 million, and he also reprinted his radio talks as pamphlets that he sent without charge to his followers. On both the airwaves and in print, Coughlin's fundamental message was the same: Jews were evil, money-hungry conspirators who were destroying every value that Christians held sacred.

Emergence of the Radio Priest

Charles Coughlin was born into a middle-class family of Irish heritage in Ontario, Canada, in 1891. He was educated in Catholic schools and received his bachelor's and divinity degrees from Toronto colleges. Ordained in 1916, he quickly earned a reputation as a dynamic orator.

In 1926, Coughlin was assigned to be pastor of a new church in a suburb of Detroit. The post was a demanding one because Royal Oak was a working-class community pockmarked with vacant lots and abandoned buildings. As an innovative means of expanding his congregation, Coughlin approached Detroit radio station WJR and asked to broadcast a weekly sermon based on the news events and issues of the day.

From the moment Father Coughlin stepped to the microphone, his experiment with the medium of radio was a glorious success. Within a few months, thousands of letters and financial contributions were flowing into Royal Oak. Detroit newsmen anointed Coughlin the "Radio Priest," and in 1930 the young cleric signed a contract to speak nationwide on CBS radio.

Because the country was in the midst of the Great Depression, he initially concentrated his discourse on economic matters. But economics soon led him into politics. His powerful voice rose in indignation as he railed against bankers for causing the country's fiscal woes. The week

Although Father Charles Coughlin could look like a gentle
parish priest, his anti-Semitic venom was harsh and hateful.
Courtesy of the Library of Congress.

Coughlin stepped into politics by criticizing President Herbert Hoover
as "the banker's friend, the Holy Ghost of the rich, the protective angel of
Wall Street," listeners so loved the potent rhetoric that they flooded Royal
Oak with 1.2 million letters.[3]

By 1932, the Radio Priest's weekly commentary had become so popular that he was employing 100 clerks to process 80,000 letters a week, and
Royal Oak had to build a post office solely to handle his mail. The young
priest was riding high on a wave of public interest in the newest mass
medium. By the early 1930s, 70 percent of American homes had radios,
and the communication medium was hailed as the "miracle of the age."
By mid-decade, Coughlin's weekly broadcast had become one of the most
popular programs on the air.[4]

People crowded around their radios partly because of the oratorical
quality of Coughlin's voice, which scholars have described as "warm,"

"inviting," "mellow," and "vibrant." The Radio Priest's ability to reach his audience was aided by other characteristics as well. One biographer wrote, "His success was a result of his extraordinary skills as a radio performer, his ability to make his sermons accessible, interesting, and provocative."[5]

Coughlin soon learned that sprinkling his script with colloquial terms such as "swell," "damn," and "lousy" made his presentation more engaging. He also spiced up his talks with ringing assertions and righteous fury, coining memorable phrases—"Christ or chaos," "the New Deal is God's deal," "Roosevelt or ruin."

His simple phrasing appealed to the masses of farmers, laborers, and industrial workers who waited eagerly for Coughlin's weekly visit into their homes. Crushed by the Depression, which had stolen their expectations of social and economic mobility, these working-class Americans responded by the millions to Coughlin's radio magnetism. By 1933, listeners were sending $5 million a year to "the messiah of Royal Oak." Having no desire to accumulate wealth for hedonistic purposes, Coughlin erected a mammoth new church with seating for 3,500.

But Father Coughlin generated controversy as well. Not every listener applauded his vitriolic attacks on the nation's political leaders and economic institutions, and persons of authority began to question the priest's tactics. Al Smith, a Catholic and former governor of New York, told the *New York Times* in 1933, "When a man addresses so great a number of listeners as Father Coughlin, he assumes the responsibility of not misleading them by false statements or poisoning their judgments with baseless slanders." Opting to avoid trouble, CBS refused to renew Coughlin's contract, and NBC declined his request to pick it up. Complaining that the networks were denying his freedom of speech, Coughlin paid for the connecting phone lines to form his own network of sixty stations stretching from Maine to Colorado.[6]

In 1935, Coughlin demonstrated that he could mobilize his followers to political action. He opposed a plan to create a World Court, saying the organization would only benefit the "satanic international bankers" he blamed for America's economic woes. Coughlin urged his listeners to block the proposal, which President Franklin D. Roosevelt supported, by contacting their members of Congress. Coughlin's appeal produced 200,000 telegrams bearing more than 1 million signatures. Congress was stunned by Coughlin's power, and the World Court proposal was defeated. Both the *New York Times* and Roosevelt credited Coughlin with killing the plan.[7]

As Coughlin's power grew, so did his dissatisfaction with Roosevelt. The solution to America's lack of money, Coughlin said, was simply to print more of it. The president opposed the inflationary proposal as shortsighted, prompting Coughlin to call FDR a pawn of the international bankers. The radio commentator then broke from the president, coining new epithets—"The New Deal is a raw deal!" and "We can't have a New Deal without a new deck!"

In 1936, Coughlin expanded beyond the radio and began committing his rhetoric to print by founding a weekly magazine. *Social Justice* published the scripts from his broadcasts along with essays and news items supporting the Radio Priest and his ideas.[8]

Coughlin had grown into a national political force. *New Republic* magazine credited him with single-handedly ousting two congressmen from Ohio. Bolstered by this success, he became the driving force behind a third political party formed to capture the White House. Ineligible for the presidency because of his Canadian birth, Coughlin chose Congressman William Lemke, a North Dakota Republican, to head the Union Party ticket. Drawing enthusiastic crowds as large as 30,000 as he campaigned from coast to coast, the Radio Priest pledged that if his party didn't win at least 9 million votes, he'd retire from broadcasting. When Lemke pulled only about one-tenth that number, Coughlin withdrew from radio.[9]

But he didn't remain silent for long. In early 1937, his golden throat again found its place on the airwaves when he created a new forty-seven-station hookup that spanned the continent. Aware that his failure in the election meant he had to find a new theme if he hoped to hold the attention of his listeners, Coughlin focused on the position that ultimately would have devastating impact on American society.

Promoting Anti-Semitism

Anti-Semitism hadn't been a mainstay of Coughlin's early commentaries, but, during the 1936 presidential campaign, he'd spoken of the "challenge of American Jewry" and had referred to Jews as "the money-changers" and "traffickers in gold." He'd also implied that Jews weren't patriotic, saying, "I challenge every Jew in this nation to tell me that he does or does not believe in the principle of 'love thy neighbor as thyself.'" *Newsweek* reported on these comments in a cover story about Coughlin.[10]

In 1938, the Radio Priest created the Christian Front. The all-male organization consisted of local chapters called "platoons," with many people flinching at the concept of a clergyman using such a blatantly military term. The Christian Front excluded Jews from its membership, which was 100 percent white and 90 percent Catholic. Local chapters in dozens of American cities organized "buy Christian only" movements. Platoons attracted thousands of frustrated people to meetings, where the major activities became drinking beer while praising Coughlin and cursing the man they condemned as the unofficial leader of American Jews—Franklin Delano "Rosenfeld."[11]

Coughlin reinforced his anti-Semitic views in 1938 when he reprinted the spurious "Protocols of the Elders of Zion" in *Social Justice*. Originally published in Russia at the turn of the century, the forged documents purported to detail a plot by Jewish leaders to destroy Christian civilization and impose financial slavery upon the world. Coughlin's first installment from the "Protocols" quoted the unnamed organizer of the plot as telling his fellow Jews, "We shall soon begin to establish huge monopolies, reservoirs of colossal riches, upon which even large fortunes of the goyim (gentiles) will depend to such an extent that they will go to the bottom together with the credit of all the States on the day after the political smash."[12]

In his comments accompanying the material, Coughlin argued that the world Jewish community's plans proposed in the "Protocols" had been carried out to create the Great Depression. Coughlin wrote, "The author of this document foresaw many years ago how to create want in the midst of plenty and how to agitate the thoughtless masses." His purpose in reprinting the "Protocols," he said, was to defend God. He stated, "The tyranny, oppression and needless poverty in the world are not of God's devising but are the results of planning by men who hate and detest the Christian principles of brotherhood."[13]

Coughlin also showed his anti-Semitism through a series of other accusations. In the first, he asserted that Jews were prime players in a global conspiracy to ensure that communism would dominate every country in the world. Then he contended that Jewish bankers had plotted and financed the 1917 revolution that had overthrown Czar Nicholas of Russia, which he characterized not as a revolt by the peasants but as a "mad slaughter of Christians."[14]

Many people responded to Coughlin's remarks with outrage. Rabbi Stephen S. Wise, leader of the World Jewish Conference, said, "Coughlinism is the deadliest form of anti-Semitism in America today." A front-page story in the *Detroit Free Press* bluntly called the priest's broadcasts a "weekly attack on the Jews" and lambasted his total disregard for accuracy, saying Coughlin suffered from a "congenital inability to tell the truth."[15]

Defending the Nazis

Coughlin next took a stand that was nothing short of fanatical—even for a man known for his extremism. In late 1938, the priest *defended* the Nazi persecution of Jews. In a broadcast, Coughlin said Jews had introduced communism into Russia, thereby propelling the Germans to devise the concept of Nazism to save Germany from this new threat. Communism, Coughlin told listeners, "was a product not of Russia, but of a group of Jews who dominated the destinies of Russia." Repeating the word "communism" a dozen times to exploit the visceral hatred most Americans felt toward the antithesis of democracy, Coughlin argued that communism had to be stopped, regardless of the price—including committing atrocities against Jews.[16]

Many radio stations that had broadcast Coughlin's shocking defense of the Nazis immediately denounced it as incendiary. WMCA in New

York was the first to protest his message. Immediately after the broadcast, the station told its listeners, "Father Coughlin has uttered certain mistakes of fact." WMCA then directed Coughlin to submit his future scripts to the station forty-eight hours before he aired them. When Coughlin refused, the station dropped him from its schedule.[17]

But most of Coughlin's followers stood by him. After he defended Nazi persecution of Jews, 6,000 New Yorkers gathered outside the WMCA studio to show support for him. The crowd cheered each time Coughlin's name was uttered and booed at every mention of Roosevelt. After the station refused to air his broadcasts, his admirers organized massive picket lines in front of the station, with 2,000 people demanding that WMCA keep their favorite radio voice on the air.

Many Catholic leaders, however, renounced him. The president of the American Bar Association, Frank J. Hogan, said, "We Catholics cannot permit men of ill will to preach bigotry and anti-Semitism without raising our voices in protest." Cardinal George Mundelein of Chicago tried to distance the Catholic Church from Coughlin. In a statement read nationwide over NBC, Mundelein said, "Father Coughlin has the right to express his personal views on current events, but he is not authorized to speak for the Catholic Church, nor does he represent the doctrine or sentiments of the Church."[18]

The number of Coughlin detractors continued to grow. The *Chicago Catholic Worker* published an open letter to Coughlin, addressing him as "the patron of prejudice" and accusing him of having become "psychotic on the question of Jews." The letter continued, "Your controversial Russian revolution statements justify a senseless, un-Christian attitude toward Mrs. Cohen, the delicatessen lady around the corner, and Meyer, the insurance collector." *Christian Century*, a Protestant weekly, condemned Coughlin for "attempting to arouse and play upon the animus of anti-Semitism" and being "Hitlerish in outlook, in method and in the effect he produces."[19]

The comparison to Adolf Hitler didn't bother Coughlin, as the priest repeatedly—in perhaps his most radical stand of all—expressed *admiration* for the demonic dictator. The priest wrote, "Hitler is to be admired.

He has made of Germany the defeated a new, united, great nation. He has brought back to his father-land the pride of industrial achievements and scientific improvements." Even after Hitler invaded Austria and Czechoslovakia, Coughlin continued to praise the German leader.[20]

"Inciting to Riot and Civil War"

In a radio commentary in July 1939, Coughlin took yet another shocking step, considering his position as a man of God, by endorsing violence as a completely appropriate response to the social ills that, according to him, Jews had instigated. He said, "The Christian way is the peaceful way until—until—all arguments have failed, there is left no other way but the way of defending ourselves against the invaders of our spiritual and national rights. And when your rights have been challenged, when all civil liberty has succumbed before the invaders, then may Christians meet force with force."[21]

Members of the Christian Front translated their leader's words into acts of intimidation and physical violence. In cities across the country, Coughlin's followers smashed the windows of Jewish-owned stores and scrawled graffiti on the front doors of Jewish homes. Young men who called themselves "Coughlin storm troopers" pushed Jews off sidewalks, battered them with verbal insults, and baited them into Nazi-like street brawls where brass knuckles and knives were the weapons of choice. Jewish parents were afraid to send their children to school because gangs of young hooligans would beat up every Jewish boy they caught alone. Police reported hundreds of cases of lone Jewish women, children, and elderly men being beaten by groups of men who proudly identified themselves as "Father Coughlin's brownshirts." For Jews, American streets and subways were no longer safe.

Coughlin's critics formed an organization called Friends of Democracy, seeking to have the priest removed from the air. They wrote the National Association of Broadcasters, saying that Coughlin's endorsement of violence was clear evidence that he was using the airwaves "for the purpose of inciting to riot and civil war, and stirring up racial prejudice and hatred among the American people." The letter continued, "We urge that provision be made immediately to cancel Father Coughlin's contracts." Coughlin's detractors argued that his commentary wasn't protected by the First Amendment because that document didn't apply to acts that incite violence.[22]

Public opposition to Coughlin intensified. By late 1939, several large radio stations refused to air Coughlin's program. Dozens of others waited until his contract with them expired and then opted not to renew it.[23]

In January 1940, FBI agents in Brooklyn arrested seventeen members of the Christian Front and charged them with conspiring to overthrow the US government. According to the FBI, the men had been plotting to murder several Jewish leaders as well as a dozen members of Congress. Instead of denouncing the arrested men, Coughlin defended them. Praising them as a "fine body of New York Christians," he said, "I freely choose to be identified as a friend of the accused. It matters not whether they be guilty or innocent; be they ardent followers of the principles of Christianity or the betrayers of them, my place is by their side. There I take my stand."[24]

By September 1940, few stations were willing to broadcast Coughlin's hate-filled diatribes, and it was no longer economically feasible for the Radio Priest to continue to broadcast. After fourteen years on the airwaves, he left radio.[25]

Translating Hate Speech into Print

Coughlin didn't, however, disappear from the scene entirely, as he continued his anti-Semitic commentary in *Social Justice*. In February 1942, with the United States fighting in World War II, Coughlin announced on the pages of his magazine that Jews had engineered the entire war. According to him, the momentum for war had begun in 1933 as an outgrowth of an alleged Jewish-communist alliance. Because Jews wanted the Communist Party to take over Germany, he said, they had created an anti-German propaganda campaign in the United States aimed at pushing America into the war. *Social Justice* stated, "A worldwide sacred war was declared on Germany not by the United States, not by Great Britain, not by France, not by any nation; but by the race of Jews." Coughlin used this chapter of his anti-Semitic crusade to argue once again that the Nazis were fully justified in persecuting Jews.[26]

Coughlin's assertion that Jews had started World War II was the straw that broke the camel's back. Since the mid-1930s, US Attorney General Francis Biddle had been monitoring Coughlin's activities, and by 1939 FBI Director J. Edgar Hoover had taken personal charge of the investigation. The findings were disturbing. The most damning piece of evidence against Coughlin was a sworn statement from a secret agent of the federal government who'd posed as an Axis agent: He claimed that Coughlin had worked for the Nazis in early 1941 to disseminate anti-Semitic propaganda in the United States.[27]

After America entered the war, men like Coughlin who'd previously been dismissed as crackpots were no longer tolerated. Because his hate-mongering undermined the war effort, federal officials took direct action to silence him. FBI agents drove a fleet of vans up to Coughlin's church and seized both his personal papers and his business records. In April 1942, Biddle charged *Social Justice* with violating the Espionage Act, and the US postmaster general barred the magazine from being sent through the mail on grounds that it was seditious.[28]

But it ultimately took authorities of the Catholic Church to stop Coughlin from making public statements. Biddle communicated with Detroit Archbishop Edward Mooney, saying that if Coughlin continued to speak, the federal government would charge him with sedition, which would lead to a high-profile and extremely embarrassing ordeal for the Catholic Church. In May 1942, Mooney ordered Coughlin to cease all nonreligious activities. *Social Justice* never appeared again, and Coughlin left the public eye.[29]

From 1942 until he retired in 1966, Coughlin served quietly as a parish priest in Royal Oak. Only the most persistent of news organizations succeeded in persuading him to make any statement whatsoever, such as when *Life* magazine managed to extract the brief quotation, "It was a horrible mistake to enter politics." Father Coughlin died in 1979.[30]

Influencing the Social and Political Landscape

Although it's not possible to establish a direct cause-and-effect relationship between Father Charles Coughlin's hate-filled rhetoric and the spread of anti-Semitism through American society, he clearly had a significant impact on the minds of the American people.

As early as 1935 and the World Court debate, Coughlin demonstrated his ability to impel millions of voters to political action. Observers of the American scene also asserted Coughlin's far-reaching influence. *Fortune* magazine wrote in 1934, "Coughlin is just about the biggest thing that ever happened to radio." The *Chicago Catholic Worker* said in its 1939 open letter to Coughlin, "You are the most powerful Catholic voice in the United States today. You are a definite, undeniable force on the American scene. Your opinions sway millions."[31]

An audience sometimes soaring to 45 million Americans gathered around the radio to hear Coughlin each Sunday afternoon from 1926 to 1940, and at least 1 million of them made the further commitment of subscribing to *Social Justice*. With such a huge and fervent audience listening to his every word, Coughlin clearly had a profound impact on American society, closing the minds and hardening the hearts of many people toward the world Jewish community. As one biographer wrote, "His crisp voice, his vibrant personality, and his message were wonderfully suited to the time in which he lived and to the new medium which was sweeping the country." More than any other man or woman of the early days of this first electronic medium, the priest perfected the formula that successfully touched his listeners. The story of how he spread anti-Semitism provides students of journalism history with a stunning example of the power of the radio to propel change—and not necessarily by appealing to the best in human nature.[32]

9

USING "ROSIE THE RIVETER" TO PROPEL WOMEN INTO THE WORKFORCE

WORLD WAR II WAS A WATERSHED EVENT IN THE EVOLUTION OF the American woman. The demands that the international conflict made on the people of the United States offered women opportunities for new and expanded roles, profoundly changing the traditional social order. Ten million working-age men donning military uniforms created a severe labor shortage in the private sector and, in particular, in the rapidly expanding defense industries. Faced with a critical need for manpower, the nation turned to *woman*power.

Women heeded the call. As millions of them entered the labor force for the first time, the iconic image of Rosie the Riveter—young and beautiful, strong and confident—aptly symbolized the phenomenon for the American public. Many women worked in industrial jobs directly related to the wartime buildup, laboring in airplane plants, shipyards, and munitions depots. Others worked in offices both inside and outside the government, serving most often as typists, secretaries, and personnel managers. Still others wore military uniforms, joining the branches of the army and navy created for women, frequently as nurses. This surge in wartime employment radically altered the face—not to mention the shape—of the nation's workforce. In 1940, 12 million American women worked outside the home; four years later, that number had jumped to 19 million—an increase of a staggering 58 percent.[1]

Such a sea change, like so many other events in American history, was aided by the Fourth Estate. Newspapers, news magazines, and radio stations gave working women unprecedented quantities of positive coverage during the early 1940s. In concert with the government's intense effort to persuade women to join the workforce, American journalism became a willing venue for what proved to be highly successful propaganda. News organizations prodded, coaxed, and cajoled the public into supporting the concept of women working outside the home—an idea that middle-class America previously had refused to embrace. Journalistic outlets abandoned all traces of their traditional adversarial role vis-à-vis the government and reminded women that their brothers, husbands, and sons were in danger of dying because they lacked the wartime goods that women could supply.

Although the primary motivation for news organizations nudging women into the workforce was to support the government and the war effort, the campaign ultimately had other beneficiaries as well. The flood of positive images of working women prompted nonworking women to expand their vision of what life could offer. This caused millions of women to consider striving to find fulfillment not in cleaning toilet bowls or ironing their husbands' shirts but in operating a fifteen-ton crane or readying a machine gun for the field.

Some scholars question the long-term impact of women joining the workforce during World War II, pointing out that many of them were forced to give up their jobs when the soldiers came home. But there's no question that the phenomenon altered the consciousness of a generation of women as well as the expectations of their daughters. Rosie the Riveter herself gained a new level of confidence because she learned not only that she could fill GI Joe's shoes but also that doing so made her feel good about herself and her new place in society. Journalist Dorothy Thompson summarized the point at the time, saying, "There is no example in which a class or group of people who have once succeeded in expanding the area of their lives is ever persuaded again to restrict it."[2]

Calling All Women

World War II was a battle of production. The Germans and Japanese had a ten-year head start on amassing weapons and wartime equipment, and the Allies suffered major material losses at Dunkirk and Pearl Harbor. The United States had to play catch-up, for victory clearly would go to the side with more airplanes, battleships, guns, and ammunition. Production was essential for victory, and women were essential for production. The *Baltimore Sun* put it succinctly by saying, "The problem of wartime womanpower is just as vital as that of wartime manpower."[3]

Encouraged by the government's propaganda machine, the nation's news media dutifully called for action. Radio proved to be a successful venue in Seattle, where the city's multitude of defense plants created an acute labor shortage. The local chamber of commerce appealed to station KJR and created a twice-weekly program called "Jobs for Women." Each fifteen-minute broadcast began with general commentary on the importance of women to the war effort and then aired descriptions of specific jobs available—listing physical requirements, location, hours, and wages. The strategy worked. After a mere four weeks, 2,200 women had joined Seattle's workforce, and city officials credited the radio station for the success.[4]

Nationwide, though, large-circulation newspapers and magazines did the lion's share of the communicating. In many cases, the headlines told the story. A typical example from the *New York Times* read "Needed: 50,000 Nurses." News magazines did their part as well, with *Time* announcing "Nightingales Needed" and *Newsweek* weighing in with "More Women Must Go to Work as 3,200,000 New Jobs Beckon."[5]

Some publications were so committed to increasing the number of working women that they raised the possibility of *forcing* women to work outside the home, either as soldiers or as part of the defense buildup. The *Washington Post* headlined one such story "Should the United States Draft Its Womanpower?" In the text of the story, the *Post* stated, "Many American women favor the drafting of women—particularly young women—for military and industrial service." To support that statement, the paper quoted the president of the International Federation of Business and Professional Women as saying, "We take men. There is no reason why we should not take women. This is war and you have to have organized effort. And that's the way to get it."[6]

The *New York Times* opted not to *tell* women readers to march onto the assembly line, but to *show* them how working women were making a difference. A typical article said of American women, "They are helping to build dive bombers for the Navy; they are making time fuses for high explosive shells in government arsenals; they are filling and sewing powder bags in a dozen newly built plants; they are turning out millions of rounds of machine-gun and small-arms ammunition." *Times* editors surrounded the copy with photos that drove home the point, showing determined women of all ages working diligently at their tasks. The images carried captions such as "For precision work, women's fingers are often defter than men's" and "Where a leak may mean death, the job must be thoroughly done."[7]

The *Times* joined the other publications in running strident pleas for women workers that read like they'd been written by government public relations flacks. One began, "Of our many war problems, one of the most acute is the need for graduate trained nurses. There are nurses now with American troops in Ireland, in Iceland and in Bataan, with fox holes dug beside their sleeping cots; there were four on Wake Island when the Japs got there. And many thousands more are needed." The recruitment brochure-style rhetoric continued, "To any working person, one of the greatest sources of satisfaction and of resultant prowess is the sense of being needed and in demand." The article was surrounded by photos of student nurses trying on their white caps for the first time.[8]

Glamorizing the "Girls"

Before World War II, a woman working outside the home generally carried the stigma of economic necessity. A man's wife or daughter bringing home a paycheck suggested that he wasn't able to provide for his family. Eliminating this deeply ingrained perception was no easy task, but the American news media tried to do just that. One of their most effective strategies was to glamorize the working woman.

A full-page article in the *Christian Science Monitor* newspaper reported that women were doing their part in the war effort by shifting "From French Heels to Slacks." That headline ran above a three-column photo that could just as easily have appeared in *Vogue* or *Glamour*. It showed a trio of beautiful young women with broad smiles on their faces as they walked confidently forward, arm in arm, above the caption, "In Jumper and Slacks They Work . . . on recess from tire-changing duties in Washington." The accompanying article continued the upbeat tone, beginning, "The American 'glamour girl' is about to have her popularity crown usurped by the woman in overalls." The article went on to wax admiringly of the millions of women who were redefining what it meant to be fashionable. "Short skirts, full blouses, and flowing bobs get caught in wheels and presses. Open-toed shoes pick up loose filings. French heels trip over cables and tools. Slack suits and low-heeled oxfords are almost a necessity in factory jobs." In another feature, the *Monitor* made assembly-line workers sound like such Hollywood stars as Betty Grable, describing them as "alluring Grable-like damsels, clad in slacks and bandannas, and oozing glamour from every pore."[9]

Papers also glamorized working women in their news stories. In an article about how women were changing factories, the *New York Times* managed to slip in the names of two of the country's top women's fashion designers. "In shops where delicate, dainty precision work is done," the story said, "Lilly Dache can design a fetching bonnet to keep the hair from catching in the machinery. Molyneux can do a dashing uniform in gay colors and light fabrics." The *Times* repeated the technique in an article reporting on the huge number of women working in arsenals and

The iconic poster featuring Rosie the Riveter communicated
that women who joined the workforce could be strong and
tough while also being feminine and beautiful.
Reprinted from the National Archives.

aircraft plants, this time creating an image that made assembly-line work
sound like applying makeup by saying, "Under fluorescent lights they
sit at benches that might well be dressing tables, and work with tools no
larger than a manicure set."[10]

News magazines did their part as well. *Life* published a photo essay,
titled "Girls in Uniform," that gushed, "The woman worker in a war industry has acquired some of the glamor of the man in uniform. In labor's social scale, she belongs to the elite. At the very top is the girl who

works in an airplane factory. She is the glamor girl of 1942." The article, surrounded by photos of beautiful working women, went on to describe America's newest glamor girl as arriving at the factory at 6:30 a.m., "her hands smooth, her nails polished, her makeup and curls in order." *American Magazine* took the trophy for glamorizing female workers via photos when it spread an image of four leggy young women across two pages to illustrate an article titled "Glory Gals." The three-paragraph article about the Women's Ambulance and Defense Corps was dwarfed by the titillating image of the women—dressed in scanty khaki shorts—frolicking in the surf as if they were contestants in the Miss America pageant.[11]

Praising Working Women

Although the glamorized descriptions gave the impression that working women looked like Hollywood stars, news outlets communicated that Rosie the Riveter was much more than just a pretty face. A *Newsweek* article about women journalists, for instance, ended with a statement clearly tailored to reassure male readers. "The younger generation of newspaperwomen," the magazine wrote, "is composed of women who can do a man's job but still look like women."[12]

The leading voices in American journalism had positive words for working women outside their field, too. By late 1942, *Newsweek* was boasting that women were working in every area of defense production, stating admiringly, "Depending on the industry, women today make up from 10 to 88 per cent of total personnel in most war plants." *Time* bragged that a female worker "can turn out half again as much work as a man," and the *New York Times* began a story with the assertion, "All responsible people connected with industry today agree that women are equal to men as far as being able to do almost any industrial job."[13]

In particular, the news media repeatedly applauded women's superior dexterity, which meant they could assemble the tiny, intricate parts that went into the airplanes and battleships that were essential to the war effort. The *New York Times* reported that women excelled in other factory jobs as well. "Women of all ages are among our best welders and shipfitters," the *Times* said. "A Danish woman welder of 53 can match the record of the best man we have found."[14]

Radio joined the newspapers and magazines in trumpeting women's abilities. A station in Portland, Oregon, sponsored a "Working Women Win Wars Week." A typical script had the announcer saying women possessed "a limitless, ever-flowing source of moral and physical energy, working for victory." After a second voice asked why the country needed female workers, the announcer responded, "You can't build ships and planes and guns without them."[15]

When it came to highlighting women's strengths, the *Los Angeles Times* reported the fact that female workers had gained a reputation for being far superior to their male counterparts when it came to paying attention to detail. "Inspection is one of the departments in which women now play an important part," the paper said. To support that statement, the *Times* went on to state, "Wright Aeronautical reports its 60 young women inspectors test 32,760,000 parts in a year."[16]

Balancing Two Worlds

Because a third of the women who joined the World War II labor force were mothers, the nation's journalists reassured the public that women could balance their responsibilities in the home with those in the workplace.

The quintessential article appeared in the *New York Times* under the headline "Woman War Worker: A Case History," although it could just as easily have read "Wonder Woman: A Case History." It began, "Alma is a pretty woman," and then proceeded to describe a wife and mother with an "extremely feminine build" who managed to excel at her war plant job while also taking care of her husband and three children—also mentioning, of course, that "Alma didn't complain much." Indeed, her remarkable daily schedule didn't allow for such luxuries.[17]

Alma began her day by arriving home from her nightshift job at the plant just in time to get Sally, Billy, and Tom Jr. off to school. After making her own breakfast and cleaning up the kitchen, she'd sleep for an hour until it was time to make lunch for the children. After feeding the six-, eight-, and nine-year-olds and washing the lunch dishes, she went back to bed until the children returned from school. Then she rose again to clean the house and prepare dinner so it would be on the table when Tom got home. After doing the dinner dishes and helping the kids with their homework, Alma slept for another hour before Tom woke her at 10 p.m. Alma survived on five or six hours of sleep a day while spending forty-eight hours a week on her job, which required her to stand and operate a large machine that spat out tiny aircraft parts. Her only day off was Sunday, which she spent doing the week's laundry.[18]

The *Times* story ended with a textbook example of a passage crafted to inspire other American wives and mothers to march into the workforce. "When Alma measures the dullness and loneliness of a housewife's job against the interest and companionship of a production job," the paper said, "she inevitably concludes she does not wish to be a housewife or a housemother. She wishes, and will fight, to be a working wife and a working mother." Melodramatic music would have provided a fitting background for the maudlin prose. "Alma is going to be present in the machine shop from here on out, come war, peace, or high water. She has the energy. She has the ability." The story had built to a time-worn cliché that was delivered in the final sentence: "Where there's a will, it finds a way."[19]

Other articles were dotted with comparably supportive statements and rosy images to reassure mothers, as well as society in general, that it was possible—as well as *patriotic*—for women to balance the dual responsibilities of home and work. Many of those stories described the child care centers that exploded in number during the early 1940s as women began working outside the home as never before. Typical was a piece in the *Chicago Tribune* that began, "The sun shone thru the candy stripe drapes and danced in its own reflection on the tiny, bright yellow tables and chairs." The story reported that this particular nursery school was one of eighty-four in Chicago serving the needs of working mothers. After praising the quality of the facilities as well as the commitment of the teachers, the *Tribune* gave the school an enthusiastic thumbs up, stating, "It is an ideal children's haven."[20]

Redefining "Women's Work"

By World War II, magazines had spent a century and a half—since the founding of *Ladies Magazine* in 1792—telling women that their "sphere" was defined by the four walls of the home. The campaign to attract women into the wartime labor force, however, required that a very different message be sent. With the fate of democracy hanging in the balance, newspapers and magazines promoted the new message with gusto, encouraging women workers to expand into myriad new directions.

American Magazine began one story by saying, "A woman, when she gets hopping mad or when she senses a peril to the things she loves, can do darn near anything." It then took the next step of showcasing the fields in which women were breaking new ground. An article titled "Amazons of Aberdeen" reported that in 1941 not a single woman had been allowed to work at the Maryland testing grounds, but, three years later, 400 women were making sure Uncle Sam's guns and ammunition were working properly before they were sent to the boys at the front. The article raved, "The girls fire big berthas, drive tanks over shell-torn terrain, toss 60-pound shells around as if they were biscuits. Tough babies, these gals? Well, hardly. Most of them are housewives, many of them mothers." Photos showed women in a variety of positions—driving a tank, operating a .30-caliber machine gun, towing a truck out of the mud.[21]

Other publications also championed women expanding into fields previously reserved for men. The *New York Times* urged forestry officials to hire more women, pointing out that their keen powers of observation meant they could spot fires better than men could. *Time* campaigned for more women doctors by reporting that only 6 percent of US medical students were women, compared to 85 percent in Russia.[22]

Another major theme in the effort to expand the definition of "women's work" was to increase the jobs open to African-American women. The war represented a second emancipation for black women, who'd always worked outside the home but, because of the increased acceptance of working women, were now able to advance beyond jobs as domestics. The drive for victory should outweigh the racism that pervaded many industries, *Newsweek* argued, as black women were as capable of working in aircraft plants and shipyards as white women were.[23]

Any list of women pioneering in new jobs during the war must include one who became the epitome of the intrepid new American woman: Margaret Bourke-White. Already highly regarded for her breathtaking 1930s *Life* magazine photos that transformed factories into Gothic cathedrals, she gained new visibility by becoming the first woman correspondent accredited to the army air force. In addition to covering the fighting, Bourke-White also served as the model for the army's first set of uniforms for women correspondents—which included a pink party dress for special occasions.

One of Bourke-White's most exciting stories came after the military brass refused to allow her to fly to North Africa, saying airplanes were too dangerous for women, and her subsequent decision to get there by sea instead. When her troopship was torpedoed, she wrote firsthand from a lifeboat. Bourke-White's *Life* article on the harrowing experience featured not only stunning photos but also a poignant description of the life-and-death realities of wartime. "We were bobbing farther away from the big ship," she wrote. "Just as a soldier let go of the raft to reach for a rope from the lifeboat, a wave flung the raft against him and cracked his skull. The skipper dived overboard, caught hold of the soldier and the two were dragged back into the lifeboat. Before the night was over, the soldier had died."[24]

Capturing the Moment in Pictures

Bourke-White's photo credit line was the most famous to appear in the nation's news publications, but it wasn't the only one. For at the same time that newspapers and magazines were using words to propel women into the workforce, they were also showcasing images for that same purpose. By the 1940s, journalists had become well aware of the ability of high-quality photos to touch the emotions of the American public. Editors filled their pages with images of thousands of dedicated women, most of them wearing Rosie the Riveter's confident expression.

Life, with its large format and status as the nation's first photo news magazine, set the standard. Bourke-White's stirring account of her rescue

Blanche Jenkins—wife, mother, welder—was one of the hundreds of American women raised to heroic status through the artistry of *Life* photographer Margaret Bourke-White.

© *LIFE magazine/Getty Images*

at sea came to life with a half-page photo at the beginning of the article. It showed a rescue plane circling above a crowded boat filled with men and women waving, cheering, and raising the V-for-victory salute.[25]

The photographer's artistry in her "Women in Steel" photo essay defied the two-dimensional limitations of a magazine. She depicted the heroic women workers as far too strong and powerful to be captured on a printed page: Florence Romanowski poured molten-hot liquid steel into molds as sparks burst like fireworks on every side. Elizabeth Laba heated the iron ingots in her oven to 2,300 degrees. Rosalie Ivy, described in the caption as "a husky Negro laborer," mixed a special mud to seal the casting hole that molten iron would flow through on its way to the blast furnace.[26]

Bourke-White was drawn to women who were rugged and robust, but most photographers of the era—the vast majority of them men—preferred more feminine beauties. For the photos to accompany his "Girls in Uniform" photo essay, *Life* photographer J. R. Eyerman focused on Marguerite Kershner, who meticulously applied rouge, eye shadow, and lipstick before arriving at the factory. "Although Marguerite looks like a Hollywood conception of a factory girl," the caption below one of her half dozen photos read, "she and thousands like her are doing hard, vital work." In keeping with journalism's commitment to glamorizing the working woman, Kershner also was shown enjoying an active social life by bowling and roller skating.[27]

Regardless of the publication, the most ubiquitous image was of a woman at her work station, focusing on her given task. Whether *Time* published a medical story debunking rumors that riveting caused breast cancer or *Newsweek* reported that a new study had found women less inclined than men to move from plant to plant, the articles came complete with images of women diligently at their posts—whether drilling in *Time* or inspecting artillery cartridges in *Newsweek*. The *New York Times* dotted its pages with close-up photos of Rosie the Riveters as well, showing women intently welding, tuning engines, and operating grinders on the assembly line.[28]

Changing the Social Order

World War II revolutionized the role of women in American society. When the international crisis created a desperate need for American workers, women responded with impressive quantities of enthusiasm, wherewithal, and—above all—ability. Between 1940 and 1944, the number of women in the workforce increased by more than half, proving to women themselves and to the public at large that "girls" were fully capable of succeeding in the workplace. What's more, they simultaneously shattered the conventional stereotypes of "women's work" and made major strides toward destroying sex labels.

The social revolution that began during the war didn't stop with the armistice. Even though a huge number of working women gave up their jobs—many against their will—at the end of the war, others remained in the workplace. In late 1946, 1 million more women were working in factories than had been there in 1940, and almost all the 2 million women who worked in offices during the war stayed at their desks when peace returned. The change was most noticeable among married women, with the percentage of American couples in which both husband and wife worked leaping from 11 percent before the war to 20 percent after it. The idea of women working outside the home clearly was becoming an accepted part of middle-class life.[29]

Numerous scholars have concluded that the news media and their powerful influence over public opinion were central to bringing about this radical change in the social order. "None of the changes in women's work could have occurred without the active approval and encouragement of the principal instruments of public opinion," wrote historian William H. Chafe. "Newspapers and magazines did their part in the publicity build-up by depicting Rosie the Riveter as a national heroine and exhorting others to join her." Other scholars have expressed similar sentiments. In her study of World War II women, Leila J. Rupp wrote, "For the first time, the working woman dominated the public image. Women were riveting housewives in slacks, not mothers, domestic beings, or civilizers." In another study, Susan M. Hartmann concluded, "Media images of women were expansive, widening the range of acceptable behavior, providing positive examples of unconventional women, and blurring traditional gender distinctions."[30]

By calling for women workers and then praising the accomplishments of the women who responded, journalism—through both words and images—contributed immeasurably to the advancement of American women. Even though the Fourth Estate's primary motivation for this proactive effort was to help the United States win the war, a byproduct of that campaign was to push women toward developing a broader and often more fulfilling role in society.

In the decades that followed, conservative forces attempting to maintain the status quo would find it no easier to turn back the emerging sense of worth and potential among women than to turn back the hands of time. Social movements advance along a continuum, with each step forward leading to the next. The working women of the 1940s, with the news media's assistance, laid the psychological groundwork—creating the mindset and arousing the consciousness—of the next generation, paving the way for the women's liberation initiatives that erupted in the 1960s.

10

STANDING TALL AGAINST JOSEPH MCCARTHY

SENATOR JOSEPH MCCARTHY'S POLITICAL CAREER WAS LIKE A Roman candle. In early 1950, he was an obscure first-term senator. But by 1952, his star had risen to national prominence as his anticommunist witch hunt helped propel the Republican Party into the White House for the first time in twenty years. In late 1953, McCarthy's career spiraled downward, careening toward the ultimate nadir that today makes the very mention of his name send a chill down the spine of any fair-minded American.

McCarthyism was a reckless political gamble to convince voters that the Democratic Party had presided over the country through two decades, not of accidents or errors—but of treason. Through a barrage of charges and countercharges, McCarthy insisted that the government was riddled with subversives working to destroy American values. Exploiting the country's Cold War fears, he destroyed the lives of thousands of innocent men and women.

The hand behind his bluff was printer's ink. Newspapers turned McCarthy's unsubstantiated charges into sensational stories that shrieked from page one. When accusations came from a US senator who claimed to be leading a campaign to save his country from evil forces, the Fourth Estate accepted those allegations as newsworthy fact.

Journalism also played a key role in bringing McCarthy down. For the force that, more than any other, ended the shameful era of McCarthyism was TV news. As other reporters shuddered at McCarthy's power, Edward R. Murrow stood tall against him. Murrow's *See It Now* on CBS first aired the story of an exemplary Air Force lieutenant who'd fallen victim to McCarthy. Five months later came "A Report on Senator Joseph R. McCarthy," the legendary journalistic triumph that exposed the demagogue while earning praise as the most important program in television history.

Another TV network then moved into the spotlight, providing gavel-to-gavel coverage of the most explosive congressional hearings in American history. For more than a month, ABC held 80 million viewers riveted to their televisions as the camera revealed McCarthy to be a rude and sadistic bully. By the time the hearings ended, McCarthyism had been discredited.

The Nightmare Decade

McCarthyism didn't develop in a vacuum. The American self-assurance won so dearly during World War II began to fade from the nation's consciousness at the end of the 1940s, with fear and uncertainty taking its place. The Cold War mentality crept into the American mind as communism consolidated its grip on Eastern Europe, as well as the Middle and Far East, to create a mood that was grim and unsettling.

The Soviet Union came to be perceived as a sinister enemy that threatened to annihilate the United States. In 1949, the Soviets flexed their muscles by detonating an atomic bomb. Even more shocking was China's fall to communism as the Nationalist Chinese forces of Chiang Kai-shek withdrew to the island of Taiwan, leaving the mainland to communist leader Mao Tse-tung. A few months later, an American public still weary from world war saw its men once again engaged in battle on foreign soil, this time in an effort to contain the spread of communism. The fighting in Korea continued for three years, claiming the lives of 54,000 US soldiers.

The pall of fear spreading across the country also caused many Americans to sense danger within their borders as a series of events shocked the nation. First, the State Department blamed internal sabotage for the failure, despite a huge infusion of financial aid, of its China policy. Next, the public learned that US diplomat Alger Hiss had passed secrets to a communist agent. Then the House Un-American Activities Committee investigated allegedly subversive activities by writers, actors, and directors in the entertainment industry. After scientists Ethel and Julius Rosenberg were convicted of wartime espionage for giving the Russians information about the atomic bomb, they were both executed. It became an era when to be accused was to be assumed guilty and when associating with the wrong people could destroy an individual's life.

The Meteoric Rise of Joe McCarthy

Joe McCarthy began his campaign in February 1950 by waving a sheet of paper in front of the members of a women's club in Wheeling, West Virginia, and bellowing, "While I cannot take the time to name all of the men in the State Department who have been members of the Communist Party and a spy ring, I have here in my hand a list of 205 that were known to the Secretary of State and, nevertheless, are still working and shaping the policy in the State Department." Neither the audience nor the nation that read the claim on the front page the next day knew that the sheet of paper didn't contain a single name.[1]

When McCarthy repeated his charges in Salt Lake City, Denver, and Reno during the next week, the specific number of communists changed each time, going to 207 to 81 to 57. Despite the inconsistencies, by the time he took his accusations to the Senate floor in late February, McCarthy had emerged as chief spokesman for a communism-in-government crusade that many Republicans recognized as the issue that could put them in the White House.

In the sport of intimidation, Senator Joseph McCarthy
was aided by his chief counsel, Roy Cohn.
© Yale Joel/Getty Images

McCarthy's flair for drama forced the Senate Foreign Relations Committee to investigate his charges. For five months, he accused various government officials of advancing the communist cause. The committee's official action, voted by the Democratic majority, was to denounce McCarthy's crusade as "a fraud and a hoax," chastising the senator for perpetrating deliberate and willful falsehoods.

Proof of the popularity of McCarthy's cause, however, came in the fall of 1950. By delivering thirty speeches, he propelled his anticommunist witch hunt into a campaign tour de force. And after the ballots were counted, political observers credited McCarthy with Republican victories in a dozen Senate races. Most notable was the stinging defeat of Millard E. Tydings, chairman of the committee that had denounced McCarthy.

The anticommunist pit bull next set his sights on the 1952 national elections. He publicly called President Harry S. Truman a "son of a bitch" and labeled Secretary of State Dean Acheson the "Red Dean"—thereby saying Acheson was a communist. The Wisconsin senator was highly sought after, stumping on behalf of candidates in sixteen states and earning a rousing ovation as a featured speaker at the Republican National Convention.

The results of the election reconfirmed McCarthy's power. He was cited as a major factor in helping the Republican Party take control of the White House. Observers also estimated that at least eight Republican senators owed their victories to McCarthy's support.

In the new Congress, McCarthy became chairman of the Permanent Subcommittee on Investigations, having wide authority to investigate government activities. What's more, he controlled a subcommittee staff, hiring as chief counsel the abrasive Roy Cohn. As subcommittee chairman, McCarthy earned a reputation as a savage inquisitor. In 1953, he initiated preliminary inquiries of 445 people.

McCarthy Exploits the Press

Although the climate of the times and Republican strategy contributed to McCarthy's rise, the single most important element was his ability to manipulate the press. Scholars have acknowledged his media savvy. In his book *Joe McCarthy and the Press*, Edwin R. Bayley concluded that McCarthy "was able to generate massive publicity because he understood the press, its practices and its values; he knew what made news."[2]

In particular, McCarthy was a master at manipulating the wire services—the Associated Press, United Press, and International News Service. Because only a handful of papers had their own reporters in Washington, these operations had enormous influence.

One of McCarthy's most successful media techniques involved the timing of accusations. He calculated the exact hour of the day he could make a claim and be sure the wire services wouldn't have time to track down a response from the accused person before stories had to be filed to meet the deadline for the afternoon papers. So the journalists, driven by competition, distributed one-sided stories. Allen Alexander of the

Associated Press recalled, "AP member newspapers also subscribing to competing UP and INS services would message frantically: 'Opposition reports that McCarthy said XXX. Where's ours?' What do you tell your superiors when they see a message like that?"[3]

McCarthy's tactics allowed him to manipulate papers into publishing dozens of lies. United Press reporter George Reedy recalled the morning McCarthy waited until 10:50 to announce he had a letter proving that Owen Lattimore, a Johns Hopkins University professor, was a spy. Reedy knew the competing news services would report the charge for the 11 a.m. deadline. "We all wanted to see the letter, but he wouldn't give it up," Reedy recalled. "So I had to go down and write the story. At 11:45 a.m., Joe let go of the letter. There wasn't a thing in it to back up what he'd said." The papers printed clarifications, but those items received far less prominence than the original accusations had.[4]

Another of McCarthy's techniques exploited the concept of objectivity. News accounts in the 1950s barred all interpretation, as the journalistic convention of the day was that news stories should provide a bare-bones recitation of the facts—nothing more. So McCarthy knew that journalists would report, without comment, any charge a US senator made.

Reporters were so fearful of allowing subjectivity to slip into their work that they wouldn't, for example, include in a story the fact that a particular accusation was the fifth or tenth or fiftieth unsubstantiated accusation McCarthy had made that week. William Theis of the International News Service lamented, "We let Joe get away with murder, reporting it as he said it, not doing the kind of critical analysis we'd do today. All three wire services were so God damned objective that McCarthy got away with everything, bamboozling the editors and the public. I'd go home literally sick, seeing what that guy was getting away with."[5]

Many reporters came to regret how McCarthy had manipulated them into being mere conduits for his lies. Reedy later said, "We had to take what McCarthy said at face value. Joe couldn't find a communist in Red Square, but he was a United States senator. So we reported whatever he said."[6]

Edward R. Murrow Redefines TV News

At the same time that print journalism was committing acts that it would later feel guilty for having allowed, TV was developing the program that was fated to become an icon of electronic journalism.

CBS introduced *See It Now* in 1951. The narrator of the thirty-minute news program was the man who ultimately would wear the mantle "patron saint of the broadcasting profession." Edward R. Murrow first won his place in journalism history while reporting for CBS radio during World War II. Speaking from the rooftops of London during bombing raids, from trenches all over Europe, and from the Buchenwald concentration camp on the day it was liberated, Murrow became the most trusted voice of the war. His masterful reporting was coupled with a superb delivery and a deep sense of humanity to create a prose style that sounded like poetry.[7]

Murrow's behind-the-scenes collaborator was Fred Friendly, a young producer whose vision and technical wizardry enhanced Murrow's on-air strengths. The Murrow-Friendly partnership began in 1950 with *Hear It Now*, a magazine program on CBS radio. When TV emerged as the electronic medium of choice, the two men transformed the program into a visual phenomenon.

See It Now offered audiences a conceit that was entirely new to the infant medium. For Murrow and Friendly created the first TV program to grapple with controversial issues, crafting segments about such provocative subjects as the quality of health care and the hazards of cigarette smoking. The explosive growth of television further aided *See It Now*'s rise to legendary status. In 1947, only 1 percent of American homes had a television; by 1953, that percentage had jumped to 80.[8]

Defending the Little Guy

In 1953, Murrow and Friendly decided the time had come for a program to show that the paranoia gripping the country had gone too far. Their search for an upstanding citizen whose rights had been violated by the government's obsession with national security led them to Milo Radulovich. The twenty-six-year-old meteorologist had spent eight years in the air force and received a commendation for his work on a secret weather station, and he'd continued to serve as a reserve officer while attending the University of Michigan. Under McCarthyism, however, he'd been classified as a security risk because he associated with people believed to be subversives—his father and sister. A military board of inquiry recommended that Radulovich be ousted from the reserves because his two family members subscribed to Serbian-language newspapers.

"The Case of Milo Radulovich, A0589839," aired in October. It began with Murrow's simple introduction, "This is the story of Milo Radulovich—no special hero, no martyr." Murrow then described the young man's impeccable military record and the high regard his neighbors in Dexter, Michigan, had for him. Murrow was sketching the American Everyman, saying, "His wife works nights at the telephone company. They live at 7867 Ann Arbor Street."[9]

Viewers next heard John Radulovich, Milo's father, say why he subscribed to the Serbian-language newspaper. "I like their Christmas calendars," he said. Margaret Radulovich then appeared, insisting that her choice of newspapers had nothing to do with her brother, stating, "My political beliefs are my own private affair." Lieutenant Radulovich made the same point, speaking quietly but with conviction. "What my sister does, what political opinions or activities she engages in, are her own affair," he said. "They certainly do not influence me."[10]

One of the program's most stunning revelations was that the newspaper Radulovich's father and sister read wasn't, in fact, pro-communist. Murrow reported that the paper consistently supported Marshal Tito, the Yugoslavian leader who five years earlier had broken with the Soviet Union and since that time had been receiving aid from the United States.

Murrow ended the broadcast with a dramatic statement delivered directly into the TV camera, "We believe that 'the son shall not bear the iniquity of the father,' even though that iniquity be proved. And in this case, it was not."[11]

Reaction was swift. Of 8,000 letters and telegrams CBS received, 7,200 supported Radulovich. Media reviews were overwhelmingly positive as well. *Newsweek* said the segment marked a "week of triumph" for *See It Now*, and the *New York Times* lauded the broadcast as "superb" and the first program in TV history to take "a vigorous editorial stand in a matter of national importance."[12]

The most potent praise came five weeks after the broadcast when the secretary of the Air Force appeared on *See It Now* and announced that Milo Radulovich would be allowed to continue to serve as an officer in the Reserves. As Friendly later wrote, that statement "established for the first time the enormous impact of television reporting."[13]

Attacking the Big Guy

The success of the Radulovich program encouraged Murrow and Friendly, in the colorful words of one observer, "to lunge for the heart of the beast." They decided to deliver a body blow to McCarthy by showing viewers exactly what kind of unscrupulous methods he used.[14]

Most of the March 1954 *See It Now* segment consisted of filmed speeches by McCarthy. The audience heard the senator contradict himself by first denouncing criticism of either major political party, for fear that such attacks would cause the decline of democracy, and then breaking his own rule by condemning the opposing party, saying, "Those who wear the label 'Democrat' wear it with the stain of a historic betrayal—twenty years of treason." The audience also was given a taste of McCarthy's malice, seeing him badger witnesses and hearing his feigned slip of the tongue in referring to the 1952 Democratic presidential nominee not as Adlai Stevenson but as *Alger*—a mean-spirited allusion to convicted spy Alger Hiss.[15]

"A Report on Senator Joseph R. McCarthy" contained incisive statements by Murrow as well. He accused McCarthy of terrorizing innocent people and lying to the American public. At one point, Murrow spoke directly to the viewers and said, "The line between investigation and persecution is a very fine one, and the junior senator from Wisconsin has stepped over it repeatedly." Murrow's voice became stern as he continued,

EDWARD R. MURROW
-1-

After challenging McCarthyism, Edward R. Murrow became the
most revered television newsman in history, with one historian
calling him the "patron saint of the broadcasting profession."

© *Michael Ochs Archives/Getty Images*

"This is no time for men who oppose Senator McCarthy's methods to keep silent."[16]

Murrow's eloquent prose, however, took a backseat to the compelling visual images that he and Friendly had chosen to depict McCarthy. Many observers who have viewed the program have attempted to transform those images into words. One said the clips portrayed the senator "as a villain and a bully" and revealed "his shoddy practices and demeanor." Another said McCarthy came across as "a giggling psychopath," and a third wrote of the senator, "Sneering, truculent and wholly evil, he rumbled his evasions and hesitations and lies. He was caught huffing and chuckling in a way that sounded as if he was just a little nutty."[17]

As soon as the program ended, network switchboards lit up with the largest flood of responses in TV history. CBS received 12,000 phone calls and telegrams, with positive reactions outnumbering negative ones fifteen to one. Even after McCarthy took advantage of *See It Now*'s offer to broadcast a half-hour rebuttal—in which the senator accused Murrow of being a communist—the mail continued to run overwhelmingly in the newsman's favor.[18]

The press response was equally enthusiastic. The *New Yorker* dubbed the program "an extraordinary feat of journalism," *Newsweek* said that "no political show so damning [has] ever been done before," and the *New York Times* called the segment "crusading journalism of high responsibility and genuine courage."[19]

With the passage of time, *See It Now*'s program on McCarthy has assumed legendary status, with many scholars calling it the single most important broadcast in television history. In particular, historians have praised the program's impact on McCarthy's career. The assessments have been legion, including, "The program was the decisive moment at which opinion turned against McCarthy," and, "Thereafter, McCarthy's fortunes went steadily down." The author of one history of the mass media wrote unequivocally, "The man mainly responsible for silencing McCarthy was Edward R. Murrow."[20]

Televised Hearings Strike the Final Blow

The climactic moment in McCarthy's downfall came two months later when the nation watched live as McCarthy reinforced what Murrow and Friendly had shown on tape: he was a sadistic bully. Thanks to television, the drama unfolded before one of the largest audiences ever to witness a major event in American history—an extraordinary 80 million viewers.

The Army-McCarthy hearings evolved out of the senator's charges that subversives had infiltrated the US Army. Military officials countercharged that McCarthy and counsel Roy Cohn had sought preferential treatment for Private G. David Schine, a young man who'd worked for McCarthy's committee before being drafted. The two warring sides then met during

Senate hearings. In April 1954, NBC aired the opening salvos, and CBS offered a nightly film summary. ABC placed considerably more emphasis on the hearings, providing continuous live coverage for all thirty-six days of the hearings—a total of 180 hours.[21]

During the hearings, thirty witnesses marched to the microphone and described how Cohn, with McCarthy's support, had tried to secure special treatment for Schine, the heir to a hotel fortune who'd developed an unusually close relationship with Cohn. According to testimony, Cohn repeatedly demanded that military officials appoint Schine to a post near Cohn in New York City, threatening to intensify the investigation of the army if the demand wasn't met. After Schine was assigned to a base in Georgia, Cohn demanded that the soldier be excused from Saturday duty and be granted extra passes so he could travel to New York every weekend.

One vivid confrontation during the hearings became imbedded in the consciousness of the American public. It pitted McCarthy against Joseph Welch, the army's special counsel. Welch was an avuncular Bostonian blessed not only with a keen legal mind and a gentle charm but also with a flair for courtroom drama. McCarthy grew to detest Welch because he had won, through the TV camera, the nation's affection. Sensing that McCarthy was about to attack Welch, CBS and NBC decided to broadcast the day's hearings live.

In the fateful encounter, Welch won point after point. Then McCarthy abruptly broke into the testimony and began a reckless accusation that history would never forget. Sneering at Welch, McCarthy accused him of "treason" because one of the associates in Welch's Boston law firm had been a member of a communist-front organization.[22]

As McCarthy began, Welch lowered his head into his hands and stared at the table in front of him. After a few minutes of McCarthy's raging, Welch slowly raised his leonine head and formed the muted word "Stop." Leaning toward the microphone, he asked the committee chair for the right to speak. As Welch began, McCarthy turned away to talk to an aide. Welch asked for his attention. McCarthy responded, laughing, "I can listen with one ear." Welch said sternly, "This time, I want you to listen with both." Welch then unleashed the first of several dramatic statements he would utter that day, "Until this moment, senator, I think I never really gauged your cruelty or your recklessness."[23]

The entire hearing room—and the nation—held its breath, silenced by the stone-cold emotion in Welch's voice. He explained that Frederick Fisher had participated in the communist-front organization when he'd been a student at Harvard long before joining Welch's law firm. Welch said he initially had wanted Fisher to assist him during the hearings in Washington but, upon learning of the young lawyer's activities in college, had decided he should remain in Boston. Welch then turned to McCarthy. "Little did I dream you could be so reckless and so cruel as to do injury to that lad. He shall always bear a scar needlessly inflicted by you." In the tone of a compassionate minister being forced to chastise a wayward soul, Welch continued speaking to McCarthy, "If it were in my power to forgive you for your reckless cruelty, I would do so. I like to think I am a gentle man, but your forgiveness will have to come from someone other than me."[24]

In a horribly miscalculated effort to win the audience to his side, McCarthy then struck back at Welch by saying he had no right to speak of cruelty. Welch turned to McCarthy and said, "Let us not assassinate this lad further, senator. You have done enough." Welch then released another of the verbal bullets that ultimately would prove fatal to McCarthy, "Have you no sense of decency, sir? At long last, have you left *no sense of decency*?"[25]

After a moment of silence, the entire hearing room exploded with spontaneous applause. Every man and woman who'd observed the heart-stopping verbal exchange knew that Welch had triumphed—and wanted to shower their approval on him.

When Welch stood to walk from the room, reporters raced to the telephones to tell the nation of McCarthy's humiliating defeat. As the gentle lawyer—now the noble defender of fairness—approached the hearing-room door, a woman laid her hand softly on his arm and, overcome with emotion, burst into tears. The TV audience saw it all.

The *New York Times* reported that McCarthy's televised performance "demonstrated with appalling clarity precisely what kind of man he is."

The story continued, "One cannot remain indifferent to Joe McCarthy in one's living room. He is an abrasive man. And he is recklessly transparent. The country did not know him before, despite all the headlines. Now it has seen him. The things that have hurt him and cost him support are his manner and his manners. The Senator from Wisconsin is a bad-mannered man."[26]

Scholars studying the iconic event have echoed the same thoughts, writing, "The close-up exposure left a feeling of distaste for McCarthy," and, "Joe came across as boorish, disruptive, and anarchic." Even Roy Cohn agreed, writing of the television coverage, "The blow was terribly damaging to Senator McCarthy. He was pictured before the nation as a cruel man who deliberately sought to wreck a fine young lawyer's life."[27]

The American people spoke as well. In January 1954, a Gallup Poll had reported that 50 percent of the people surveyed had a favorable response to McCarthy. After the Murrow program and the hearings, however, that figure plummeted to 34 percent.[28]

Media critics lavished praise on ABC for broadcasting the hearings, particularly because the action cost the network dearly. All the revenue that sponsors would have paid for the huge block of air time was lost, as sponsors weren't willing to be associated with programming that could harm McCarthy. Airing the hearings cost ABC more than $500,000.[29]

The coverage led to action. Immediately after the hearings, senators began efforts, in earnest, to silence McCarthy. They ultimately censured him, marking only the fourth time in two centuries that the Senate had taken such severe action. In December 1954, the senators voted sixty-seven to twenty-two to strip McCarthy of his power, subjecting him to public disgrace. McCarthy's life came to an abrupt end three years after the Senate action. A heavy drinker, he died of liver disease associated with alcoholism. He hadn't yet reached his fiftieth birthday.

Trial by Television

Beginning in 1950 and continuing for three years, Senator Joseph McCarthy became a fierce presence in America. Stopping him required a power of great might. That valiant savior of the democratic way of life began to emerge when Edward R. Murrow committed *See It Now* to attacking the senator, first with the Radulovich segment and then with the program crafted to reveal McCarthy as a malicious and mean-spirited bully. ABC joined the campaign by airing live coverage of the Army-McCarthy hearings—including Joseph Welch's gripping verbal assault. The entire drama, thanks to the TV cameras, unfolded in the living rooms of 80 million Americans.

It took a force of immense potential and proportion to tame a power as diabolical as the Roman candle known as Joe McCarthy. But in the early 1950s, the infant institution of TV news distinguished itself—in its finest hour—by demonstrating that it was fully equal to such a formidable task.

11

PUSHING CIVIL RIGHTS ONTO THE NATIONAL AGENDA

BY THE 1950S, SLAVERY HAD BEEN OUTLAWED IN THE UNITED States for nearly a century, but southern racists had devised other forms of tyranny to keep black Americans in their "place." Poll taxes, grandfather clauses, unfairly administered literacy tests, and various acts of intimidation denied African Americans the right to vote, and the concept of "separate but equal" deprived them access to public facilities and decent educations.

In 1954, the US Supreme Court pronounced six words that forever altered the legal status of black Americans: "Separate educational facilities are inherently unequal." The *Brown v. Board of Education* decision prompted African Americans to challenge unjust laws and discriminatory practices, spawning the Civil Rights Movement. The initial challenges largely failed, though, because of the wall of bigotry that segregationists had constructed—they ruled the American South the way kings had ruled feudal estates.[1]

And then came television. By covering the movement's various events, TV news awakened people throughout the country to the realities of

African-American oppression in the South. By pushing those reprehensible actions into the face of the American people everywhere, TV news propelled the Civil Rights Movement into public consciousness and onto the national agenda. Northern newspapers such as the *New York Times* and *Boston Globe* also covered the movement, but TV news had much more impact.

Journalists and scholars alike have praised the vital role that television played in advancing race relations during the late 1950s and early 1960s. CBS producer William Peters said, "The Negro revolution of the 1960s could not have occurred without television coverage." Among the scholars who have lauded TV's role in mobilizing the nation to end segregation is William Wood. In his book *Electronic Journalism,* Wood wrote, "The on-the-scene coverage of intimidation and bestiality in the old South made indelible impressions on many who had been oblivious to or indifferent over home-grown, American brutality and injustice. Suddenly men and women all over the country were as close as across the street to the crucible of revolution. Whites everywhere were awakened."[2]

As the TV cameras showed African Americans being cursed, spat upon, attacked by police dogs, and blasted with firehoses merely for trying to exercise the rights they were guaranteed by the Constitution, those images became imbedded in the American mind. Public opinion then galvanized in support of civil rights.[3]

The First Great TV News Story

By the late 1950s, television news was competing with newspapers on a daily basis, and the Civil Rights Movement was the first great TV story. NBC newsman Bill Monroe wrote, "When you *see* and *hear* a wildly angry man talking, whether he is a segregationist or integrationist, you can understand the man's anger, you can feel it—the depth of it, the power of it. But if you *read* a description of what the man said, you find that, by comparison, the words are dried-up little symbols through which only a fraction of the story comes."[4]

That the Civil Rights Movement was a great TV story didn't mean, however, that the South wanted network journalists to report it. The stability of African-American oppression rested on local control of information, with many southern papers refusing to publish articles that might disturb the existing racial pattern. When segregationists realized that TV was disrupting the system, they saw reporters as outside agitators—and enemies. Dan Rather of CBS recalled looking for a motel to stay at when covering a story in Mississippi and being greeted by a sign in a window that read "NO DOGS, NIGGERS OR REPORTERS ALLOWED."[5]

Segregationists didn't stop with making signs, as dozens of correspondents were injured while covering the movement. When NBC's Richard Valeriani was reporting from Alabama in 1965, he was struck from the back with the wooden handle of an ax, sustaining a severe head wound that kept him in the hospital for several days. Valeriani recalled how law enforcement officials responded, saying, "A state trooper saw the whole thing. He took the ax handle away from the guy, telling him, 'You've done enough damage for one night.' But that was it. The trooper didn't even arrest the guy."[6]

Knocking Down Walls in Little Rock

Observers point to a Gothic-style high school in Arkansas as the backdrop for the first chapter in TV's epic coverage of the Civil Rights Movement. CBS correspondent Robert Schakne said, "Little Rock was the first case where people really got their impression of an event from television. It was the event that nationalized a news story that would have remained a local story if it had just been a print story."[7]

During the summer of 1957, African-American leaders in Little Rock challenged the segregated school policy by enrolling nine black students in the city's most highly regarded public high school, which was all white. In early September, network cameras were on hand to show the nation that the students walked gravely toward Central High School—the girls in white blouses, the boys in pressed trousers—but then were turned away,

Television cameras captured in vivid images the curses and hateful venom that became part of Elizabeth Eckford's daily life as one of the "Little Rock Nine."

© AP Photo/Arkansas Democrat Gazette/Will Counts

blocked by Arkansas National Guardsmen. Governor Orval Faubus had ordered the soldiers to stop the students from entering the school.[8]

Every image that day was gripping, but one stood out from all the rest. Black leaders had arranged for the youngsters to be brought to the school in a police car for protection. But one student, Elizabeth Eckford, didn't have a telephone, so she hadn't been notified of the plan. The petite fifteen-year-old, therefore, arrived at the school alone. Confronted by angry segregationists, the tiny figure was captured on film as the crowd screamed, "Lynch her! Lynch the nigger bitch!" Clutching her school books and trying desperately not to cry, the girl was shown surrounded by thousands of sneering whites towering over her. The camera continued to focus on the lone girl until she finally escaped onto a city bus.[9]

The cameras remained in Arkansas throughout the month, as President Dwight Eisenhower in Washington struggled with what to do. No crusader for racial equality, Eisenhower wanted states to resolve their own issues. But this time the governor had gone too far. His refusing to allow the students to attend the school was in open defiance of the Supreme Court's desegregation ruling—and played out, thanks to TV, in front of the entire country. After three weeks of indecision Eisenhower placed the Arkansas National Guardsmen under federal control, ordering the soldiers to protect the "Little Rock Nine."

Cameras were in front of Central High School the next morning as the students again attempted to enter the building. The African-American youngsters were dwarfed by throngs of angry segregationists who covered the school grounds, chanting, "Two-Four-Six-Eight! We don't wanna integrate!" The soldiers—with their bayonets drawn—surrounded the frightened African-American students and inched their way through the angry sea. The faces were contorted as the white crowd jeered and screamed, "Go home, nigger!"[10]

Coverage continued throughout the school year. The cameras documented uniformed soldiers marching through the streets of Little Rock and the barrage of curses and threats spewed onto the African-American students. Each morning, viewers around the country saw the caravan of military jeeps in front of and behind the station wagon escorting the nine teenagers from their homes to the school; each afternoon, the cameras recorded the return trip taking them home again.[11]

Breaking Barriers at the University of Georgia

By early 1961, the country had a youthful new president, and civil rights leaders savored new hope that John F. Kennedy's administration would provide more support for their march toward racial equality.

Testimony to the new optimism came the same month as Kennedy's inauguration, when a federal court ruled that the University of Georgia had to admit African-American students. The two young people were Hamilton Holmes and Charlayne Hunter. Their admission unleashed a

maelstrom of hatred, and the TV networks rushed to Georgia to document it.[12]

The attention centered on Hunter because she, being female, was required to live in a dormitory, while Holmes, being male, was allowed to
move off campus. Then a frightened eighteen-year-old, Hunter appeared
nightly on the TV screen for days on end, looking toward the ground as
white students screamed and spat at her. One piece showed the world how
students taunted Hunter, as the film captured a white girl walking up to
Hunter, tossing a quarter on the floor and sneering, "Here, nigger. Here's a
quarter. Go change my sheets."[13]

Although the students' contempt for Hunter initially must have
seemed beyond belief to many northern viewers, similar images became
commonplace in the next few years. The same scenes unfolded time
and time again as educational institutions in the South—including the
University of Mississippi later in 1961 and the University of Alabama in
1963—gradually and fitfully became desegregated.

Riding Buses for Freedom

The next phase of coverage evolved from a Supreme Court decision banning segregation in interstate travel. To test the new law, in May 1961 a
racially mixed group of college students bought bus tickets to take them
from Washington, DC, to New Orleans. When the students were dubbed
"freedom riders," TV had its next story.[14]

NBC cameraman Moe Levy boarded one of the buses with the students, capturing their images on film. The young men and women who
boarded the first two buses in Washington were well dressed and well
groomed. One slender young African-American woman wore a tailored
suit and carried a white patent leather purse. The young man beside her
wore a dark suit and striped tie, with a carefully folded handkerchief pro-
truding from his breast pocket.[15]

As the freedom riders traveled south through Virginia and the Car-
olinas, segregationists occasionally taunted them, but those acts were
forgotten once the buses crossed into Alabama. The state police had

promised to escort the buses, but at some point along the way the police cars vanished. So when the buses pulled into the Montgomery station, a mob of 2,000 segregationists—armed with bricks, baseball bats, and lead pipes—attacked the students. Although no images of the blood-bath were filmed because the mob smashed Levy's camera, the networks broadcast footage of the bruised and bloodied students in their hospital beds. The young men and women lost teeth and suffered broken bones, many of them beaten so severely that they were disfigured for the rest of their lives. Levy was repeatedly clubbed, and one of his legs was permanently injured.[16]

Defying the Power Structure in Birmingham

In the early 1960s, Alabama's largest city became a notorious battlefield in the civil rights struggle. For it was in Birmingham that 3,000 black men, women, and children were arrested in one seething spring. TV cameras sent images of the event throughout the country, and viewers saw footage they'd never forget.[17]

In 1963, the Reverend Martin Luther King Jr. targeted Birmingham for a series of nonviolent protests aimed at overturning the city's white power structure. The campaign began in April, with demonstrators pick-eting stores and conducting sit-ins at lunch counters. In week two, the campaign expanded to marches. As the arrests climbed, demonstrators from other cities streamed into Birmingham.[18]

Television showed that many protesters were in their twenties but others were middle-aged women wearing dresses, hats, and white gloves. The only violence portrayed on film was by whites. Footage would be-gin with blacks walking quietly up to a lunch counter and sitting on the stools. As the waitresses ignored them, the African Americans gazed for-ward, some of them lost in prayer. The serenity was soon shattered by a white segregationist approaching from the rear and pouring a bottle of ketchup over a peaceful protester's hair. The blacks remained poised as the whites pointed their fingers and laughed at the ketchup dripping onto the protester's shirt or blouse. In some scenes, the whites became enraged by the victim's lack of reaction and pushed him or her off the stool. Then a white police officer would enter the picture, arresting the blacks while allowing the whites to go free.

During the next several weeks, as the daily dramas continued to play out on the evening news, the eyes of the nation turned to Birmingham. The black community's ability to unite and the protesters' willingness to be injured and arrested increasingly frustrated and angered Police Commissioner "Bull" Connor and the other racist authorities. The protest had now continued for a full month, the city jail was overflowing, and the protesters were clearly succeeding in their efforts to shine the spotlight on Birmingham. Tension was high.

In early May, protesters introduced a daring new strategy to win the nation's compassion: having school children join the demonstrations. Thousands of African-American boys and girls, many still in elementary school, took to the streets for a massive march through downtown. The children celebrated the "Black and Glad" aspect of the movement, laughing and dancing while they sang simple freedom songs to a jazz tempo— creating dynamic images.[19]

Connor wasn't amused. He arrested 700 youngsters and ordered his officers to become more *physical*. Protesters were stunned when the police began using high-pressure firehoses that were so powerful that even the strongest of men couldn't stay standing against them. The officers manning the hoses pushed women and children to the ground and pinned them against buildings as if they were animals.

The second instrument of domination Connor authorized was even more startling. German shepherd police dogs, trained to attack dangerous criminals, were brought to the scene. The ferocious animals snarled and pulled at the leashes the officers used to control them. Many of the children were so frightened they cried hysterically and tried to escape. Connor responded by ordering the dogs forward as he yelled proudly, "Look at those niggers run!"[20]

Television captured the terror. And that night on their TV screens, the American people witnessed a level of police brutality far beyond anything they'd ever imagined could take place in the United States. Viewers saw,

A Birmingham police officer held this young man in place so
the attack dog could rip into his stomach—and the television
networks saw to it that the whole world was watching.

© *Associated Press/Bill Hudson*

for example, a middle-aged woman being held to the ground by five white
police officers, one with a knee across her throat. Those same viewers also
watched as a dignified woman, dressed in high heels and a pearl necklace,
kneeled in prayer amid the chaos on all sides of her.[21]

The specific scene from that day that caused the most reaction was
of a police dog, with its fangs bared, tearing at the stomach of a black
schoolboy. The officer controlling the dog grabbed the young man's
sweater, holding him in place so the dog could maul him. One historian
went so far as to credit the success of the Birmingham campaign to that
one image, writing, "If there was any single point at which the 1960s
generation of 'new Negroes' turned into a major social force, the appearance of that photograph was it. Intense pressure on President Kennedy
to initiate federal action began to be applied the moment that image
appeared."[22]

An editorial in the *New York Times* spoke for millions of TV viewers when it stated, "The use of police dogs and high-pressure firehoses to subdue school children in Birmingham is a national disgrace." Americans around the country demonstrated their solidarity with the protesters by organizing public marches in forty cities.[23]

In Alabama, negotiations that previously had failed now succeeded. The day after the images of the firehoses and police dogs were televised, Kennedy sent a Justice Department official to Birmingham to mediate between city officials and the demonstrators. And exactly one week after the shocking images had aired, the leaders reached an agreement that allowed, for the first time, African Americans to shop at city stores and eat at city restaurants.[24]

The TV images prompted action on the national level as well, propelling Kennedy to propose civil rights legislation of a scope and boldness that a few months earlier wouldn't have been possible. In a speech televised live during prime time, the president said what African Americans had been waiting generations to hear, "We preach freedom around the world, but are we to say to the world—and much more importantly, to each other—that this is the land of the free, except for the Negroes? The time has come for this nation to fulfill its promise."[25]

Marching on Washington

Building on the momentum the Birmingham images had created, civil rights leaders took their crusade to the power center of American government. And as they planned the March on Washington, organizers kept foremost in their minds that the event had the potential to become a television spectacle—a promise that was fully realized.[26]

Network coverage of the August 1963 event began early. NBC led its rivals with the network's *Today* morning program kicking off with a thirty-minute report, followed by updates throughout the day, a two-hour recap in the afternoon, and a final report during prime time. ABC hopped in and out with coverage as the day progressed, and CBS carried the speeches live for three hours in the afternoon, then ran a special in the evening. The networks received exuberant praise for their coverage. A *Washington Post* story began, "As a TV spectacular, the March on Washington was a program without parallel."[27]

And a great event it was. With heads high and chests forward, 200,000 Americans marched, some spending their life savings to make the pilgrimage to the nation's capital. The demonstrators showed well on television, especially when the networks took their cameras high into the Washington Monument for panoramic shots. The images showed marchers carrying signs that demanded "Decent Housing Now" and "Jobs and Freedom Now."

The main speaker of the day was a man the TV camera loved—and helped boost to his preeminent stature in the movement. Martin Luther King Jr., with his broad face and muscular neck and shoulders, filled the television screen with a sense of physical as well as spiritual power. In his rich baritone voice, the thirty-four-year-old Baptist preacher spoke the moving words that generations of African-American boys and girls would commit to memory, "I have a dream that my four little children will one day live in a nation where they will not be judged by the color of their skin, but by the content of their character."[28]

Television took a step toward that dream a few days later when NBC produced *The American Revolution of '63*, a news special that's been described as the magnum opus of civil rights coverage. The *New York Times* called the program "a turning point in TV's journalistic evolution. Never before has so much valuable prime time been accorded to a single domestic issue in one uninterrupted stretch."[29]

It was particularly courageous for NBC to air the three-hour program because sponsors refused to support it, fearing segregationists would boycott any products advertised during the show. The network stood firm, canceling its entire evening of commercial programming to show the special and thereby losing $500,000 in revenue in a single night.[30]

The program profiled cities that had played key roles in the movement up to that point, giving the network a chance to replay images of terrified students in Little Rock and ferocious police dogs in Birmingham. The introductory statement was as stirring as the footage, "Did this American

Revolution begin this year in Birmingham? Or did it begin in 1954 with a Supreme Court decision? Some of its roots reach back to 1776 to an independence declaration—even back to the year 52 when the Apostle Paul, preaching in Athens, said, 'God hath made of one blood all nations of men.'"[31]

Some Americans, however, still adamantly opposed the civil rights revolution—and the medium that was propelling it onto the national agenda. Mississippi Governor Ross Barnett said, "Fellow Americans, you are witnessing one more chapter in what has been termed the 'Television Revolution.' The TV networks have publicized and dramatized the race issue far beyond its relative importance in today's world. The three-hour special program and the degree of coverage accorded to the August 28 March on Washington underlined the fact that the American public is being propagandized by overemphasis."[32]

Barnett wasn't the only segregationist who chastised television for supporting the movement. After NBC canceled its telecast of the Blue-Gray college football game because African Americans weren't allowed to play in it, Alabama Governor George Wallace denounced the decision as "irresponsible." And when CBS president Frank Stanton testified at a Senate hearing, South Carolina Senator Strom Thurmond attacked him for devoting too much coverage to civil rights, asking Stanton point blank, "Don't you care about white people?"[33]

Seeking Voting Rights in Selma

In 1964, civil rights leaders turned their attention toward blacks being denied the vote, focusing specifically on Selma, Alabama, where Americans of African descent comprised 57 percent of the residents but less than 1 percent of the registered voters. Martin Luther King Jr. set out to change that statistic by asking supporters from around the country to come to the city and undertake a voter registration campaign.[34]

The supporters heeded the call, as did network correspondents. Typical of the images they broadcast was one showing a tall, distinguished-looking African-American man in a suit and tie being taunted by white hooligans at the registrar's office. The teenage boys pushed the middle-aged man out of line and then chased him down the street, yelling obscenities at him. When one of the thugs knocked off the man's hat and he leaned over to pick it up, the boys kicked him. The TV camera showed the episode in its shameful entirety.[35]

King's most daring idea for drawing attention to the voter registration drive was to lead a fifty-mile march from Selma to the state capitol in Montgomery. The event would end with the protesters delivering a petition to Governor Wallace, even though the legendary racist publicly opposed the event.[36]

On Sunday, March 7, 1965, some 600 men and women started walking down US Route 80. But after marching 300 yards, they found the highway blocked by state troopers. The men were led by James Clark, Selma's quick-tempered sheriff. After the marchers refused to disperse, Clark and his men attacked them in full force.

TV images of the event showed clubs flying in all directions as African-American men and women screamed and fell to the ground while the officers continued forward, stomping on the people who lay on the pavement. Then the film showed officers running after particular marchers, striking them without mercy. A middle-aged woman in a head scarf hunched down on her knees, but an officer struck her on the head with his nightstick. When the woman collapsed on the ground, another officer ran into the picture and kicked her in the stomach and clubbed her again.[37]

Officers being mounted on horses added another memorable dimension to the scene. Looking like Cossacks overpowering the peasants, the mounted men spurred their horses and charged into the crowd with nightsticks swinging and steel-toed boots kicking at the protesters. Meanwhile, hundreds of whites stood on the edge of the highway whooping and cheering.[38]

Scenes on TV became even more horrifying when clouds of tear gas filled the screen. As the white officers covered their faces with gas masks, African-American men and women fell coughing and sputtering to the ground. State troopers raced from one person to the next, striking each one again and again with their nightsticks. The cameras moved in for close-ups of some of the bloody figures lying motionless, and still the officers continued to beat and kick them.[39]

The incident—dubbed "Bloody Sunday"—ignited a powder keg of protest across the country. Members of Congress, governors, and clergymen denounced the brutality. Michigan Governor George Romney led 10,000 marchers in a demonstration in Detroit, 15,000 New Yorkers protested in Harlem, and thousands of other indignant Americans snarled traffic in Chicago, Los Angeles, and Washington.

Like much of the nation, President Lyndon Johnson found the images appalling. After Governor Wallace flew to Washington to meet with the president, Johnson announced, "I told the governor that the brutality in Selma last Sunday must not be repeated." When another Selma march was conducted two weeks after the first, the crowd swelled to 3,000 protesters from across the country. With Johnson insisting that Wallace provide protection for the marchers, the event unfolded without violence.[40]

But LBJ's more important activity that month was a televised address to Congress. The speech, which Johnson delivered with visible emotion, was in preparation for a voting rights bill he submitted two days later—which was enacted within four months. Johnson said, "Many of the issues of civil rights are complex and difficult. But about this there can be no argument: Every American citizen must have an equal right to vote."[41]

Television Images Nourish a Social Revolution

Congress ultimately passed two pieces of legislation that became the most important tangible products of the Civil Rights Movement. The Civil Rights Act of 1964 established the Equal Employment Opportunity Commission and prohibited restaurants, hotels, and other facilities of public accommodation from turning away any person on the basis of race. The Voting Rights Act of 1965 banned all barriers to Americans exercising the right to vote.

In the same breath that journalists, historians, and activists speak of these landmark pieces of legislation, they also describe the pivotal role TV news played in gaining support for the measures. In particular, observers point to the televised images of police brutality in Birmingham and Selma. NBC commentator Edwin Newman said, "When the people around this country saw people being beaten by hoodlums while they were seeking the right to vote, there was a sense of righteous indignation. The effect of these scenes, brought into our homes via television, was one of shock. We saw civil rights marchers and children being bitten by police dogs. The Civil Rights Act suddenly had the support it needed. Those images changed history."[42]

From a historian's viewpoint, Gary Orfield wrote of the images from Birmingham, "Anyone watching TV could understand what it felt like to have a dog, capable of tearing a man apart, lunge at him during a peaceful march. One image of a woman held down by five policemen was worth a million pious words. Brutal use of powerful firehoses to knock down demonstrators made the crisis clear in homes across the country." And John Lewis, who in 1965 led the voting rights march in Selma and today is a member of the US Congress, said, "If it hadn't been for television on that day, we wouldn't have gotten the Voting Rights Act of 1965. The Civil Rights Movement in this country owes a great deal to television."[43]

Newspapers and magazines can communicate information about an event, but TV news can make viewers feel like they are *part of* that event. For two centuries, citizens committed to advancing the cause of African American civil rights had struggled to convince the public that their cause was just. During the late 1950s and early 1960s, television allowed that minority to succeed by bringing a simplicity and a moral clarity to the issue. The bigotry of the segregationists and the determination of the African Americans, so vividly expressed on screens across America, spoke louder than any printed page. The images that TV news conveyed to its viewers moved the conscience of a nation and helped propel the people of the United States to take concrete steps toward leveling the racial playing field in this country.

12

BRINGING THE VIETNAM WAR INTO THE AMERICAN LIVING ROOM

TV NEWS BECOMING A MAJOR FORCE COINCIDED NOT ONLY WITH the Civil Rights Movement but also with the US military buildup in Vietnam. Network evening news programs expanded from fifteen minutes to half an hour in 1963; the first ground troops were sent to Indochina in 1965. The Vietnam War, therefore, became the first televised war. It also eventually became the least successful foreign war in American history.

Many media and political experts have argued that by bringing grisly images of battle into the American living room, TV news played a key role in turning the public against the Vietnam War and, ultimately, in hastening the end of that conflict. Although those observers are divided on whether ending the war was the right or wrong decision, they agree that TV showed the raw horror of war in ways that print journalism couldn't. Violence, carnage, and human suffering were depicted in withering reality, while topics such as politics and strategy, which weren't easily translated onto film, were downplayed. So TV viewers were left to conclude that the Vietnam War was costing American lives but wasn't justified.

Numerous scholars and journalists have made this point. In the book *The Vietnam Legacy*, Edward Shils wrote, "Television gave the American people vivid images of certain aspects of the war in Vietnam which they could never have gotten from reading newspapers and periodicals. It made them see the war as a meaningless destruction of lives." And veteran NBC commentator Edwin Newman concluded, "Television brought the Vietnam War into our living rooms on a nightly basis. They produced close-up, sensational images of war. American viewers saw the real experience of war transformed into theatrics on the twenty-one-inch screen. And they recoiled."[1]

America's Longest War

President Truman initiated US involvement in Vietnam in the early 1950s by sending military aid to the French colony. Truman and the men who entered the White House after him hoped to stop Vietnam from following China, its neighbor to the north, into communism. In 1954, Vietnam was divided in half—Ho Chi Minh's communist government in the north was headquartered in Hanoi, and the prodemocracy government in the south was centered in Saigon. American involvement continued under both Republican and Democratic administrations, with President Eisenhower dispatching military advisers to South Vietnam and President Kennedy increasing the number of those advisers. President Johnson took an even stronger hand against the communists, committing the first troops to Indochina.

Vietnam moved onto most Americans' radar in 1964. US military personnel announced that North Vietnamese patrol boats had fired on American destroyers in the Gulf of Tonkin, prompting Johnson to order a retaliatory strike that destroyed twenty-five boats and an oil depot. At LBJ's request, Congress passed the Gulf of Tonkin resolution, assuring its support for "all necessary action" to defend US forces in Southeast Asia.

In 1965, Johnson ordered offensive bombing raids and sent ground troops, with the number of GIs in Vietnam reaching 175,000 by year's end. Although the Americans were better equipped than the North Vietnamese, they weren't familiar with the style of warfare practiced by the rebel Viet Cong guerrilla fighters. Time after time, the enemy evaded the Americans by *melting* into the jungle. Determined to defeat the communists, Johnson continued to escalate the war effort. By 1967, the number of US troops exceeded 500,000.

Ultimately, the United States paid a high price for fighting in Vietnam, with more than 58,000 Americans dying in the war. The number of Southeast Asians who died isn't known, with estimates generally ranging from 1 million to 3 million.

The Most Powerful Medium in History

Although television existed during the Korean War, it hadn't yet evolved into a major news medium. By the mid-1960s, however, more people were receiving their news from TV than from newspapers. And as the Vietnam War continued, that balance increasingly shifted toward television. By 1972, two out of three persons surveyed named television as their major news source.[2]

At the height of the war, the evening news programs were drawing huge numbers of viewers. ABC, CBS, and NBC attracted a combined audience of 35 million per night. One of the most committed of those viewers was President Johnson, who was so obsessed with television news that he had three TV sets in the Oval Office, one for each network.

Television correspondents in Vietnam, as well as their print counterparts, were free to go wherever they wanted and report whatever they found, for this was the first—and last—American war without military censorship. During the early years of fighting, journalists were such committed cheerleaders for the government that officials felt voluntary guidelines were fully adequate. Those rules identified fifteen categories of information, such as troop movements, that were off-limits. Violation of the rules meant a reporter would lose his or her accreditation, but that happened only four times during the entire war.

Through 1967, television coverage was overwhelmingly favorable to US policy. After the Tet Offensive in early 1968, however, TV's portrayal of the war became much more critical.

Technological advances boosted the capabilities of TV news. New, lightweight cameras combined with jet air transportation and communication satellites meant that, for the first time, film from the front became a regular part of daily news coverage. Further advances meant that black-and-white images were transformed into color ones—blood could be seen in all its horrific brilliance.

Exposing the Horrors of War

From the moment ground troops arrived in Vietnam in 1965, television presented viewers with the most realistic battlefront images possible. TV defined the reality of war as, in a word, *blood*.

Typical was a 1967 piece in which NBC's Greg Harris joined a platoon of GIs. "In the first twenty-six days of the present operation," Harris reported on air, "this particular unit killed 270 VC while suffering only three wounded Americans." Film then showed US soldiers charging into a village, bayonets drawn. Harris continued, "Today the Viet Cong lost the use of Cong Phu. Tomorrow they will lose the use of another village, then another." As Harris wrapped up his report, the film showed the huts in the village burning.[3]

Dozens of such reports aired day after day, week after week. Each told of a unit burning a village, with film often showing dead bodies—many of them charred. NBC correspondent Jack Perkins said matter-of-factly during one report about a village being burned, "There was no discriminating one house from another. There did not need to be. The whole village was destroyed."[4]

Although lurid images of dead and wounded Vietnamese soldiers and civilians often filled the screen, the most sought-after film was of blood flowing from the veins of American GIs. An NBC News vice president said at the time, "It's not a Vietnamese war; it's an *American* war in Asia. And that's the only story the American audience is interested in." He told

Television coverage brought the reality of the battlefield—such as this image
of First Cavalry Division medic Thomas Cole enduring his own suffering while
trying to care for his wounded buddies—into the American living room.

© Associated Press/Henri Huet.

his correspondents to concentrate on providing graphic images of US soldiers engaged in combat.[5]

The bloody scenes were often featured as dramatic close-ups, with flames engulfing thatched roofs and black smoke billowing into the sky serving as backdrops. Typical was a heart-wrenching NBC sequence that showed a young GI screaming in anguish, "It hurts! It hurts!" as medics rushed him past the eye of the camera, his right leg reduced to a bloody stump.[6]

A Zippo Cigarette Lighter Ignites a Firestorm

The most controversial story of the early years of the war was by Morley Safer of CBS. One day in 1965, Safer was having coffee with some Marines when one of them asked if he'd like to join them on a field operation the next day. Safer jumped at the chance. After an amphibious carrier took them to Cam Ne, the men marched single file into the village and, in orderly fashion, burned every hut to the ground. The film was riveting. As the huts burst into flames, the Marines could be seen warning the Vietnamese peasants to run. But the film also showed that the warnings were useless because they were in English, while the confused looks on the women's and children's faces communicated that they understood only Vietnamese. The most poignant detail on the film, however, evolved from what the Marines used to ignite the thatched roofs: Zippo cigarette lighters.

When the film arrived in New York, network executives recognized the explosive nature of a report that depicted American soldiers cavalierly destroying a Vietnamese village by pulling lighters out of their pockets. Fred Friendly, the producer who'd piloted Edward R. Murrow through his battles with Joseph McCarthy ten years earlier, was awakened in the middle of the night. Friendly agreed to run the footage.

Safer's narrative for the story began with a recitation of facts—"The day's operation burned down 150 houses, wounded three women, killed one baby, and netted these four prisoners"—as Safer pointed to four elderly men. The correspondent, clearly shocked by the horror he'd witnessed, then added his own highly critical comments, "Today's operation is the frustration of Vietnam in miniature."[7]

Friendly didn't go home after the "Zippo segment" aired. Instead, he went to his office and began answering the phone calls from hundreds of angry Americans who cursed CBS for portraying GIs as heartless killers.

Among those callers was President Johnson. The leader of the free world called Frank Stanton, president of CBS News. Johnson's first question was as vivid as the film itself—"Frank, are you trying to *fuck* me?" Letting loose with the full fury of his monumental temper, Johnson continued, "Your boys just shat on the American flag."[8]

Tet Stuns a Nation

The single most significant military action in the war erupted in late January 1968 when the North Vietnamese orchestrated the Tet Offensive.

Named for the Lunar New Year holiday that coincided with it, this ambitious attack included simultaneous assaults on more than 100 sites—virtually every city, town, and military base in South Vietnam. The most dramatic action was by a Viet Cong suicide squad on the US Embassy in Saigon, killing five American soldiers. That action ended after a few hours, but heavy fighting continued throughout the south for another ten days.

Tet's repercussions were enormous. On the communist side, following an initial advantage gained from the surprise factor, the ground taken was lost again. The offensive was, in short, a military failure. Because of the reaction in the United States, however, the Viet Cong could claim a major psychological victory. Tet shocked the American public, which had believed that success in Vietnam was imminent. The offensive seriously damaged the credibility of the Johnson administration, as the American people were suddenly impatient with this prolonged war. And in a presidential election year, the public had a direct means of expressing its dissatisfaction.

The role television news played in the Tet Offensive was momentous. Just as Vietnam was America's first TV war, Tet was America's first TV superbattle. The story had drama, suspense, and enormous public interest. With the communists acting offensively and taking the US military by surprise, the very future of democracy seemed to be on the line. Television news pulled out all the stops to cover the story.

The US Embassy was the focal point of coverage for three days, as an ongoing gun battle on the grounds provided a live-action bonanza for TV crews. Barrages of automatic weapon fire, scenes of men running for cover behind trees, and the lifeless bodies of two fallen GIs made for some of the most eye-popping news images in American military history—as exciting as a Hollywood blockbuster.

CBS and NBC quickly produced news specials on Tet. Alarmist in tone, the programs portrayed the offensive as a brutal bloodbath, with lengthy footage that was unmatched in its sheer volume of gore and carnage. The prime-time spectacles strongly reinforced the message that Tet was a devastating defeat for the United States.

At the same time that the networks filled their TV screens with portraits of havoc and an American military run amok, they also filled the ears of the public with words of pessimism. Jeff Gralnick of CBS told his audience, "The Viet Cong proved they could take and hold almost any area they chose." ABC's Joseph Harsch expressed a similar skepticism toward US forces when he reported, "Best estimates here are that the enemy has not yet, and probably never will, run out of the manpower to keep his effort going. It is the exact opposite of what American leaders have, for months, been leading us to expect."[9]

In the midst of the crisis, it was understandable that the networks had initially reported incomplete or inaccurate information. Impossible to excuse, however, was the fact that ABC, CBS, and NBC all continued to portray Tet as a Viet Cong victory even after American officials provided indisputable evidence that the offensive had failed. Despite those facts, the networks neglected to set the record straight, allowing their hasty judgments to stand.

Later in 1968, field producer Jack Fern proposed that NBC undertake a three-part series showing that Tet had, in fact, been a military failure for the Viet Cong. Network executives rejected the proposal, saying such a series would only confuse viewers. The executives told Fern, "Tet was already established in the public's mind as a defeat, and, therefore, it *was* an American defeat."[10]

The Shot Felt Around the World

The TV image that, more than any other, burnt the brutalities of war into the consciousness of the American people was the filmed execution of a Vietnamese man on a Saigon street a few days after the Tet Offensive began.

NBC correspondent Howard Tuckner and his cameramen were standing on a street near the An Quang Pagoda, a center of government opposition, on the fateful morning. At the far end of the block, they saw several South Vietnamese soldiers with a prisoner wearing casual civilian clothes—plaid shirt, black shorts, no shoes. The soldiers walked toward the newsmen to present the prisoner to General Nguyen Ngoc Loan. The cameramen began filming the prisoner, showing that his hands were tied behind his back and that he'd been beaten.

The prisoner was marched down the street toward Loan, who then drew his snub-nosed .38 revolver. The prisoner stood three feet from the general, his eyes downcast. Without speaking to the man, Loan lifted his right arm and stretched it out straight as his index finger squeezed the trigger. There was the crack of a shot and a grimace on the prisoner's face as the bullet slammed into his brain. The dead man's legs folded under him. As he fell to the ground, blood spurt from his head.[11]

Tuckner cabled NBC in New York: "THIS STORY IS COMPETITIVE. CBS AND ABC WERE THERE BUT WE ARE THE ONLY ONES WHO HAVE FILM OF THE EXECUTION." Tuckner ended the cable by flagging the fact that there could be "BLOOD SPRAYING OUT" of the prisoner's head and then referring to the cameraman: "IF HE HAS IT ALL, IT'S STARTLING STUFF."[12]

He had it all. He also had a huge audience. Because of the excitement that the Tet Offensive had created, the NBC audience watching that night's program had jumped from 15 million to a staggering 20 million. And the color images of the execution made history: a televised death.

Robert Northshield, executive producer of the *NBC Huntley-Brinkley Report*, aired the film, cutting it immediately after the gunshot to spare viewers from the spurting blood. Northshield "went to black" as soon as the man hit the ground and then kept the screen empty for three seconds to provide a buffer between the stomach-wrenching image and the commercial that followed. Even so, the producer later acknowledged, "It was the strongest stuff American viewers had ever seen."[13]

Tuckner's narration was terse. He merely said who the men in the images were—although the victim wasn't identified by name—and let the film roll. "Government troops had captured the commander of the Viet Cong commando unit. He was roughed up badly but refused to talk," Tuckner said. "A South Vietnamese officer held the pistol taken from the enemy officer. The Chief of South Vietnam's National Police Force, Brigadier General Nguyen Ngoc Loan, was waiting for him."[14]

The American public was shocked by the image of a South Vietnamese general—a man supported by the United States—assassinating a Viet Cong officer on a Saigon street.

© *Associated Press/Eddie Adams.*

Viewers were horrified. More than a thousand of them called NBC to complain that the film was in bad taste, particularly because it was aired during the early evening when children might be watching. Tuckner defended airing the chilling scene, saying, "The film showed, at a time when all eyes were on Saigon, that although the United States went over there ostensibly to keep South Vietnam free from communism and the communists were accused of atrocities, that a leading figure of the Saigon government killed a man in the street without a trial."[15]

The film had a huge impact on the American public. *Time* magazine said, "That picture lodged in people's memories" because it showed a South Vietnamese government official "cold-bloodedly executing" a thin, frightened man by "blowing the suspect's brains out." In his study of the impact of television on American society, NBC's Edwin Newman said,

"This film revolted the nation. 'What was this war turning us into? What kind of people allowed such things to happen?' Television pictures were disturbing. Public opinion was moving. Television caused the change."[16]

Exposing the War as Unwinnable

The man who set the tone for TV coverage after the Tet Offensive was Walter Cronkite. The avuncular CBS anchor, with his kind and gentle manner, had shepherded the nation through many momentous events, including the 1963 Kennedy assassination. The anchor of the country's most-watched news program, Cronkite had supported the American military's effort in Vietnam during the early and mid-1960s. President Johnson, aware of Cronkite's prestige and power, called him to the White House three times during 1966 and 1967 for private meetings.

But all of that was before Tet. Like other Americans, Cronkite was shocked by the first news reports of the communist offensive. On that fateful night, he was in the CBS newsroom in New York. As the news flashes from Saigon came clattering across the teletype, Cronkite ripped a page from the machine and screamed incredulously, "What the hell is going on?" Reading on to discover that communist forces had penetrated the US Embassy compound, he cried out the same refrain that people all across America would soon echo, "I thought we were *winning* this war!"[17]

Cronkite decided to find out what, indeed, was going on in Vietnam. It was a risky step, as it meant shedding his mantle of impartiality and sharing his personal impressions about the most important story of the era. But at this moment when the public was utterly confused, Cronkite decided it was his duty as the signature figure in the country's largest network news operation to clarify the situation for his viewers.

So Cronkite went to Southeast Asia to interview soldiers and visit battle sites. Then the anchorman—the person that polls identified as the most trusted man in America—broadcast the most influential program of his life. Footage on *Report from Vietnam by Walter Cronkite* showed him wearing a steel helmet and flak jacket as he walked through the rubble of warfare.

Cronkite began, "Who won and who lost in the great Tet Offensive against the cities? I'm not sure. The Viet Cong did not win by a knockout, but neither did we." Cronkite went on to predict other standoffs in the fighting, "It seems now more certain than ever that the bloody experience of Vietnam is to end in a stalemate."[18]

He then told America exactly where he, personally, stood on the future of the war. "It is increasingly clear to this reporter that the only rational way out, then, will be to negotiate—not as victors, but as an honorable people who lived up to their pledge to defend democracy, and did the best they could." His final expression that lingered on the screen combined pained acceptance with solid resolve.[19]

The country's most influential newscaster had determined that, for the first time in two centuries, the United States wasn't able to win a foreign war. Rather than continue to sacrifice human lives, he said, American officials should negotiate a peace settlement and leave Vietnam.

Cronkite's assessment had unprecedented impact. For among the millions of Americans who put great stock in what the anchorman said was Lyndon Johnson. And when the program ended, the commander in chief said sadly, "If I've lost Cronkite, I've lost the war." Opinion polls confirmed Johnson's fear. In one of the most dramatic shifts of public opinion in history, within six weeks after the Tet Offensive began, one American in five switched from supporting the Vietnam War to *not* supporting it. This meant that for the first time since the war began, a majority of Americans opposed the war.[20]

A month after Cronkite's special, Johnson shocked the nation with a double-barreled announcement. He wouldn't run for reelection, and he would begin reducing US participation in the war.

Observers have pointed to Cronkite's program and Johnson's subsequent decision to downsize the war as a clear example of the news media's mighty power in shaping history. David Halberstam of the *New York Times* wrote, "Cronkite's reporting changed the balance; it was the first time in American history a war had been declared over by an anchorman."[21]

Because Cronkite's assessment coincided with the news media's portrayal of the Tet Offensive as a Viet Cong victory, the impact of the two events can't be separated. What is clear, though, is that coverage changed radically. Before January 1968, editorial comments by TV journalists had run four to one *in favor of* US policy. But after that point, comments ran two to one *against* US policy.[22]

Contributing to the negative tone of the coverage were two high-profile revelations related to Vietnam. In November 1969, freelance journalist Seymour Hersh reported the My Lai massacre. During that event, which had occurred a year and a half earlier, American soldiers had destroyed an entire Vietnamese village, killing between 200 and 500 civilians. My Lai dealt a devastating blow to the US military, with Lieutenant William Calley being convicted of mass murder. The second revelation exposed the shocking realities of what forces had driven US policy toward Vietnam. In June 1971, the *New York Times* and *Washington Post* began reporting on secret government documents, known as the Pentagon Papers, that showed American military action often hadn't been guided by humanitarian concern but by the political benefit of an administration fighting a war. Although the government attempted to block publication of the material, the US Supreme Court sided with the newspapers, saying the material didn't endanger national security—it merely embarrassed the government.

Television News Helps End a War

The many journalists and scholars who argue that TV images were a major force in turning the American people against the war in Vietnam are on solid ground. The process began in the mid-1960s, when the blood of dead and wounded American GIs, as well as that of Vietnamese soldiers and civilians, first began to flow across the television screen.

Then came Tet. Television images of the Viet Cong penetrating the US Embassy compound, with bodies of GIs lying in camera range, showed the American people that—regardless of what the politicians and military brass were saying—the United States wasn't winning the war. And then viewers witnessed a South Vietnamese officer—a man fighting on *our* side—shooting an untried prisoner in cold blood. After those images and Walter Cronkite's bleak assessment, American public opinion shifted. People were finally willing to say that they'd been supporting a hideous and inhuman war. And they refused to continue.

For a book with the goal of documenting the impact that the news media have had on American history, it's sufficient to establish that TV coverage of the Vietnam War played a key role in bringing the fighting to an end. When the discussion includes not only a divisive war but also how the news media should cover future conflicts, however, that discussion seems incomplete without taking the final precarious step of questioning whether TV news hastening the end of the Vietnam War was a positive or a negative contribution to history.

Both journalists and government officials have identified the central issue. Nationally syndicated columnist Bob Greene wrote, "The argument can be made that any war—even World War II—shown in the gory, close-up way in which television showed Vietnam, is destined to lose the public's support; that once they have seen the videotape, all they will want is out." Dean Rusk, who served as secretary of state in the 1960s, made the same point, saying that the impact of Vietnam battle scenes on the ordinary citizen every day was powerful. "One can reflect upon what might have happened in World War II if Dunkirk had been on television," Rusk said. "So I think we need to do a good deal of thinking about whether or not an armed conflict can be sustained for very long if the worst aspects of it are going to be reflected on television every day. There may have to be certain kinds of censorship."[23]

When television news brought the "worst aspects" of the Vietnam War into the American living room, it was doing its job. As long as a free press remains fundamental to the democratic form of government, the news media's accurate depiction of reality—no matter how vivid or horrifying that reality may be—is a positive contribution to that country. TV news showed the American people exactly what their military was doing halfway around the world, and, knowing that information, the people chose not to continue.

At some point, the men and women elected to positions of national leadership in this country may succeed—as Rusk suggested—in limiting what freedom of the press means. But until that loathsome day, there's no question that reporting the realities of war is both the duty and the responsibility of the American news media. If the people of the United States are willing to send men and women into battle, they also must be willing to acknowledge that death, destruction, and human suffering are byproducts of that decision.

13

EXPOSING CRIMINAL ACTIVITY IN RICHARD NIXON'S WHITE HOUSE

At 2:30 on the morning of Saturday, June 17, 1972, three Washington, DC, police officers caught five men attempting to place listening devices inside Democratic National Committee offices in the Watergate complex in the nation's capital. The men wore business suits and rubber surgical gloves.

That event opened Pandora's box on a scandal that ultimately revealed that the Richard Nixon White House was at the center of the most widespread system of political corruption ever revealed to the American people. The break-in led to revelations about misuse of campaign contributions, laundered money, political sabotage, deception, immorality, and any number of illegal activities. After two years of actions by the judicial, legislative, and executive branches of the US government, President Nixon was forced to resign from office.

The stunning abuses of power didn't expose themselves through their own volition. The *Washington Post* and two young reporters who worked for it demonstrated, perhaps more clearly than at any other time in history, the value of the Fourth Estate joining the official branches of the government to serve the American people.

More than a Third-Rate Burglary

By sheer instinct, the *Washington Post* placed the burglary story on page one—Washington is a political town, and it was an election year. That initial story didn't speculate on the larger significance of the break-in, but, by noting the bizarre details, the story hinted that perhaps this was more than a routine crime. "The men had with them at least two sophisticated devices capable of picking up and transmitting all talk, including telephone conversations. In addition, police found lock picks and door jimmies, almost $2,300 in cash, most of it in $100 bills with the serial numbers in sequence." The story also reported that the men carried forty rolls of unexposed film, two cameras, and three pen-sized tear gas guns.[1]

Two days later, White House Press Secretary Ron Ziegler refused to comment on what he dismissed as a "third-rate burglary." Ziegler's statement prompted the *Post* to editorialize—with what ultimately proved to be remarkable prescience—that although it was possible that the break-in was the work of a foreign government, "the finger naturally points, in a time of intense and developing political combat, to the Democrats' principal and natural antagonist; that is to say, it points to somebody associated with or at least sympathetic to—we may as well be blunt about it—the Republicans."[2]

The *Post* assigned two reporters to the Watergate story. Bob Woodward, twenty-nine, had graduated from Yale and spent five years in the navy before focusing on a career in journalism. *Post* editors farmed him out to a suburban weekly until the persistent reporter started calling a *Post* editor at work, at home, and on vacation. The *Post* hired Woodward as a local reporter in 1971. Carl Bernstein, twenty-eight, had worked as a copy boy at the *Washington Star* and then dropped out of college to come to the *Post* in 1966, assigned to cover suburban Virginia.

Woodward was sent to the arraignment of the Watergate burglars and sat in the front row of the courtroom when the judge asked James

Because of their coverage of the Watergate scandal, Carl Bernstein, left, and
Bob Woodward, right, were propelled to the status of journalistic icons.

© *Associated Press*

McCord, one of the defendants, what he did for a living. When McCord
whispered "CIA," Woodward's antennae began to quiver. From that moment on, the reporting duo never let up. Bernstein later recalled, "We just
very logically, through many hours, did the kind of reporting they teach
in J-school, the kind that when I was a copy boy I watched other reporters do—that is, not to let anything fall through the cracks." The dogged
reporters held on tight to the biggest story of the era—a story that not
only made them journalistic legends but also changed the course of
American history.[3]

Flushing Out the Evidence

Woodward and Bernstein—who soon became known informally as
Woodstein—got their first break when they found that the address books

of two of the burglars contained the name E. Howard Hunt. In one book, the letters "W. H." came after Hunt's name, and, in the other, "W. House" followed the name. With some fancy telephoning, Woodward connected the burglary to the White House. His *Post* story gave readers a glimpse of how the resourceful reporter's detective work had caught the White House consultant off guard, stating, "When Hunt was asked by a reporter yesterday why two of the suspects had his phone number, he said, 'Good God!' He then paused and said, 'In view that the matter is under adjudication, I have no comment.' He then hung up the telephone."[4]

It was the first of a series of page-one stories the *Post* published, beginning two days after the break-in and reaching a climax in late October, only a few weeks before the presidential election.

- In early August, Woodstein reported that the burglars had been paid with Nixon campaign funds: "A $25,000 cashier's check, apparently earmarked for President Nixon's re-election campaign, was deposited in April in a bank account of one of the five men arrested in the break-in."[5]
- By mid-September, the intrepid reporters implicated the former US attorney general, the country's top law enforcement official, who had by then become Nixon's campaign manager: "Funds for the Watergate espionage operation were controlled by several principal assistants of John N. Mitchell and were kept in a special account of the Committee for the Re-election of the President."[6]
- In early October, Woodstein exploded the story into something far larger than a mere burglary. They reported that Nixon's entire reelection strategy was based on playing "dirty tricks" on Democratic presidential contenders, including fabricating slanderous letters about both heterosexual and homosexual affairs: "The Watergate bugging incident stemmed from a massive campaign of political spying and sabotage conducted on behalf of President Nixon's re-election and directed by officials of the White House."[7]

- By mid-October, the tenacious reporters connected White House aide Dwight Chapin, who met daily with the president, to the political espionage: "President Nixon's appointments secretary served as a 'contact' in the spying and sabotage operation against the Democrats."[8]
- And, finally, in late October, Woodstein showed that both the Watergate burglary and the campaign of political sabotage were financed by a secret fund controlled by the president's closest aide. In short, they had traced the trail of political corruption to the very doors of the Oval Office: "H.R. Haldeman, President Nixon's White House chief of staff, was one of five high-ranking presidential associates authorized to approve payments from a secret Nixon campaign cash fund."[9]

After four months of nonstop investigation, the newsmen had uncovered solid evidence that what the White House had dubbed a "third-rate burglary" was, in fact, the tip of the iceberg in the most astonishing abuse of power in the history of the presidency.

Pushing the Limits of Investigative Reporting

None of the bombshells came easy. Observers who've studied Woodstein's reporting have praised the men's energy, creativity, and tenacity.

When *Post* editors initially forced the independent young reporters to become a team, neither danced on the top of his desk. They were, indeed, a journalistic odd couple. Woodward was a registered Republican who drove a Karmann Ghia and shopped at Brooks Brothers, while Bernstein was as close to the counterculture as a reporter could get and still keep his job at a somewhat stodgy newspaper—shoulder-length hair, rumpled clothes, loose tie.

The techniques they used were those of all good journalism. Bernstein said, "You knock on a lot of doors; you make a lot of telephone calls." One of their key steps was obtaining a list of the names and home addresses of the 300 men and women who worked for the Committee for the Reelection of the President. The reporters then visited some fifty CREEP staff members at their homes. "The big factor is going out and talking to people," Woodward said. "If you call somebody at the White House on the telephone and ask for an appointment, they'll tell you no. But if you're standing out there on their front porch, facing them, they may let you in."[10]

Potential sources, most of them committed members of the Republican Party, resisted talking to the reporters. One pleaded, "Please leave before they see you." Another said, "I know you're only trying to do your job, but you don't realize the pressure we're under. Please go." The persistent reporters often returned half a dozen times before they finally gained the trust of reluctant sources. Indeed, Bernstein said he had so many doors slammed in his face that he felt like a door-to-door magazine salesman—"For every sale, you had 50 rejects."[11]

The aggressive reporters begged, lied, badgered sources, and, on occasion, broke the law. While a grand jury was hearing charges against White House officials, for example, Woodward went to the court clerk's office and asked to see the names of the jurors. He was legally permitted to read the names but not to take notes. So Woodward memorized the names and then went to a men's room and wrote them down. The reporters called one of the jurors at home, which was against the law. The juror refused to discuss the case with them, but Federal Judge John J. Sirica later wrote, "Had they actually obtained information from that grand juror, they would have gone to jail."[12]

Although the reporters never depended on a whistle-blower for insider information, they relied heavily on the most famous anonymous source in the history of American journalism: Deep Throat. A good friend of Woodward before the Watergate break-in, he was described as an executive branch official with "extremely sensitive" antennae that picked up every murmur of conspiracy at the country's political nerve center. Deep Throat, named after a pornographic film popular at the time, never gave the reporters any new information, but he confirmed dozens of facts that Woodward and Bernstein had heard elsewhere but needed to verify with a second source before printing. Deep Throat also steered the reporters away from various false leads.

Woodward and his mysterious source met dozens of times, often in the wee hours of the morning to avoid detection. They developed an elaborate system of signals right out of a spy novel. When the reporter wanted to initiate a meeting, he moved a flowerpot with a red flag in it to the rear of his apartment balcony, meaning the two men would meet at 2 a.m. in a specific underground parking garage. When Deep Throat wanted to set up a meeting, he drew clock hands indicating the rendezvous time on page 20 of Woodward's morning copy of the *New York Times.*

Deep Throat's identity remained a secret for three decades, as it wasn't until 2005 that W. Mark Felt publicly identified himself as the iconic source. Felt had been, during the period when Woodstein was investigating Watergate, the second highest official in the FBI. When he finally identified himself as Deep Throat, Felt was ninety-one years old and had lost much of his memory after having suffered a stroke.[13]

Going It Alone

The *Washington Post* played a key role in exposing the Watergate scandal, and the journalistic triumph was essentially a solo performance. Throughout the first six months after the break-in, the *Post* was virtually the only news organization to commit its investigative might to uncovering the details of the story. Indeed, many of the nation's leading newspapers, news magazines, and TV networks not only didn't follow the story themselves but also accused the *Post* of overplaying it. "For months we were out there alone on this story," said *Post* Managing Editor Howard Simons. "We used to ask ourselves: 'Where are the AP, the UPI, the *New York Times*, *Newsweek*?' It was months of loneliness."[14]

Why didn't other news organizations pick up on the burglary's implications earlier? Most Washington reporters were playing what critics call "mouthpiece journalism"—writing stories based on the official statements from the government's army of public relations flacks. In one scathing assessment of correspondents covering the president, Bill Moyers, President Johnson's press secretary, said, "The White House press corps is more stenographic than entrepreneurial in its approach to news gathering. Too many of them are sheep."[15]

Television news did a particularly abysmal job of covering Watergate. Unlike the Civil Rights Movement and the Vietnam War, this story didn't translate easily into visual images. Most elements of the Watergate story involved backroom strategizing that lent itself only to headshots of the presidential aides involved—not good television. "It's not the kind of story we do best," said Frank Jordan, NBC's Washington bureau chief. "It's not visual, and it's also very complicated."[16]

Critics pointed out that the most serious repercussion of most news organizations downplaying Watergate was that it didn't become a major issue in the 1972 presidential election, which Nixon won by a landslide.

Standing Firm

From June 1972 until January 1973, the only journalists investigating the Watergate story seemed to be working inside a beige brick building on 15th Street in Washington, DC. That commitment extended far beyond Woodward and Bernstein. Indeed, the two persons who ultimately bore the hefty burden of responsibility for the *Washington Post*'s relentless pursuit of the story were executive editor Ben Bradlee and publisher Katharine Graham.

Bradlee, buoyant and personable, had built the *Post* into one of the best newspapers in the world; Graham, soft-spoken and genteel, was the stereotypical iron butterfly—she never flinched. The executive editor and publisher formed their own mutual-admiration society. Bradlee said of his boss, "She's got the guts of a burglar." Graham said of her top editor, "Ben Bradlee had never let me down. I had no reason not to have confidence in him."[17]

Continuing to support the Watergate investigation became increasingly difficult, however, because, throughout the months immediately after the break-in, the White House admitted nothing, denied everything, and fought back—first with verbal attacks and then by calculated efforts to punish the *Post*.

Graham was shocked at the vehemence of Nixon's attack. "The most astonishing thing was the vindictiveness in the government—sometimes at the personal level—to me or Ben. You know, 'We're going to get you!'— it really got rough." A graphic image illustrating that roughness came in a telephone conversation between Bernstein and Mitchell on the night before the *Post* was to publish the story implicating the former attorney general in the burglary. Bernstein called Mitchell at home to ask him if he wanted to make any statement for the story. Mitchell responded angrily, "Are you going to run this? If you are, Katy Graham's *tit* is going to get caught in a wringer."[18]

The attacks intensified after the *Post* reported that Chief of Staff Haldeman had participated in the political corruption—the story that came closer than any other to implicating Nixon himself. Vice President Spiro T. Agnew, a fierce media critic, responded to the charge by lambasting the *Post*'s Watergate reporting as "journalistically reprehensible" and stating, "I deny that there is any secret fund."[19]

This was the point at which Bradlee's and Graham's trust was tested most gravely, because Woodward and Bernstein had, in fact, made a mistake. In the lead sentence of the Haldeman story, they said he was authorized to approve payments from a secret fund, according to "sworn testimony before the Watergate grand jury."[20]

Wrong.

The reporters were right in stating that Haldeman was authorized to approve payments from the fund, but the allegation hadn't been made before the grand jury. "It was a mistake," Woodward later admitted. "It was the worst moment in all of this." The error had evolved from a hasty conversation with the treasurer of CREEP, who'd resigned when he'd learned of the committee's sordid political antics; the treasurer's information was accurate, but he hadn't given it as testimony because the grand jury hadn't asked him to. Five days after publishing the erroneous detail, the *Post* corrected its mistake in a page-one story.[21]

It was a crippling error because fellow journalists who hadn't been keeping up with the Watergate story now used the mistake to criticize the *Post*. Referring to "sensational disclosures" and Republican denials of the existence of any secret fund, the *New York Times* grouched, "There has been no public indication that either the President or any of his close advisers played roles in or had advance knowledge of an illegal assault upon the opposition party."[22]

White House officials began the punishment phase of their anti-*Post* campaign immediately after the election. The paper's society reporter was excluded from important White House events, and *Post* reporters on various national beats found once-cooperative sources no longer willing to talk to them. Nixon administration officials also began to feed stories to the *Post*'s competition, including granting the *Washington Star* exclusive interviews with the president.[23]

Meanwhile, behind the scenes, Nixon was using—actually *mis*using— the power of his office to retaliate against the *Post*. His target was two Florida television stations owned by the Washington Post Company, and his vehicle was the Federal Communications Commission, the governmental organization that licenses TV stations.

According to secret Oval Office tape recordings that later became public, the president instructed his aides, three months after the *Post* began its Watergate investigation, to have political supporters in Florida try to block the license renewal of the two stations, claiming they weren't providing the community-service programming the FCC required. Nixon told Haldeman, "The *Post* is going to have damnable— *damnable*—problems out of this one. They have television stations, and they're going to have to get them renewed."[24]

Shortly after that conversation, Nixon supporters formally challenged the two stations' license renewal applications. The finance chairman for Nixon's 1972 campaign in Florida filed the challenge against WJXT-TV in Jacksonville; partners of a close friend of Nixon's best friend, Bebe Rebozo, filed the challenge against WPLG-TV in Miami. Both stations ultimately had their licenses renewed, but only by spending a great deal of time and money documenting that they had, in fact, fulfilled the community-service requirements.[25]

In the taped Oval Office conversation, Nixon also directed his aides to use his presidential powers to retaliate against the *Post*'s lawyer. Nixon said, "I would not want to be in Edward Bennett Williams's position after this one. We are going to fix that son of a bitch." Nixon said he was willing to spend all of the $5 million left in his campaign treasury "to take the *Washington Post* down," adding, "I don't care how much it costs."[26]

By the first of the year, the *Post* began feeling the impact of the White House campaign—in its pocketbook. The value of a share of *Post* stock dropped from $38 in December to $21 by May. Katharine Graham couldn't prove that the White House was putting pressure on Wall Street, but the publisher suspected exactly that.[27]

The Press Joins Forces with the Other Estates

Though the *Washington Post* deserves enormous praise for its efforts, the Fourth Estate alone didn't expose the Watergate scandal. The political corruption was of such monumental proportions that it demanded the combined effort of all four arms of government—unofficial as well as official.

The judicial branch's opening salvo came in September 1972 when the five burglars plus their two bosses—E. Howard Hunt and G. Gordon Liddy—were indicted. And Judge Sirica publicly announced that he was "not satisfied" that the seven indictments told the full story. James McCord then broke ranks with his fellow burglars and told Sirica he wanted to talk in exchange for a lighter sentence. McCord's testimony confirmed much of Woodward and Bernstein's reporting.

Other crucial activities by judicial officials included a federal grand jury indicting Nixon's closest aides—including Mitchell, Haldeman, and Chief Domestic Affairs Adviser John D. Ehrlichman—while naming Nixon a "coconspirator," followed by Sirica demanding that he be allowed to hear Nixon's secret Oval Office tape recordings, and then the US Supreme Court supporting Sirica.

The legislative branch's role in exposing Watergate first rose to prominence in February 1973 when the Senate voted to establish a committee to investigate charges of corruption in the 1972 election. The Senate's role in the revelations dominated the country from May to August 1973 as hearings were televised live for thirty-seven days.

It also was the legislative branch that brought Watergate to a climax when the House of Representatives Judiciary Committee voted three articles of impeachment in July 1974, charging Nixon with obstruction of justice, abuse of power, and contempt of Congress for defying committee subpoenas.

Although the executive branch was the last to become actively involved in the Watergate scandal, its participation was the most dramatic because the president himself stood at the head of executive departments and agencies. In May 1973, Attorney General Elliot Richardson appointed a special prosecutor, Harvard law professor Archibald Cox, to investigate Watergate. The executive branch then soared into the eye of the Watergate hurricane in October 1973 with what was later dubbed the "Saturday Night Massacre." Judge Sirica wanted to hear the White House tapes, but Nixon refused to release them. When an appeals court ruled in Sirica's favor and Cox indicated he'd continue to seek the tapes, Nixon told Attorney General Richardson to fire Cox. Richardson refused and resigned. When Nixon next ordered Deputy Attorney General William Ruckelshaus to fire Cox, Ruckelshaus also resigned. Nixon then named Solicitor General Robert Bork acting attorney general, and Bork fired Cox.

The executive branch in the state of Maryland also played a role in the historic events when the federal attorney in Maryland informed Vice President Agnew in August 1973 that he was being investigated on charges of committing bribery, extortion, and tax fraud while he'd been governor. Agnew eventually resigned, admitting that he'd falsified his income taxes, and House Minority Leader Gerald Ford was appointed vice president.

The White House Collapses

The dam broke in early 1974. A panel of experts named by Judge Sirica said eighteen and a half minutes in one of the tape recordings had been erased. The gap occurred three days after the break-in, prompting critics to accuse Nixon of destroying evidence that would have proven that he'd known about the break-in before it occurred.

When Nixon was finally forced to release the tapes, the American people heard that their president was a mean-spirited, lying, foul-mouthed

In August 1974, Richard Nixon became the only president in American
history to resign from office. He is shown here saying farewell to his staff
as his daughter Tricia and her husband, Edward Cox, look on.

*Reprinted courtesy of the Richard Nixon Presidential Library
and Museum/The National Archives and Records Administration.*

bigot. Although the tapes didn't prove that Nixon knew about the break-in
in advance, they left no doubt that he helped plan the cover-up. This was
the "smoking gun" that stilled all doubts that Nixon had broken the law.
Before the impeachment process could be completed, Nixon, on August 9,
1974, became the only US president in history to resign from office.

Reporters as All-American Heroes

Watergate was a disturbing tale of political corruption in which President
Nixon and the men around him orchestrated a massive effort to subvert
both the election process and the presidency. Nixon and his aides were
revealed as amoral villains who, to feed their hunger for power, came dan-
gerously close to destroying the democratic form of government.

The American people, however, prefer happy endings to sad ones. So as the nation struggled to put the dark days of Watergate behind it, people searched through the rubble for heroes. They ultimately found their white knights in the form of two youthful reporters.

Newsweek dubbed Woodward and Bernstein the "Dynamic Duo," and the media criticism journal *Columbia Journalism Review* praised two of its own as the "Davids who slew Goliath." The rise to fame by the All-American heroes clearly produced dividends for the news media as an institution. As opinion polls confirmed, it was clear that the public felt new respect for reporters. Schools of journalism around the country burst at the seams with Woodstein wannabes, and, more than at any other time in US history, journalists were lauded as the saviors of democracy.[28]

Fame is often accompanied by wealth, and Woodward and Bernstein quickly realized that tradition. Before Watergate, the annual salaries of the pair of local reporters totaled less than $30,000. Two years later, their combined incomes had soared beyond the $1 million mark. Their first money-making venture was writing *All the President's Men*, the best-selling book about their Watergate experiences. Even more profits—and more fame—followed when Robert Redford, one of the most popular film stars of the day, read the book and dubbed it "the greatest true detective story of all time!" Redford, a Democrat known for supporting liberal causes, urged Warner Brothers to transform the book into a major motion picture. In the 1974 box office hit, Redford starred as Woodward while Academy Award winner Dustin Hoffman portrayed Bernstein.[29]

The *Washington Post* was honored with the Pulitzer Prize. According to the citation, "The *Washington Post* from the outset refused to dismiss the Watergate incident as a bad political joke, a mere caper. It mobilized its total resources for a major investigation, spearheaded by two first-rate investigative reporters, Carl Bernstein and Robert Woodward."[30]

At no time in US history had the importance of the news media been more dramatically illustrated than during the bleak chapter that began on that early morning in 1972 when five men broke into the Watergate office complex—and the country would never be the same.

14

FAILING THE AMERICAN PUBLIC WITH 9/11 COVERAGE

Journalism students learn in their first reporting course that the standard formula for writing a news story is to answer the five Ws: who, what, when, where, and why. When America's leading news organizations covered the biggest event of the early 2000s, they dutifully reported answers to the first four of these questions. The titans of the journalism world faltered, however, when it came to answering the fifth question relevant to 9/11: *Why* did terrorists attack the World Trade Center and the Pentagon?

Americans were bewildered and looking for answers as to what had motivated a group of men to strike out against the United States in such a horrific way. But although the news media gave their readers and viewers a great deal of information about what had happened—as well as who was involved, along with when and where the attacks occurred—and although the public was hungry for more, news organizations fell short because they allowed that motivation question to go largely unanswered. That missing information was essential for people not only to understand the event but also to help them decide how their country should respond to the attacks.

Answering the why question required the news media to provide the public with substantive material about a number of complex and multifaceted international issues and historical relationships, as well as information about the cultural and religious differences that were related to those issues and relationships. To do this, reporters needed to consult with Middle East experts and diplomats, along with leaders of countries in the region.

The news media's failure to rise to the challenge of giving the public this content immediately after the attacks had enormous consequences. For when the nation's journalists left the why question unanswered, George W. Bush gave his explanation for the attacks—an explanation that was driven by political strategy.

By the time the nation's news organizations finally began, in earnest, to answer the why question with the depth and nuance it required, a critical mass of the American public had already accepted Bush's easy-to-understand explanation for the 9/11 attacks. The president then built on this narrative to justify leading the country into the Iraq War.[1]

Mainstream Journalism Answers the First Four Ws

One way to begin an assessment of how mainstream journalism covered 9/11 is to look at how the most influential news organization in the country reported on the event. Examining the *New York Times*'s treatment of this particular story also makes sense because the most dramatic of the attacks occurred in the paper's hometown.

On the morning after the terrorists turned four commercial jetliners into weapons of mass murder, the front page of the *Times* was dominated by a heart-stopping photo of a ball of fire exploding outward from the south tower of the World Trade Center. Surrounding that image were four more photos and four lengthy news stories that contained a total of 8,000 words.

On the morning of the terrorist attacks, America's
television networks broadcast images of smoke billowing
out from the twin towers of the World Trade Center.

© Dan Howell/Shutterstock

The writing on page one was compelling, with the lead story beginning, "Hijackers rammed jetliners into each of New York's World Trade
Center towers yesterday, toppling both buildings in a hellish storm of ash,
glass, smoke and leaping victims."[2]

Throughout its coverage, the *Times* focused on the human loss. "The
area around the World Trade Center resembled a desert after a terrible
sandstorm," the lead story stated. "Parts of buildings, crushed vehicles and

the shoes, purses, umbrellas and baby carriages of those who fled lay covered with thick, gray ash, through which weeping people wandered in search of safety, each with a story of pure horror."[3]

A second article highlighted the human toll—the number of deaths ultimately totaled almost 3,000—by quoting three dozen men and women who'd been at Ground Zero when the attack had occurred. "For several panic-stricken hours yesterday morning, people in Lower Manhattan witnessed the inexpressible, the incomprehensible, the unthinkable. 'I don't know what the gates of hell look like, but it's got to be like this,' said John Maloney, a security director for an Internet firm with offices in the trade center. 'I'm a combat veteran from Vietnam, and I never saw anything like this.'"[4]

Second on the list of the most important organizations to consider when evaluating the news media's coverage of the huge story is the *Washington Post*, the dominant journalistic voice in the geographic area where the attack on the Pentagon took place.

The *Post* placed considerable emphasis on the issue of safety. "Amid all the sadness and all the carnage," the paper stated, "there were questions about lax security and inadequate intelligence, as Americans tried to fathom how such a catastrophe could happen with no apparent warning. On at least two of the airliners, according to federal officials, the hijackers were armed with nothing but knives. How did they get away with it?"[5]

Though the *Times* and *Post* covered myriad dimensions of the story on the day after the attacks, neither paper reported on the terrorists' specific motivations. The closest they came was the *Times* saying that the scale of the multi-targeted operation "led many officials and experts to point to Osama bin Laden, the Islamic militant," as the perpetrator, and the *Post* reporting that "federal officials suspect the involvement of Islamic extremists with links to fugitive terrorist Osama bin Laden and his terrorist web, known as al-Qaeda."[6]

The front pages of other major papers followed the same general pattern. The *Chicago Tribune, Los Angeles Times,* and *Wall Street Journal* were praised for their 9/11 coverage. The papers were lauded for documenting the human dimensions of the tragedy in vivid detail while also asking tough questions about why the US intelligence community had been caught off-guard.[7]

TV news received accolades for its coverage of the attacks as well. Particularly powerful, media critics observed, were the network broadcasts on the morning of the event—especially the dramatic live shots of the second jetliner hitting the World Trade Center's south tower and the two iconic buildings collapsing, as if the scene had been created by the special effects artists at a Hollywood movie studio.[8]

Despite the praise, however, the fact remains that, in the immediate aftermath of the attacks, none of the Brahmins of the news world told their readers or viewers what specific grievances had motivated bin Laden and his operatives.[9]

The White House Answers the Fifth W

Although the nation's journalistic outlets failed to say what drove the terrorists, George W. Bush did. Many observers had attributed the president's pre-9/11 political success partly to his ability to transform complex issues into black-and-white terms. He was soon displaying that talent on live television, stating that bin Laden had attacked the United States because terrorists are bad and Americans are good.[10]

"Today our nation saw evil, the very worst of human nature," Bush said within hours after the terrorist assault. The president followed that brief, simple, and easy-to-understand statement with, in his next breath, what amounted to a declaration of war. "The search is under way for those who are behind these evil acts," Bush said. "I have directed the full resources of our intelligence and law enforcement communities to find those responsible and to bring them to justice."[11]

By the end of that history-making day, Bush and his advisers had already crafted a clear message that they would repeat many times in the next several months and years, "Freedom itself was attacked this morning, and freedom will be defended."[12]

The president's message was much the same a week later when he spoke before a joint session of Congress—as well as a national TV audience.

After the collapse of the World Trade Center's twin towers, firefighters and journalists milled around the area that soon became known as Ground Zero.

© *Anthony Correia/Shutterstock*

"On September the 11th, enemies of freedom committed an act of war against our country," he said. "Freedom itself is under attack." Later in that speech, Bush stated point blank the question that mainstream journalists had failed either to ask or to answer: "Why do they hate us?" Immediately after asking the question, Bush gave an answer that was clear and decisive, saying, "They hate our freedoms—our freedom of religion, our freedom of speech, our freedom to vote and assemble."[13]

In a masterful move, the president also used that speech before Congress, with the whole world watching, to initiate what would prove to be a highly effective campaign to paint the war on terrorism as a broad initiative that would target an entity that he labeled "the global terror network." Bush didn't name the specific countries he believed to be members of that network, saying only, "Every nation, in every region, now has a decision to make. Either you are with us or you are with the terrorists. From this day forward, any nation that continues to harbor or support terrorism will be regarded by the United States as a hostile regime."[14]

Despite Bush's assertion that he was telling the public what had motivated the terrorists to attack the United States, he made no mention of Osama bin Laden's criticisms of American foreign policy.

The country's leading news organizations didn't point out the president's failure to articulate bin Laden's grievances. Indeed, some of the most widely respected names in American journalism soon went out of their way to echo the same messages the president had been sending—and that were resonating with the American public. The *New York Times* wrote, "The terrorists who organized and carried out the attack did it solely out of hatred—hatred for the values cherished in the West as freedom, tolerance, prosperity, religious pluralism and universal suffrage." *CBS Evening News* anchor Dan Rather went on his network's late-night talk show to express his views, which also seemed to parallel the president's. When *Late Show* host David Letterman asked Rather what had motivated the terrorists, the newsman said, "Who can explain madmen, and who can explain evil? They see themselves as, 'We should be a great people, but we're not,' and it drives them batty. That's the only explanation."[15]

The Internet Takes a Leap Forward

When journalism failed to report the specific grievances that had motivated the terrorists, many perplexed Americans turned to alternative sources of information by going to a platform that 9/11 played a major role in moving onto the global radar screen: the Internet.

The news media criticism magazine *Columbia Journalism Review* would later report that the terrorist attacks provided the Internet's "great leap forward" as a source of information. "Many people were not satisfied with what they read and saw in the mainstream media," the magazine wrote. "Or it was all the 'Why do they hate us?' sort of teeth-gnashing. There was a deep dissatisfaction with that."[16]

One document that legions of Internet users found when they sought answers to the why question was a statement bin Laden had issued in 1998. The "Jihad Against Jews and Crusaders" had initially been published by an Arabic newspaper based in London, but by 2001 it had been reproduced on any number of websites, many of them accompanying the statement with commentary. The manifesto made it clear that bin Laden saw himself not as a terrorist but as a heroic defender of Muslims who wanted to fend off what he believed was a Western invasion that threatened his faith and culture much the way the Christian Crusades had done some 900 years earlier.[17]

The most chilling sentence in the document was bin Laden's interpretation of how the Islamic prophet Mohammad would have responded to the actions of the United States. "In compliance with Allah's order," he said, "we issue the following fatwa [religious ruling] to all Muslims: To kill the Americans and their allies—civilians and military—is an individual duty for every Muslim."[18]

According to the manifesto, the single most significant factor leading to the call for mass murder was the American military's continued presence on Arab soil. "For over seven years," the document stated, "the United States has been occupying the lands of Islam in the holiest of places, the Arabian Peninsula: plundering its riches, dictating to its rulers, humiliating its people, terrorizing its neighbors." This statement referred to the 15,000 US soldiers who had remained in Saudi Arabia after the end of the Persian Gulf War in 1991. Some Muslim leaders saw America's operation of military bases in Saudi Arabia as a deliberate desecration of holy sites because two of Islam's most sacred places—Mecca and Medina—are located in that country.[19]

A second specific grievance cited in the "Jihad Against Jews and Crusaders" involved US support of Israel. "The Americans' aim," bin Laden stated, "is also to serve the Jews' petty state." According to experts whose comments accompanied the manifesto on many websites, bin Laden believed that America's long-term strategy was to make Israel the dominant power in the Middle East, at least partly to control the region's oil reserves. He alleged, therefore, that the United States was using its economic and military might either to weaken the other countries in the region—such as Iraq, Saudi Arabia, Egypt, and Sudan—or to make those nations puppet regimes that would do America's bidding.[20]

A third major criticism of US foreign policy articulated by the manifesto focused specifically on Iraq. The document stated that by 1998 the "crusader-Zionist alliance" had brought about the deaths of more than 1 million Iraqis, most of them civilians. Americans had targeted that particular country for "horrific massacres," bin Laden wrote, because Iraq had been, before the Persian Gulf War, the strongest country in the Arab world and, therefore, the biggest obstacle the United States faced in its quest to make Israel the region's dominant force.[21]

Many of the sites that reproduced the grievances questioned the statements in the manifesto. One that described itself as having been created "expressly to expose the evil of bigotry, extremism and hatred found in radical Islam," for example, challenged bin Laden's assertion that the United States was responsible for the deaths of 1 million Iraqis. "Nowhere can I find evidence to back that number up," the site's creator said. "Various sources estimate the Iraqi civilian and military casualties from the Gulf War at between 10,000 and 205,000."[22]

Why Not the Why?

Because bin Laden's grievances against the United States were readily available on the Internet but news organizations such as the *New York Times* and *Washington Post* didn't report them, a logical question to ask is: Why didn't they?

One possible answer to that question came in the news media criticism magazine *American Journalism Review*. After criticizing reporters and editors for not identifying the motivations of the terrorists immediately after 9/11, the magazine wrote, "During this time of national trauma, they feared putting forth anything smacking of criticism of the U.S. government. There were real concerns that, in the days immediately following the attacks, stories that explored the roots of anger toward the U.S. would appear to rationalize or excuse the tragedy."[23]

In other words, news organizations steered clear of identifying the terrorists' motivations because they were afraid that doing so might be interpreted as both unpatriotic and as an effort to justify the attacks.

Based on the firestorm of criticism that one liberal intellectual received after publishing an essay in the *New Yorker*, that fear was well founded. "Where is the acknowledgement that this was not a 'cowardly' attack on 'civilization' or 'liberty' or 'humanity' or 'the free world,'" Susan Sontag asked in the piece, "but an attack on the world's self-proclaimed superpower, undertaken as a consequence of specific American alliances and actions?"[24]

Peter Carlson of the *Washington Post* instantly condemned Sontag. He called her piece "belligerent, self-righteous, and anti-American— astonishingly wrongheaded." Carlson went on to say, "Regular people can be dim at times, but it takes a real intellectual to be this stupefyingly dumb." Charles Krauthammer, whose syndicated column appeared in 150 newspapers across the country, also denounced Sontag, writing, "What she is implying is that because of these 'alliances and actions,' we had it coming. The implication is disgusting."[25]

Building a Case for War

More important than speculating on why the news media didn't report bin Laden's grievances immediately after 9/11 is documenting what journalism's failure allowed the White House to do. Propelled by his success at convincing the public that the attacks were motivated by the terrorists being evil and America being good, President Bush set out to build on that idea to justify going to war with Iraq.

The initial fighting began less than a month after 9/11 when US and British forces launched a bombing campaign in Afghanistan, the country where bin Laden was living at the time of the attacks. The stated purpose of the strikes was twofold: first, to weaken al-Qaeda, the network of Islamist militants that bin Laden had created to end foreign influence on the Muslim world, and, second, to weaken the Taliban, the repressive movement that prevented Afghan women from working and Afghan girls from receiving an education. After bombing the camps where al-Qaeda and the Taliban trained new recruits, US and allied troops took control of Afghanistan's largest cities.[26]

During his State of the Union address in late January, the president said, "Our war on terrorism is well begun, but it is only begun." The specific statements from his speech that received the most attention were that America's enemies included all "regimes that sponsor terror" and that those rogue nations represented an "axis of evil." When it came time for the president to name nations on that list, number one was Iraq, followed by Iran and North Korea.[27]

Vice President Dick Cheney was soon sending strong messages as well. In March 2002, he said of Iraqi President Saddam Hussein, "This is a man of great evil. And he is actively pursuing nuclear weapons." Five months later, Cheney updated that statement, saying, "Saddam Hussein now has weapons of mass destruction. There is no doubt that he is amassing them to use against our friends, against our allies, and against us."[28]

Cheney took the lead in communicating a second message that was even more central to the campaign to take the country to war: Iraq had been involved in 9/11. The vice president stated on NBC's *Meet the Press* in September 2002, "There is a pattern of relationships going back many years between Iraq and al-Qaeda." Cheney said the lead hijacker, Mohamed Atta, had traveled to Czechoslovakia to meet with an Iraqi man to plot the attacks. "We have reporting that places Atta in Prague with a senior Iraqi intelligence official," Cheney said, "five months before the attack on the World Trade Center."[29]

That statement by the vice president was a key factor in propelling both houses of Congress to pass a joint resolution authorizing the president to use force in Iraq. The vote was 296 to 133 in the House, 77 to 23 in the Senate.[30]

Bush later followed in Cheney's footsteps by also connecting Iraq to 9/11. The president stated, "Iraq has sent bomb-making experts to al-Qaeda," and another time he said, "Iraq has aided, trained and harbored terrorists, including operatives of al-Qaeda." Bush also made the link by repeating Cheney's assertion that "The lead hijacker met with an Iraqi intelligence official to plot the attacks." And in an address to the nation, Bush not only conflated Iraq with the 9/11 terrorists but warned the public that another attack could occur at any time, saying, "The danger is clear: Using chemical, biological, or nuclear weapons obtained with the help of Iraq, the terrorists could fulfill their stated ambitions and kill hundreds of thousands of innocent people in our country."[31]

Although by the early spring of 2003 it was clear that the nation was on a course to war, at least one online news outlet spoke out against that action. *Slate* magazine quoted Czech President Vaclav Havel as saying that he'd told the White House there was no evidence that Mohamed Atta had ever met with an Iraqi intelligence official. *Slate* also opposed the United States going to war with a country struggling with enormous internal conflicts. "The Bush administration is in no shape—diplomatically, politically, or intellectually—to wage war with Iraq," the magazine stated. "How is the administration going to handle Iraq's feuding opposition groups, Kurdish separatists, and myriad ethno-religious factors?"[32]

On March 19, 2003, the Iraq War began.

America Pays a High Price

President Bush was soon boasting that US forces had defeated Iraq after a mere forty days of fighting and with only 139 American casualties. "Major combat operations in Iraq have ended," he said. "Iraq is free." He made that announcement while dressed in a flight suit and standing on the deck of the *USS Abraham Lincoln* against a backdrop of a huge banner that read "Mission Accomplished."[33]

In fact, the war was plagued with problems from the outset. No weapons of mass destruction were found, and bin Laden escaped capture on numerous occasions. The 9/11 Commission concluded that the Prague meeting that Cheney and Bush had used to link Iraq to helping al-Qaeda plan the terrorist attacks had never taken place and that bin Laden, in fact, disagreed with Iraqi secularism so fundamentally that he never would have cooperated in any way with Saddam or his followers. A Gallup Poll found that, by early 2005, a majority of Americans believed Bush had "deliberately misled the American public" about the reasons the country should go to war. And as the insurgents proved to be both large in number and effective in strategy, many observers began comparing the growing quagmire the United States was facing in Iraq to the one it had faced thirty years earlier in Vietnam.[34]

One of the darkest days for the White House came in January 2004 when Bush's former treasury secretary revealed that the president had been fixated on attacking Iraq more than eight months *before* 9/11. "From the start, we were building the case against Hussein and looking at how we could take him out," Paul O'Neill said, "to show the world what U.S. policy is all about." This former member of Bush's inner circle said, in other words, that the president had gone to war not to avenge the deaths of 3,000 innocent Americans but to advance a preconceived and highly politicized foreign policy agenda.[35]

Dramatic evidence that the public was dissatisfied with the Bush presidency came in the 2006 midterm election when control of both houses of Congress shifted, after a dozen years, from the Republicans to the Democrats. Exit polls showed that voters were concerned because economists estimated the Iraq War could eventually cost as much as $2 trillion and because the fighting had already taken the lives of 3,000 US soldiers.[36]

Although there was no national election to document dissatisfaction with the country's news organizations, myriad critics were saying that journalists should have done more to block the White House effort to build support for invading Iraq. *American Journalism Review* sniped, "Prominent critical articles were rare," and *Columbia Journalism Review* wrote, "The American media failed the country badly," and "The success of Bush's PR war was largely dependent on a compliant press that uncritically repeated almost every fraudulent administration claim."[37]

While the critics denounced mainstream news organizations, they had positive comments about both the paid journalists and the unpaid observers who had raised their voices on the Internet. *Slate* magazine was praised, for example, for having pointed out, in advance of the war, that the White House wasn't prepared for the level of hatred among the opposition groups within Iraq that eventually became a major problem in the war. In addition, *American Journalism Review* commended the bloggers who'd called it a "sorry spectacle" that reporters hadn't challenged Cheney and Bush when they'd made the spurious connection between Iraq and 9/11.[38]

Still more praise went to the online magazine *Salon* for publishing critical comments about the president that mainstream news outlets labeled "sour grapes" and refused to print because they came from Al Gore, the man Bush had defeated in the 2000 election. "President Bush and his administration have been distorting America's political reality by force-feeding the American people a grossly exaggerated fear of Iraq that was hugely disproportionate to the actual danger," *Salon* quoted Gore as saying. "There is now voluminous evidence that the powerful clique inside the administration that had been agitating for war against Iraq seized upon the tragedy of 9/11 as a terrific opportunity to accomplish what they had not been able to do beforehand: Invade a country that had not attacked us and didn't threaten us."[39]

Another Internet venue that critics applauded was YouTube, the website that allows users to upload, view, and share video clips. After Cheney repeatedly denied that he'd ever said there was a connection between Mohamed Atta and an Iraqi intelligence official, YouTube began replaying the video of the vice president saying exactly that.[40]

Too Little, Too Late

Although the country's major news organizations failed to report bin Laden's grievances against the United States immediately after 9/11, it should be acknowledged that they eventually discussed the topic—though generally neither directly nor prominently.

Three weeks after the attacks, the *New York Times* ran a profile of bin Laden that included the statement that he had grown to "hate an America that, as he saw it, had used its power to oppress the people of Islam." That profile appeared on page five of the newspaper's second section. Likewise, a full ten days after the attacks, the *Washington Post* reported that bin Laden considered the presence of US troops in Saudi Arabia "an intolerable affront to 1,400 years of Islamic tradition, dating back to an injunction from the prophet Muhammed that there 'not be two religions in Arabia.'" That statement in the *Post* appeared in the twelfth paragraph of a story that was published on page twenty.[41]

The specific dates on which those stories were published are significant. For the references to bin Laden's grievances didn't appear until many days after President Bush had already stated and then repeatedly reinforced his "terrorists are bad and Americans are good" explanation—which appeared on the front pages of newspapers and as the lead stories on network and cable news programs—that he presented both as the reason for the attacks and as justification for going to war.[42]

Because this chapter has been built around criticizing early news accounts of 9/11 for failing to answer the why question, it seems appropriate that the chapter should speak to another question related to that fifth of the Ws: *Why* was George W. Bush so determined to go to war with Iraq?

Several reasons have been suggested. The president may have wanted, as he's said, to bring freedom to the people of Iraq. Or he may have wanted to control the production and distribution of the world's oil supply. Or he may have wanted to weaken one of Israel's fiercest enemies. Or he may have wanted to finish the job that his father, President George H. W. Bush, had started with the Persian Gulf War in 1991. Or he may have wanted to use what he believed would be an easy US victory in Iraq to intimidate other hostile nations around the globe.[43]

Whichever of these factors or combination of them served as Bush's motivation, he failed the American public by starting the Iraq War, much as the news media failed the American public in their coverage of 9/11.

15

ELECTING AN AFRICAN-AMERICAN PRESIDENT

FOR THE FIRST 220 YEARS OF THIS COUNTRY'S NATIONAL ELECTIONS, no major political party nominated a person of color for either president or vice president. That changed in 2008 when the Democrats not only placed an African American at the top of their ticket but also succeeded in electing him with a commanding 365 electoral votes to his opponent's 173.

Several factors contributed to Barack Obama's victory, including an extremely well run campaign, an unpopular Republican incumbent, and an economic meltdown that a critical mass of voters blamed on the Republican Party. But many observers pointed to another force as playing an instrumental role in Obama's success as well: the American news media were smitten by him.

Time magazine's senior political analyst stated, "It was extreme bias—extreme pro-Obama coverage," and National Public Radio's senior Washington editor said, "The media fell in love. There's no question about it. He was a favorite—he was a favorite beyond favorites." An ABC News reporter came to the same conclusion, characterizing the news media's favoritism toward Obama as "appalling" and then saying, "Republicans are justifiably foaming at the mouth over the sheer one-sidedness of the press coverage of the two candidates and their running mates." The Project for Excellence in Journalism also indicted the news media, documenting that Obama was consistently portrayed in a "favorable light" while John McCain, the Republican nominee, was cast in a "substantially negative one."[1]

Creating a Modern-Day Messiah

The junior senator from Illinois moved onto the nation's radar screen in 2004 when he delivered the keynote address at the Democratic National Convention. His speech was so impressive that the *Washington Post* published a story headlined "Barack Obama Is the Party's New Phenom."[2]

Four years later, MSNBC news analysts who reacted to the presidential candidate's acceptance speech at the 2008 convention took a giant step beyond praising him when they anointed Obama a modern-day messiah. Keith Olbermann began the accolades by gushing, "For forty-two minutes, not a sour note—and spellbinding throughout." Chris Matthews then moved the analysis into the biblical realm by comparing Obama's speech to the others given earlier in the evening, saying, "In the Bible, they talk about Jesus serving the good wine last. I think the Democrats did the same." In another hosanna to the nominee, Matthews stated point blank, "He inspires me."[3]

That wasn't the first time the American public had heard the Democratic candidate being described as a modern-day messiah, as Oprah Winfrey had done it a year earlier during a campaign stop in Des Moines, Iowa. The talk show host—and a source of news for millions of TV viewers—had formally endorsed her fellow African American by saying, "I am here to tell you, Iowa, he is *The One.*" Speaking in an excited tone designed to rouse the crowd, Winfrey then shouted, "He is *The One*—Barack Obama!" NBC later led its evening news program with a story about Winfrey promoting the Democratic candidate, including a clip in which she said, with great emotion, "For the first time, I'm stepping out of my pew because I've been inspired. Dr. King dreamed the dream, but we don't just have to dream the dream anymore. We get to vote that dream into reality."[4]

From the beginning of Obama's campaign, journalists had failed to treat him with the detachment that's supposed to be part of their job. *Washington Post* editor John Harris later recalled how reporters at the paper had reacted to the candidate soon after he announced he was in the race. "You would send a reporter out with Obama," Harris said, "and it was like they needed to go through detox when they came back—'Oh, he's so impressive, he's so charismatic.'" Harris then described how he and the other veteran editors responded to the star-struck reporters. "And we're kind of like, 'Down, boy.'"[5]

Campaigning for a Historic First

As to why the news media favored Obama, observers point—above all else—to the fact that having a candidate of color on the national ticket of a major political party was unprecedented. Reporters and others in the news business are always drawn to a big story, and this one was huge—electing him would be more enormous still.[6]

"The first African American serious contender for the presidency was a great story," said Charlie Cook, a widely respected journalist who publishes the nonpartisan *Cook Political Report*. "And a lot of people in the media absolutely loved it. I think you can say that the media had a finger—more than a finger—on the scale on the Democratic side." Stuart Rothenberg, another longtime Washington journalist and founder of the *Rothenberg Political Report*, echoed that sentiment. "I agree completely with Charlie," he said. "I'm sure journalists preferred Obama. They liked Obama. Obama got better treatment."[7]

One occasion when news organizations pulled out all the stops in portraying Obama's campaign as a history-making one came in June 2008 when he won a marathon primary battle to place his name—rather than New York Senator Hillary Rodham Clinton's—at the top of the ticket. News outlets around the country made the unique nature of Obama's success the focus of their coverage. The online magazine *Slate* splashed the single word "History!" above its story, while the *Boston Globe* highlighted the point in the first two words of its story, which read, "Making history

During his presidential campaign, Barack Obama
promised voters that he'd bring about unprecedented
change if they elected him to the White House.
© Action Sports Photography/Shutterstock

and promising change for the future, Barack Obama clinched the Democratic nomination last night."[8]

TV news also played up the historic angle. The night Obama secured enough delegates to defeat Clinton, NBC's Tim Russert said, "Barack Obama, who says he's a skinny black kid from the South Side of Chicago, has defeated the Clinton machine to be the first African American nominated for president by a major party. It is an extraordinary night." Byron Pitts of CBS also veered away from the reporter's role as detached observer when he said, "Barack Obama and his wife Michelle walked into history's arms last night. One of America's oldest and ugliest color lines has been broken, and there's a new bridge for a new generation."[9]

Online publications jumped on the let's-make-history bandwagon as well. Early in the primary campaign when Obama bested his opponents in the Iowa caucuses, *Huffington Post* founder Arianna Huffington sounded more like a publicist than a journalist. "Even if your candidate didn't win tonight, you have reason to celebrate. We all do," she told her readers. "Barack Obama's stirring victory in Iowa—down home, folksy, farm-fed, Midwestern and 92 percent white Iowa—says a lot about America."[10]

The historic nature of Obama's campaign spawned any number of articles based on interviews with African Americans about what his nomination meant to them on a personal level. A piece in *USA Today*, for example, quoted one woman who said, "This is up there with the Emancipation Proclamation," and another who added, "We're definitely tearing down a racial boundary that has existed for years. He's really the new face of America."[11]

By the fall, reporters were routinely using the three-word phrase "historic Obama campaign" in their stories. It's impossible to gauge the impact of this element of the race, but there's no question that it added a momentum to the Democrat's quest for the White House that his Republican opponent didn't enjoy.[12]

Supporting the First Internet President

Another reason many journalists backed Obama involved his comfort level with technology. In 2008, the Internet was in the midst of transforming the field of communication, and the thousands of reporters and editors on the front lines of that revolution appreciated that the tech-savvy Democratic candidate was on the vanguard with them. Indeed, many of them were tempted to join their non-journalistic techies and buy one of the baseball caps, sold on an enterprising website, that carried the slogan "Geeks for Obama '08."[13]

One memorable step Obama took to show how important technology had become was to announce his choice for vice president not at a news conference but via a text message sent to his supporters. The *New York Times* highlighted Obama's method of communicating the news by showcasing his action in the lead paragraph of its story about who would be in the number-two spot. The piece also reproduced, word for word, the text message the Obama campaign had sent: "Barack has chosen Senator Joe Biden to be our VP nominee. Watch the first Obama-Biden rally live at 3pm ET on www.BarackObama.com. Spread the word!"[14]

Another indication of the value the Democratic candidate placed on technology came when he created MyBarackObama.com. Affectionately known as MyBO, the website allowed supporters to build lists of like-minded friends, contribute blog posts, share photos, and—most important—meet fellow Obama fans in their area to organize local events and mobilize fund-raising efforts for their candidate. MyBO users could get text-message updates on their cell phones and download an Obama widget to stay current on campaign news.[15]

Obama's campaign innovations vis-à-vis new media stood in stark contrast to his opponent's position. McCain admitted, in fact, that he didn't understand computers and couldn't send an e-mail without help.[16]

The *Washington Post* was among the long list of news organizations that praised Obama and his staff for their tech savvy. "No other major campaign has put technology and the Internet at the heart of its operation," the paper wrote. When the *New York Times* lauded Obama's effective use of new media, it focused on his embracing of social networking sites such as YouTube and Facebook. In March 2008, the *Times* reported, "Mr. Obama has about one million 'friends'"—six times as many as McCain—and also told its readers, "A musical version of Mr. Obama's campaign speech called 'Yes We Can' made by the singer will.i.am was released on YouTube. The video has been viewed more than 17 million times."[17]

Other news voices also rushed to praise the Democrat's use of new media. In January 2008, blogger Jeff Jarvis said on buzzmachine.com, "I wonder whether, quietly, Barack Obama is to become the first candidate elected by the Internet." *Wired*, the bible of the tech world, reported that "The Obama campaign has the most sophisticated organizing apparatus of any presidential campaign in history." *Advertising Age* wrote, "Digital tools have allowed the [Obama] campaign to communicate directly with voters on an unprecedented scale," supporting that statement by pointing out that he'd raised a stunning $500 million through online donations.[18]

Downplaying a Questionable Relationship

The titans of American journalism demonstrated their fondness for the Democratic candidate not only by praising him but also by downplaying an issue that could have derailed his campaign: his relationship with his longtime pastor.[19]

Questions about the Reverend Jeremiah Wright surfaced in *Rolling Stone* in February 2007. The candidate had described Wright—who had officiated at Barack and Michelle Obama's wedding and had baptized their two daughters—as his mentor. But Wright often dotted his sermons, the magazine reported, with incendiary statements such as "Racism is how this country was founded and how this country is still run!" and "We believe in white supremacy and black inferiority. . . . And God has got to be SICK OF THIS SHIT!"[20]

Rolling Stone's article had revealed that Obama's pastor held radical views that were far outside those of mainstream America. And yet, after the magazine broke the story, the country's major news outlets ignored it, with none of the leading newspapers or TV networks running follow-up stories.[21]

Unfortunately for Obama, the World Wide Web wasn't so cooperative. Various sites aired video clips from Wright's sermons, including the quote "No, no, no, not God bless America. God *damn* America!" Bloggers also picked up on the story, repeatedly asking questions such as: Why did Obama continue to be mentored by a man who made such inflammatory accusations against the United States? Why did Obama attend a church for twenty years that was led by a race-baiting demagogue? How could a candidate for president who refused to denounce Wright and his outlandish statements be considered a patriot?[22]

After the Wright story took fire on the web, the nation's leading news organizations had no choice but to cover it. In mid-March, ABC finally aired a segment on Wright. Reporter Brian Ross focused much of his attention on a sermon in which Wright accused America of being under the influence of the Ku Klux Klan—the minister called the country the "U.S. of KKK-A."[23]

Obama responded by delivering a high-profile speech on race relations that condemned the pastor's views on race as a throwback to an earlier time. "For the men and women of Reverend Wright's generation, the memories of humiliation and doubt and fear have not gone away; nor have the anger and the bitterness of those years. That anger may not get expressed in public, in front of white co-workers or white friends. But it does find voice in the barbershop or around the kitchen table. And occasionally it finds voice in the church on Sunday morning, in the pulpit and in the pews."[24]

News organizations that previously had avoided talking about Jeremiah Wright now exploded with praise for how Obama had dealt with the issue. Leading the pack was the *New York Times*, which published an editorial—titled "Mr. Obama's Profile in Courage"—that compared the speech to inspirational addresses by Abraham Lincoln and Franklin Roosevelt. The *Times* described the Wright issue as a test of character for the candidate and concluded, "It is hard to imagine how he could have handled it better."[25]

Minimizing a Major Weakness

When a detached observer assessed Obama's qualifications to be president, his major weakness was that he possessed scant experience for the job. The news media dealt with this concern by burying it under a mountain of personal strengths they attributed to the candidate.

Obama had served less than four years in the US Senate, spending much of that time running for president, and six years in the Illinois senate. And so, even compared to other youthful presidents, Obama had a thin résumé. John Kennedy, for example, had served six years in the US House of Representatives and four in the US Senate, and Bill Clinton had been a governor for twelve years and, before that, a state attorney general for two.[26]

Criticism of Obama's limited experience began during the primaries. Most famously, Joe Biden had said of his fellow Democrat during an early debate, "I think he can be ready. But right now, I don't believe he is." After Biden dropped out of the presidential race and Obama chose him to be the vice presidential nominee, the McCain campaign reminded the public of that earlier statement through TV ads. One warned voters that the country couldn't afford to entrust its highest office to "one of the least experienced people ever to run for president."[27]

When the country's leading news voices made their editorial endorsements, however, they found Obama's limited experience to be barely worth mentioning. The *New York Times* stated, "Senator Barack Obama has proved that he is the right choice to be the 44th president. Mr. Obama has met challenge after challenge, growing as a leader and putting real flesh on his early promises of hope and change." Other outlets pointed to additional attributes they saw in the Democratic candidate. The *Los Angeles Times* praised Obama for exhibiting "thoughtful calm and grace under pressure," and Long Island's *Newsday* lauded his "intellect," "judgment," and "uncommon ability to explain and inspire."[28]

Most of the endorsements said nothing whatsoever about Obama's brief résumé. When the point was mentioned, the reference was brief and followed immediately by more praise. The *Houston Chronicle* wrote, "It is true that Obama served less than a term in the U.S. Senate and that his previous elective experience is confined to the Illinois legislature. However, during that public service and his previous role as a community organizer on the streets of Chicago, he has developed an appreciation and understanding of the real-life concerns of middle- and low-income Americans."[29]

Online publications generally didn't endorse any presidential candidate, seeing the practice as too "old school." Nevertheless, some of the most high-profile of the digital outlets made it clear that Obama was their man. For example, when former Secretary of State Colin Powell broke from the Republican Party and announced that he'd be voting for his fellow African American, the *Huffington Post* gave the news prominent play. The site first ran a story that quoted Powell as calling Obama a "transformational figure" and then kept Powell's decision in the news by repeatedly publishing follow-up stories.[30]

Vilifying John McSame, John McOld, and John McOut of Touch

At the same time that the news media downplayed factors that could have derailed Obama's quest for the White House, they gave ample and prominent coverage to the weaknesses of his Republican opponent.[31]

Many of the editorial endorsements of the Democratic candidate characterized his Republican rival as "John McSame"—in other words, saying that electing McCain would be tantamount to reelecting the unpopular George W. Bush to a third term. The *Atlanta Journal-Constitution* wrote, "McCain has yet to explain how most of his proposed policies and approaches differ from those of the current president," and the *New York Times* said, "Mr. McCain offers more of the Republican every-man-for-himself ideology, now lying in shards on Wall Street and in Americans' bank accounts." Similar words came from the *Boston Globe*, which argued, "John McCain would try to solve the country's problems by going back to the same Republican set of tools: tough talk abroad, tax cuts for the richest at home."[32]

A second theme in McCain's coverage was that he was too old to be president. "John McCain, 71, will be the oldest president ever elected if he goes on to win the White House in November," *Newsweek* observed early in the campaign. The news weekly later continued the "John McOld" theme by running a piece titled "How Old Is Too Old?" The story stated, "While the old mandatory retirement age of 65 has been largely junked, there are still age limits for jobs like airline pilot or police officer, the kinds of jobs that require some of the same skills as the presidency—unwavering mental acuity and physical energy." *Time* magazine weighed in on the "John McOld" theme, too, saying, "He has suffered serious skin cancers over the years," and, "His age and health, therefore, are of legitimate concern to voters."[33]

As damaging to McCain as what news outlets had to say about his age may have been how the topic was treated on *The Daily Show*. Jon

Stewart commented, after one debate, that the Republican candidate had wandered across the stage while muttering to himself and searching for his little dog "Puddles"—a not-so-subtle suggestion that McCain was incontinent.[34]

A third McCain weakness gained prominence in the news media as the global economic crisis grew increasingly severe. The issue first arose in August 2008 when a reporter asked the candidate how many houses he owned. McCain failed to answer the question, saying, "I will have my staff get back to you on that." Reporters instantly jumped on the comment, saying the answer was seven while also pointing out that many Americans weren't able to pay their mortgage on even one house. This prompted journalists to add another denigrating nickname for McCain to their list: "McOut of Touch." They slammed him again a month later when he said, as part of a much longer statement, "The fundamentals of our economy are strong." The treatment by *CBS Evening News* was typical, with anchor Katie Couric saying, "Despite Wall Street woes, John McCain said that the fundamentals of the economy are strong. And that prompted Barack Obama to mock him as out of touch."[35]

The Pew Research Center analyzed news coverage of the campaign and found that the negative stories about McCain outnumbered the positive ones by a ratio of four to one.[36]

Playing Favorites in the Vice Presidential Race

When the presidential nominees chose their running mates, journalists again showed a clear preference for one candidate. They showered the Democratic nominee with praise while exposing the Republican nominee's shortcomings.[37]

News organizations immediately embraced Joe Biden as a solid choice for the number-two spot. "Mr. Biden is the chairman of the Senate Foreign Relations Committee and is familiar with foreign leaders and diplomats around the world," reported the *New York Times*. The online publication *Politico* added that the Delaware senator's other pluses included his "working-class roots" and his "36-year tenure in Washington."

When Barack Obama made his first public appearance after it
became clear that he'd won the presidential race, he was joined
by his wife, Michelle, and their daughters, Sasha and Malia.
© *Everett Collection/Shutterstock*

RealClearPolitics made the case that Biden, unlike McCain, wasn't a
wealthy man but one who lived off his salary as a senator.[38]

News outlets went a very different route when McCain picked Sarah
Palin to be his running mate. The *New York Times* called Palin's selection
"a desperate, cynical and dangerous choice," saying McCain had tapped
the first-term Alaska governor in hopes of capturing the votes of "dis-
appointed supporters" of Hillary Clinton and in an effort to appeal to
the socially conservative base of the Republican Party that he'd failed to
capture up to that point. The online magazine *Salon* dismissed Palin as a
"Christian Stepford wife in a 'sexy librarian' costume."[39]

Further evidence of the news media's opposition to the candidate began when *Politico* reported that the Republican National Committee had
spent $150,000 to spruce up the Palin family's wardrobe. The McCain

campaign tried to downplay the revelation as "trivial," but journalists produced an avalanche of stories on the topic. Some publications highlighted details about the candidate's purchases, such as the *Daily Beast* reporting, "Nearly half of that money was spent on a single shopping spree at a Minneapolis Neiman Marcus." Other news venues stressed the political ramifications, with the *Huffington Post* writing, "It creates a huge PR headache for the McCain ticket as it seeks to make inroads among voters worried about the current economic crisis."[40]

Raising Unrealistic Expectations?

Two weeks after Election Day, one of the country's leading media reporters pointed out that journalists had played a role in getting *candidate* Obama elected but that their favorable coverage might ultimately work against *President* Obama succeeding. Howard Kurtz of the *Washington Post* went on to say that the news media had created unrealistic expectations for the man who was about to move into 1600 Pennsylvania Avenue. "Obama's days of walking on water won't last indefinitely," Kurtz wrote. "His chroniclers will need a new story line. And sometime after Jan. 20, they will wade back into reality."[41]

Kurtz had it right.

News organizations that previously had been unstinting in their praise of Obama soon began criticizing him. The *Huffington Post* was one of the first; when Bill Maher said he wasn't happy with the president's lack of progress on climate change, the website gave prominent play to the late-night-TV host's comment, "This is not what I voted for." MSNBC news analysts were soon trashing Obama as well; after the president gave a speech about the BP oil spill in the Gulf of Mexico, Keith Olbermann dismissed the address as meaningless because it contained "nothing specific at all," and Chris Matthews said it made him want to "barf."[42]

The criticism escalated as Obama's presidency continued. *Politico* made much of the fact that his pre–White House résumé had been so thin, saying, "Obama came to office with less executive experience—precisely none—than any president since Gerald Ford." The online publication said this dearth of managerial expertise was one reason the rollout of Obamacare was a debacle, even though it was the president's signature initiative. The *New York Times* was even tougher on the man it had favored during the campaign, sniping, "he may not always be as good at everything as he thinks he is" and "even those loyal to Mr. Obama say he tends to overestimate his capabilities." The *Times* made those disparaging comments in a front-page story that railed against the president's "unfulfilled pledge that he would be able to unite Washington" and "his claim that he would achieve Israeli-Palestinian peace."[43]

Political historians weren't surprised when the news media's relationship with the president soured, as a similar process had played out many times in the previous two centuries. That is, the nation's journalists often had reported when residents of the White House failed to deliver on the promises they'd made while campaigning. What was different this time, though, was the degree of disappointment that millions of Americans felt when the actions they'd been hoping for didn't materialize. In this instance, the promises hadn't been made merely by the candidate, which was expected, but also by the news media that had been so smitten.

The news media's change of heart regarding *The One* became dramatically clear when he sought a second term. Several major papers that had endorsed Obama in 2008 gave their editorial support to Republican nominee Mitt Romney in 2012. The *Houston Chronicle*: "We were captivated by the Illinois senator's soaring rhetoric and energized by his promise to move American politics beyond partisan gridlock. It hasn't happened." The *Des Moines Register*: "Barack Obama rocketed to the presidency from relative obscurity with a theme of hope and change. A different reality has marked his presidency." *Newsday*: "Had Barack Obama done the job of president with the same passion and vision he displayed in seeking it, he would likely deserve another term. He did not."[44]

In explaining their decisions to oppose the president's reelection, these papers focused much of their criticism on the country's continued financial woes. The *Chronicle*, for example, said, "We do not believe four more years on the same plodding course toward economic recovery is the best path forward." That wasn't the only fault, however, that the journalistic voices pointed to. The *Register* denounced Obama's inability to achieve any degree of bipartisanship, saying, "Early in his administration, the president reached out to Republicans but was rebuffed. Since then, he has abandoned the effort, and the partisan divide has hardened." *Newsday* went beyond naming one or two failures and created a long list of what it called the president's "broken promises," including that Obama hadn't carried through on his pledges to slow climate change, reform immigration policy, reduce the national debt, or increase government transparency.[45]

Because this chapter's thesis is that the nation's news outlets were overwhelmingly pro-Obama during the 2008 election campaign, it seems logical to ask whether that happened again when he sought reelection. The answer to that question, according to experts, is a resounding "No." After studying the two elections, one political science scholar wrote, "Obama's coverage in 2012 was notably less sympathetic than in 2008," and the authors of a book about the Obama/Romney contest said, "News coverage of both candidates was balanced" and "Neither was covered more positively or negatively than the other." Anyone who's inclined to believe that news organizations learn from their past behavior, therefore, may conclude that journalists came to realize that they'd treated Obama too favorably during his initial race for the White House—and chose not to repeat their error four years later.[46]

16

SUPPORTING GAY AND LESBIAN RIGHTS

DURING THE TWENTIETH CENTURY, THE AMERICAN NEWS MEDIA'S coverage of gay men and lesbians was overwhelmingly negative. In 1950, newspapers routinely referred to gay people as "perverts," with headlines such as "Perverts Called Government Menace" in the *New York Times* and "Sex Perverts Called Risks to Security" in the *San Francisco Chronicle*. Journalism's penchant for making disparaging comments about gay people remained intact through the final decade of the century. In 1993, for example, the *Chicago Tribune* told its readers that pedophilia was rampant in the gay community, saying, "Homosexual men are much more likely than heterosexual men to incorporate boys into their sexual practices"—even though experts insisted that this wasn't true.[1]

In the early years of the twenty-first century, however, news organizations changed dramatically vis-à-vis how they treated gay people. As the US Supreme Court and Congress considered a series of cases and issues involving this increasingly visible segment of society, the nation's news media committed their editorial might to leading the public toward a more enlightened attitude toward a person's sexual orientation.[2]

Legalizing Gay Sex

Journalism's change of heart became clear in 2003 when the nation's highest court heard a case involving sex between two men.

The circumstances of the case had unfolded on a night in 1998 when someone called the police in Houston, Texas, and complained that "a man with a gun was going crazy" at a particular residence. When officers responded to the complaint and entered John Lawrence's home, they didn't find a gun or a disturbance but, instead, saw two men having sex. Lawrence and Tyron Garner were arrested and convicted of engaging in "deviant sexual intercourse." (The man who'd called the police was later identified as Garner's boyfriend. He was eventually found guilty of filing a false police report and was sent to jail for thirty days).[3]

Lawrence and Garner appealed their conviction, and the case made its way to the US Supreme Court. *Lawrence v. Texas* attracted national attention as a test of state sodomy laws. Up through the 1960s, every state had such a statute, but, by 2003, many of the laws had been eliminated. In Texas and a dozen other states, though, sodomy laws remained on the books.[4]

After the Supreme Court heard oral arguments in the case, news outlets urged the justices to decriminalize sodomy nationwide. The *New York Times* wrote that such a ruling would keep pace with other countries that hadn't just legalized gay sex but also had either approved same-sex marriage—such as Belgium, Canada, and the Netherlands— or had enacted laws banning employment discrimination against gay workers—including all countries in the European Union. "When it comes to protecting the basic civil liberties of all people, including lesbians and gay men," the *Times* wrote, "the United States should lead the world, not lag behind it."[5]

In June 2003 when the justices announced their decision in *Lawrence v. Texas*, every major news organization in the country gave prominent play to the six-to-three vote that did away with all remaining state sodomy laws. The *Washington Post* wrote, "The decision represents an enormous breakthrough in the struggle of gay men and lesbians." *Time*

The lawsuit filed by John Lawrence, left, and Tyron Garner, right, led to a
landmark Supreme Court ruling that legalized gay sex. They are shown
here celebrating the victory with their lawyer, Mitchell Katine, center.

© *Reuters/CORBIS*

magazine went so far as to say the ruling was comparable to the 1954
Brown v. Board of Education decision that had desegregated the country's public schools.[6]

Among the broadcast journalists who praised the *Lawrence v. Texas*
decision was ABC reporter Michel Martin. "The court has closed a long
and painful chapter in the nation's past when gay men and lesbians were
not treated with respect," she said on the news program *Nightline*. Martin
showed clips from the *Ellen* and *Will & Grace* TV shows before stating,
"The court is catching up to the public—catching up with present reality."[7]

Legalizing Same-Sex Marriage in Massachusetts

Five months after the US Supreme Court legalized gay sex, the highest
court in Massachusetts ruled that barring gay people from marrying violated the state constitution. As soon as local officials had time to prepare

for the gleeful brides and grooms coming their way, same-sex marriages in the state began.[8]

The country's news outlets applauded the action in a flurry of editorials. "Offering an institution as important as marriage to male-female couples only was discriminatory and had to end," said the online magazine *Slate*, while the *Boston Globe* argued that if same-sex couples in the state were only allowed to join together in civil unions but not to marry, that would have "created an odious 'separate but equal' version of partnerships under the law."[9]

Statements of approval weren't confined to editorials, as news and feature stories also were sending positive messages—starting with the fact that same-sex couples were stable. "When Gloria Bailey and Linda Davies first pledged their commitment to each other," *USA Today* reported, "their love and union were a secret." The paper then quoted Bailey as saying, "We had a private ceremony, just the two of us, 33 years ago." Her marriage to Davies in 2004, Bailey continued, was "the culmination of a lifelong dream." State officials in Massachusetts didn't keep statistics on how long same-sex couples had been in relationships before they'd been allowed to make them legal, so the *San Francisco Chronicle* did it. The paper interviewed 400 brides and grooms and then reported that they'd been together an average of twelve years. "Gay couples clearly can and do stick together," the *Chronicle* wrote. "And legalizing marriage will lead to even more such stable relationships."[10]

Another recurring message the news media communicated was that couples were sexually faithful. A front-page *New York Times* article reported that Dolores Trzcinski and Marie Auger, together for twenty-five years, "represent an often-overlooked slice of gay America: the monogamous homebodies more likely to have met at Bible study than a bar." The piece also gave details about two men. "Jeffrey Manley found Jusak Bernhard by posting a note in an online chat room from a man looking to share his life with another Christian man," the *Times* wrote. Bernhard was quoted as saying, "Our relationship is faith-based. We do our prayers and Bible readings together and depend on our faith to carry us through difficult times." The online magazine *Salon* ran a profile of a lesbian couple who'd been monogamous for fifty-one years—"Fidelity Was Their Path" read one subhead. "We were too busy to have affairs," Phyllis Lyon said, while Del Martin added, "We love each other. That's all it takes."[11]

News outlets also communicated that gay couples make excellent parents. A front-page article in the *St. Louis Post-Dispatch* quoted a sociology professor as saying that children with parents of the same sex "are every bit as likely to be well-adjusted and psychologically stable as kids who have a father and a mother." Later in the piece, a mother named Lisa Mandel said, "Being a parent is so huge that it completely overshadows being a lesbian. It doesn't matter how much money I make or what sexual orientation I am—I'm a parent first." CBS made a similar point in a *60 Minutes* segment. When a correspondent interviewed Carol Adair and Kay Ryan, he asked what impact having two mothers had on their daughter. Adair's response was articulate as well as thoughtful. "People who are raised in homes that are non-traditional are more flexible," she said. "And flexible people are strong, while rigid people are weak. People who can bend and look and think—they have an easier time finding their own ethical center."[12]

Fighting for Hate Crime Protections

In 2007, the battle for lesbian and gay rights shifted to the US Congress and a campaign to pass legislation that had previously failed to win approval.

Efforts to expand hate crime protections to include actions based on sexual orientation had begun in 1998 after two high school dropouts had tortured and killed a University of Wyoming student named Matthew Shepard. They'd singled out Shepard because he was gay, and the details of the brutal crime—which included beating the victim and then tying him to a fence and leaving him to die—made headlines throughout the world.[13]

At the time, hate crimes were defined as violent acts in which victims were targeted specifically because of their race, color, religion, or national origin. Under federal provisions, state and local law enforcement agencies received extra resources to investigate and prosecute such cases. Gay activists attempted, after Shepard's murder, to persuade Congress to extend the definition to include crimes that had been prompted by a victim's sexual orientation. Legislation was introduced but didn't pass.[14]

Supporters in 2007 had two reasons to hope that progress now could be made. First was the momentum coming from the *Lawrence v. Texas* decision, and second was same-sex marriage having been approved in Massachusetts.

Opposition from Republican congressional leaders and President George W. Bush, however, killed the legislation. One recurring argument against the bill was that people would be prosecuted for committing a hate crime if they criticized homosexuality, an objection that the bill's proponents refuted by pointing out that hate crimes are legally defined as physical acts.[15]

Lesbian and gay activists tried again in 2009. This time, they came armed with statistics showing that more than 12,000 crimes based on a victim's sexuality had been committed in the previous decade.[16]

Many news organizations championed the proposed legislation. The *Minneapolis Star Tribune*, for example, wrote, "Including gay men and lesbians in hate-crime laws reflects America's greater understanding that sexual orientation is no reason to deny basic human rights." Other proponents of the bill included *Politico*, which said it would be "unconscionable" for Congress not to approve the measure, and the *Huffington Post*, which wrote, "It's a no-brainer that hate-crimes laws should be expanded to cover sexual orientation."[17]

When the bill came up for debate in the House, the country's two openly gay members of Congress, Barney Frank of Massachusetts and Tammy Baldwin of Wisconsin, made powerful speeches on its behalf. The legislation then passed both houses by substantial majorities.[18]

CNN's story about President Barack Obama signing the bill reported that it was "the first major federal gay rights legislation" ever approved by Congress.[19]

Experiencing a Series of Setbacks

Every development involving gay people wasn't positive, as the era saw plenty of disappointments.

The biggest of the setbacks came when members of Congress introduced the Defense of Marriage Act in 1996. The bill—widely referred to as DOMA—defined marriage nationwide as a union between a man and a woman. This meant that options such as filing joint federal tax returns and receiving a spouse's Social Security benefits wouldn't be available to same-sex couples, even if their marriage was legal in the state where they were living.[20]

News organizations denounced the proposed bill. The *Boston Globe* said the legislation "does not deserve to pass," and the *New York Times* called it "unfair and unconstitutional." *Slate* wrote, "DOMA is an effort to deny a class of citizens a fundamental civil right."[21]

Despite the protests, the House passed the bill 342 to 67, and the Senate followed suit with a vote of 85 to 14. President Bill Clinton then signed DOMA into law.[22]

The next major setback was a reaction to Massachusetts legalizing same-sex marriage. After that action, social conservatives across the country began pushing for their states to amend their constitutions to block the same-sex marriage initiative from expanding.

When Missouri state legislators introduced such an amendment, the *St. Louis Post-Dispatch* asked its readers to "reject discrimination and vote no." Likewise, when Michigan and Georgia legislators proposed amendments, the *Detroit News* wrote, "Locking into the constitution a permanent ban against same-sex marriage ignores the changing nature of attitudes," and the *Atlanta Journal-Constitution* asked, "Why enshrine discrimination and hostility toward gay Georgians into the constitution, a document designed to expand liberties, not restrict them?"[23]

But the editorial statements repeatedly fell on deaf ears. By the end of 2008, thirty states—including Missouri, Michigan, and Georgia—had passed constitutional amendments banning same-sex marriage.[24]

Another disappointing battle played out in Congress with efforts to pass the Employment Non-Discrimination Act. At the time, thirty-three states had no statutes protecting gay workers, which meant that employers could reject job applicants or fire current employees solely because of their sexual orientation.[25]

The measure that was drafted in 2007—abbreviated to ENDA—would ban such actions by all government agencies and by private employers with fifteen or more workers.[26]

News outlets threw their editorial heft behind the proposal. "The right to work is among the most basic of American rights," wrote the *Washington Post*, "and it should no longer be off-limits to gay men and lesbians." The *Huffington Post* called the legislation a "vital measure," and the *Pittsburgh Post-Gazette* said, "This bill would make a historic statement about tolerance."[27]

Barney Frank introduced the bill in the House but soon ran into a major complication. He informally polled his colleagues and learned that the legislation had a good chance of passing if it covered gay men, lesbians, and bisexuals but that it would fail if it also covered transgender workers. So Frank removed language from the bill to protect employees from discrimination based on their "gender identity."[28]

Many activists were furious, accusing Frank of discriminating against an important segment of the community. The congressman defended his decision, telling the *New York Times*, "There is a tendency in American politics for the people who feel most passionately about an issue to be unrealistic in what a democratic political system can deliver, and that can be self-defeating."[29]

Frank's bill, without the phrase "gender identity," was passed in the House, but it died in a Senate committee.[30]

Yet another setback came in the country's most populous state. The California Supreme Court had approved same-sex marriage in May 2008, but opponents quickly began an effort to overturn the ruling through a voter referendum known as Proposition 8.[31]

All ten of California's largest-circulation newspapers spoke out against the initiative. The *Los Angeles Times*: "By banning same-sex marriage,

Prop. 8 would create second-class citizens." The *San Diego Union-Tribune*: "We urge a No vote on Proposition 8." The *Orange County Register*: "We recommend a 'no' vote on Prop. 8."[32]

On Election Day, however, 52 percent of California voters supported the initiative. Analysts later said the referendum had succeeded because the leaders of the Catholic Church and Mormon Church had united, while also reaching out to African-American congregations.[33]

Allowing Lesbian and Gay Soldiers to Serve Openly

A CNN interview helped propel a new issue into the spotlight in 2009. The man being questioned was former chair of the Joint Chiefs of Staff Colin Powell, and the topic was "don't ask, don't tell." Under that policy, American military officials didn't *ask* soldiers about their sexual orientation, which meant lesbians and gay men could serve in the military as long as they didn't *tell* their superiors about their sexuality.

When CNN anchor John King asked Powell about the "don't ask, don't tell" policy, the general said it was time for a change. "The policy that came about in 1993 was correct for the time," Powell said. "Sixteen years have now gone by, and a lot has changed with respect to attitudes within our country, and therefore I think this is a policy that should be reviewed."[34]

News outlets responded with editorials calling for lesbian and gay soldiers to be open about their sexuality. "Repealing the ban on gays serving in the military is long overdue," the *Philadelphia Inquirer* insisted, while *USA Today* said point blank, "The policy is simply wrong." The *Daily Beast* website made its case against "don't ask, don't tell" by profiling ten exemplary soldiers who'd been discharged because of the policy, including a lesbian who'd graduated at the top of her class from the Naval Academy and a gay man who'd been honored as the Marine of the Year.[35]

The combination of Powell's statement and the many editorials prompted politicians and military leaders to think seriously about the issue. In President Obama's 2010 State of the Union address, he said, "This year, I will work with Congress and our military to finally repeal the law that denies gay Americans the right to serve the country they love." Department of Defense officials then undertook a comprehensive review of the policy.[36]

After the study was completed, news outlets turned the results into major news. TV anchors who summarized the findings on the news programs implied that the policy's days were definitely numbered. Diane Sawyer of *ABC World News* said, "Today, the Pentagon released its long-awaited study on 'don't ask, don't tell' and how the troops will react if gays can serve openly in the military. After seeing the study, top brass are reaffirming it's time for a change." Brian Williams of *NBC Nightly News* sent the same message, saying, "Today at the Pentagon, this nation's top military commanders said the time has come for gay Americans to serve openly in their nation's armed forces." [37]

The biggest takeaway from the study was that allowing lesbians and gay men to serve openly wouldn't damage military effectiveness. Specifically, most active-duty soldiers said they didn't foresee any problems if the ban was lifted. Indeed, 69 percent of them said they'd already worked with fellow soldiers they believed to be gay or lesbian and that fact hadn't caused any problems whatsoever.[38]

Even more news outlets then called for repealing "don't ask, don't tell." *Salon* condemned it as a "loathsome" policy, while *Politico* went with a more pragmatic argument, saying, "Enforcement has resulted in 13,000 service members—volunteer soldiers that this nation needs—being hounded out of the ranks. This is a loss that a nation fighting two wars can ill afford."[39]

Both houses of Congress voted, by the end of the year, to repeal the policy. President Obama then signed the bill into law.[40]

Advancing Toward Marriage Equality

By 2012, same-sex marriage had moved back onto the nation's radar screen. This was partly because several more states had made it legal for pairs of brides and pairs of grooms to tie the nuptial knot—the total had climbed to ten plus the District of Columbia—but mostly because two court cases had the potential to move marriage equality forward on the national level.[41]

The broader of the two cases involved Edie Windsor and Thea Spyer. They'd become a couple in 1967 and had shared a life for forty years. A low point for them came in 1980 when Spyer was diagnosed with multiple sclerosis, while a high point came in 2007 when they traveled to Canada and were married. When Spyer died two years after the wedding, she left her estate to her wife. Windsor didn't have to pay state inheritance tax because New York recognized the couple's marriage. She was denied that benefit on the federal level, however, because the Defense of Marriage Act said the term "spouse" only applied when a marriage was between a man and a woman. So Windsor had to pay $363,000 in estate taxes.[42]

Windsor then sued the federal government, seeking a refund and saying DOMA discriminated against same-sex couples. By the end of 2012, her case had progressed through the legal system and was scheduled to be heard by the US Supreme Court.[43]

The second case revolved around the California voter referendum that had halted same-sex marriages in that state. In 2009, two couples had filed a federal lawsuit, claiming that Proposition 8 was unconstitutional. By the end of 2012, the US Supreme Court had agreed to hear their case.[44]

Any number of news organizations weighed in on the two lawsuits, with the editorial statements consistently favoring the gay and lesbian plaintiffs.

"The Supreme Court has the opportunity to advance human rights" by ruling for Edie Windsor, wrote the *Boston Globe*, while the *Washington Post* labeled DOMA "indefensible—a law that relegates the nation's gay and lesbian citizens to second-class status. One of the most notable statements came from CNN, which broke from the tradition among TV news outlets by taking a firm editorial stand on *Windsor v. United States*. "The Court needs to do the right thing and end discrimination against gay couples," the network stated on its website. "The social and civil discrimination that persists as long as our federal government does not recognize same-sex marriage is inexcusable."[45]

News outlets also urged the Supreme Court to side with the two California couples. "The day Proposition 8 is overturned can't come too soon," wrote the *San Jose Mercury News*. The *New York Times* agreed, saying,

The crowd erupted in spontaneous applause when Edie Windsor appeared at the annual Pride Parade in New York City in 2014.
© *lev radin/Shutterstock*

"There are 18,000 same-sex couples in the state who were married before Proposition 8 was passed, and their presence does not seem to have damaged relationships between men and women." The *Daily Beast* didn't focus on the couples but on the 40,000 California children living with either two moms or two dads, arguing that "the children of same-sex couples need their parents to have full recognition and full status."[46]

When the Supreme Court heard oral arguments on the cases in March 2013, the news media provided saturation coverage. The story led the network and cable TV news programs and ran on the front page of every major paper and news website in the country. One of the most frequently reproduced quotes came from Justice Ruth Bader Ginsburg. Comparing how DOMA treated opposite-sex couples and same-sex couples, she said, "There are two kinds of marriages—the full marriage and then the sort of 'skim milk' marriage."[47]

News organizations made sure to report the benefits that married lesbian or gay couples weren't currently receiving but that they'd have if the justices struck down DOMA. These included that couples would be allowed family hospital visitation rights and that a husband or wife who was a citizen of another country could remain in the United States with his or her spouse.[48]

Three months after the oral arguments, news outlets pulled out all the stops when they reported that the justices, by a pair of five-to-four votes, had struck down DOMA and had said marriages could resume in California. Headlines in the country's most influential news organizations communicated the celebratory tone that flavored the coverage. The *New York Times*: "Victory for Equal Rights." The *Washington Post*: "Equality Triumphs." *Slate*: "Anti-Gay Is Yesterday."[49]

Journalistic voices had another chance to show their support for lesbian and gay rights in October 2014 when the Supreme Court chose not to rule on the question of whether state prohibitions on same-sex marriage violate the Constitution. "By passing on that debate," the *Huffington Post* gleefully announced, "the court gave a final legal stamp of approval to marriage equality in five states." Later in its story, the online publication— which by this point was the most popular political website in the country, with 110 million unique visitors each month—described the development as "a monumental achievement for the gay rights community."[50]

Two popular sites that focus on polling data quickly pointed out that the court's action would legalize marriage in several more states as well. This reality prompted *FiveThirtyEight* to place the upbeat headline "Same-Sex Marriage Is Now Legal for a Majority of the U.S." above its story. *RealClearPolitics* expressed its pleasure with the milestone in the text of its story, reporting, "Activists across the country were elated by what now appears to be a clear path to a nationwide victory in the coming months and years."[51]

Securing New Rights—with the News Media's Help

Gay men and lesbians had, by a decade and a half into the new millennium, made stunning progress in their campaign for equal rights. Most notably, sex acts between two men or two women had been legalized, lesbian and gay soldiers were serving openly, and the nation's highest court had ruled that two women or two men who had the right to marry in their home states are entitled to federal benefits.

After the June 2013 ruling in the Edie Windsor case, a long list of additional states legalized same-sex marriage. Each time the issue came up for debate, news organizations spoke in favor of marriage equality. As Illinois lawmakers were considering legislation, for example, the *Chicago Tribune* said they should "Make a firm declaration that same-sex marriage is in the best interest of the state and its residents because the law would strengthen families, protect the interests of children and affirm personal freedom"; two weeks later, Illinois gay and lesbian couples had the right to marry. Likewise, after a federal judge in Pennsylvania ruled in May 2014 that the commonwealth's ban on same-sex marriage was unconstitutional, the *Philadelphia Inquirer* pleaded with the governor to let the decision stand, saying, "It is time to give gay couples the ability to enjoy the same legal status as heterosexual couples"; soon after that, Pennsylvania couples were walking down the aisle.[52]

Judicial officials and lawmakers at the national and state levels clearly had played key roles in the various advancements that had taken place since 2003, as they were the institutions that made the rulings and passed the laws establishing that lesbians and gay men should no longer be treated like "skim milk" citizens. Another important force deserving credit is the army of activists who worked to persuade the justices, legislators, and American public that discrimination based on sexual orientation was unfair.

A close look at the journalism produced during the early years of the twenty-first century shows that the news media also used their formidable resources on behalf of the cause. Whether it was bringing attention to an issue by placing it at the top of a national newscast or nudging a particular initiative forward by publishing strongly worded editorials backing it, news organizations relentlessly adopted the position that these stigmatized and marginalized men and women were fully entitled to the same rights that straight Americans enjoyed.

In the next breath after acknowledging the progress that's been made, however, it must be pointed out that the struggle hasn't ended. As of 2015, many states still have constitutional amendments banning same-sex marriage, and Congress hasn't passed the Employment Non-Discrimination Act—which means that gay workers in half the nation are still being denied jobs because of their sexual orientation. What's more, precious few of the actions that represent milestones toward equality for gay men and lesbians have improved the lives of transgender Americans.

It's impossible to know for certain, because of the shifting tides of politics, the degree to which future judicial officials and lawmakers will help secure additional rights. The consistent record of support provided by journalism, however, should assure concerned observers that the news media will continue to do whatever they can to champion the cause.

17

FOCUSING ON HOW

THE NEWS MEDIA HAVE SHAPED AMERICAN HISTORY. ABSO-
LUTELY. Boldly. Profoundly.

From the 1760s when patriots created the "Journal of Occurrences"
to propel the colonists toward the American Revolution through the
present as news outlets continue to champion gay and lesbian rights, the
Fourth Estate has been a central force in determining how this nation
has evolved. Between those two events, thousands of journalists and news
organizations have served as catalysts for social movements as well as
landmark events that have defined this country's history. The news media
often have used their might as a positive force—but sometimes not.

Now that I've piloted the reader through two and a half centuries
of American journalism shaping the nation's history, in this concluding
chapter I want to focus on one final and fundamental point: *How*? To answer this question, I've looked closely at the major players in the sixteen
episodes I've highlighted in this book. Specifically, I've examined the news
outlets and their actions with an eye toward identifying the common
characteristics they've shared. The following list of ten recurring traits,
then, suggests some of the methods the news media have used while helping to shape this country.

1. The news organizations that have influenced important events have been willing to set the agenda. They've approached the news media as an institution that leads society, not as one that merely records facts. None of the news organizations profiled in the previous chapters defined its role so narrowly that it passively chronicled the news without comment or interpretation. None of them, in short, was willing to function as a stenographic service.

Examples abound. *McClure's* magazine didn't produce its legendary exposé of Standard Oil Company by asking Ida Tarbell to reproduce the prepared statements mouthed by John D. Rockefeller; Tarbell pored over court documents, wooed inside sources, and listened to disgruntled competitors until she understood the inner workings of the ruthless monopoly. Half a century later, network correspondents weren't welcomed into the segregated South to cover the Civil Rights Movement; the correspondents faced signs reading "NO DOGS, NIGGERS OR REPORTERS ALLOWED." Likewise, news outlets of the 2000s haven't sat quietly and waited for the country's lawmakers and judicial officials to decide whether lesbians and gay men deserve equal rights; in 2009 when Congress was considering legislation that would extend hate-crime laws to cover sexual orientation, the *Huffington Post* bluntly said, "It's a no-brainer."

2. For many of the journalists and their news organizations, standing tall has meant standing alone. They spurned the concept, known as pack journalism, in which throngs of reporters swarm like honey bees onto the story of the moment and then buzz off, in unison, to the next communal hot spot. The journalists who've helped build this country into what it is today did so partly by consciously and fearlessly breaking from the pack, despite what were often severe consequences.

When the *Liberator* began advocating the end of slavery in the early 1830s, other editors lambasted William Lloyd Garrison as a "scoundrel" and a "toad eater," with proslavery groups offering monetary rewards to the bounty hunter who captured him. A century later, a triumvirate of courageous newspapers spoke out against the Ku Klux Klan even though the majority of the nation's journalistic voices stayed silent on the subject. In the early 1950s, wire services and newspapers were one of the major forces that propelled Joseph McCarthy onto the national stage, until the CBS program *See It Now* showed the demagogue to be a mean-spirited bully. Twenty years later, the same network allowed anchor Walter Cronkite to break from his detached role and urge the nation to bring its soldiers home.

3. Journalists who have stood up to the countless villains in American society have often placed themselves in harm's way. That is, courageous newsmen and newswomen have been threatened with physical danger—some of them ultimately carrying the scars for the rest of their lives and others dying before their time.

When Thomas Nast refused to stop publishing bruising editorial cartoons against "Boss" Tweed in the late 1860s, the death threats became so frequent that the artist had to relocate his wife and children to ensure their safety. During the Civil Rights Movement, TV correspondents were spat upon, clubbed, and kicked right along with the African-American men, women, and children whose protests they were filming—NBC cameraman Moe Levy was among those disabled for the rest of their lives.

The most dramatic acts of physical violence were against abolitionist editors and writers. William Lloyd Garrison was stoned and placed within a hairsbreadth of being lynched; Maria Stewart's fiery discourse netted her a barrage of insults—as well as rotten tomatoes. Abolitionist editor Elijah Lovejoy lost four printing presses to proslavery mobs before he finally paid the supreme price, giving his very life to the cause and thereby becoming America's first martyr to freedom of the press.

4. Many of the news organizations that have shaped American history have placed journalistic principle above financial gain. Time and time again, these publications and broadcast voices have—to preserve their integrity and do their job—suffered serious economic setbacks that have threatened their survival.

When *Harper's Weekly* refused to end its crusade against New York's nefarious Tweed Ring, city officials canceled the Harper Brothers Publishing Company contract to provide textbooks for the school system. When *Collier's* announced it wouldn't accept any more ads from patent medicine companies, the magazine's revenues dropped a dramatic

$80,000 in a single year. And when the *Washington Post* refused to allow the Watergate story to die, the value of a share of *Post* stock plunged from $38 to $21 in six months—thanks to President Nixon's friends on Wall Street.

TV journalists also have endured financial strains. When NBC couldn't find sponsors for its prime-time *American Revolution of '63* news special about the Civil Rights Movement, the network lost half a million dollars of revenue in a single night.

5. Perhaps the least admirable characteristic of the news organizations that have helped to shape American history has been a tendency among many of them to ignore or malign historically underrepresented segments of society. For much of its history, the Fourth Estate was a bastion of white, Protestant men who weren't interested in improving the lives of the disenfranchised.

One example came when *Ladies Magazine* and other periodicals of the 1700s communicated that women didn't possess the ability to function beyond the domestic sphere, and then the Brahmins of nineteenth-century journalism used their power to block women's march toward equality. The *New York World* denigrated Susan B. Anthony as being "lean, cadaverous; with the proportions of a file," and the *Philadelphia Ledger and Daily Transcript* published the appalling statement: "A woman is nobody. A wife is everything."

A second instance of this regrettable tendency followed a century and a half later when Father Charles Coughlin used his golden radio voice to attack people of the Jewish faith. The Radio Priest went so far as to say, in 1942, that World War II hadn't been caused by Germany "but by the race of Jews."

6. Another important characteristic of many of the news organizations that have influenced American history has been an eagerness to harness the power of visual images. Magazines and newspapers often have used editorial cartoons as effective weapons in their journalistic crusades, and TV news has lifted the power of visual images to unparalleled heights.

Harper's Weekly showcased Thomas Nast's devastating cartoons to loosen the Tweed Ring's stranglehold on the citizens of New York City during the late 1860s. The *New York Journal* followed the same path at the end of the century, though to a very different end, when the paper made use of Frederic Remington's artistic talents as part of its campaign to push the United States into war with Spain, including a misleading drawing of the *USS Maine* being destroyed by a Spanish mine. In the 1920s, the Memphis *Commercial Appeal* published searing cartoons as the centerpiece of its courageous campaign against the Ku Klux Klan. Twenty years later, photos brought Rosie the Riveter to life as both a "glamour girl" and a strong, resourceful factory worker who helped the United States win World War II.

The compelling nature of visual images was central to making television the most potent medium of communication in the history of humankind. In an impressive series of events beginning in the 1950s, TV news repeatedly demonstrated that its images could move the nation. In television's finest hour, CBS exposed the despicable actions of Senator Joseph McCarthy, and then the three major networks combined forces to propel civil rights onto the nation's front burner and to help end the Vietnam War.

7. As the title of this book suggests, the news organizations that have taken leading roles in shaping this country have consistently recognized that the pen can be mightier than the sword—and mightier than tyranny or demagoguery or political corruption. The instrument of communication has varied from a quill pen in the eighteenth century to websites and blogs in the twenty-first, but the communicators highlighted in this book have proven that the combination of writing talent and driving passion can be potent. The episodes described in the previous pages repeatedly have shown that this pairing can stir the emotions of the American people at crucial moments.

During the 1770s, Tom Paine's muscular prose helped transform lukewarm patriots into fiery revolutionaries. Half a century later, the suffering that defined the early lives of Maria Stewart and Frederick Douglass inspired them to write with a depth of feeling that helped turn the nation's conscience against slavery. In recent years, print, broadcast, and online news outlets have joined forces to help secure new rights for gay and lesbian Americans.

8. Many of the journalistic campaigns chronicled in this book have been led by forward-thinking news organizations that have embraced, often earlier than their more staid competitors, the technological advances that have occurred during their eras. Central to the success of the muckrakers during the late 1900s was the eagerness of S. S. McClure to adapt to the changing technology vis-à-vis printing and paper production. That allowed the publisher to aim the articles in *McClure's* toward low-paid office clerks and shop girls who could afford to buy mass-circulation magazines. Likewise, one of the reasons that TV news of the 1960s and early 1970s was able to hasten the end of the Vietnam War was that correspondents willingly hoisted new, lightweight cameras onto their shoulders and made use of the air transportation and communication satellites that allowed them to make their warfront images part of daily news coverage for the first time. And in the early 2000s, innovative online news voices such as *Politico, Slate,* and *RealClearPolitics* played important roles in supporting lesbian and gay rights.

9. Throughout its history, journalism has remained an endeavor in which a person—if endowed with talent, determination, and wherewithal— can make a difference, though not always a positive one. From Tom Paine stirring ideas in colonial America to Ida Tarbell taking on the biggest monopoly in the country and from William Randolph Hearst helping to start a war to Margaret Bourke-White creating the "Women in Steel" photo essay to glamorize female factory workers, individual men and women who've joined the Fourth Estate have, for more than two centuries, been actively shaping history.

10. Ultimately, perhaps the most important characteristic that has allowed news organizations to influence the country's evolution has been an acceptance not of the power of the news media but of the limitations of that institution. Although the journalists and news organizations profiled in this book cherished the Fourth Estate's role as watchdog over the official branches of government, none of the historic events described here was brought about solely by the news media. News articles, broadcasts, and web content often served as catalysts, but not in a single instance did journalists function in a vacuum. The news media may have placed a particular topic on the agenda, but the support and commitment of other institutions was always essential for meaningful change to occur.

Harper's Weekly and the *New York Times* exposed Tweed's wrongdoing, but the citizens of New York had to band together before the political corruption was finally ended and the wayward city officials wore prison stripes. The muckrakers fearlessly shined the bright light of truth into the dark corners of America, but it took other institutions to enact reform measures—the Supreme Court to dissolve the Standard Oil monopoly, Congress to pass the Pure Food and Drug Act, the American public to vote corrupt senators out of office. Television brought the grisly images of battle into the American living room, but President Johnson, responding to the pressure of public opinion, ultimately had to bring the troops home from Southeast Asia.

Watergate is the paramount example of the limited role the Fourth Estate can play. The *Washington Post* revealed the dimensions of the immorality of the Nixon White House, but then the Justice Department investigated the charges, the Supreme Court demanded the White House tapes, and Congress voted the articles of impeachment that toppled a president.

Although the previous chapters—as well as this list of ten characteristics describing *how* the news media have shaped American history—are all products of the past, I feel compelled to end this book with a few comments about the future. American journalism today is struggling. The rise of the Internet is the primary factor in the difficulties facing the nation's news organizations. Millions of readers who once paid to subscribe to a daily paper are now, instead, turning to online sources they can access for free. Another element contributing to the crisis involves the classified ads that, just a few years ago, accounted for 40 percent of a newspaper's revenue—until they were replaced by eBay, Craigslist, and other low- or no-cost websites. Financial woes have led papers to lay off large numbers of reporters and editors. Some papers have closed, and many others are severely threatened. Commercial TV news has also lost much of its audience, advertising revenue, and reporting resources to online sources and cable news channels.[1]

Newspapers and network TV news aren't going to disappear altogether, but their roles will continue to diminish as digital journalism reinvents how news is reported and distributed. Although the changes are frightening to many journalists and admirers of the traditional news media, the transformation isn't all bad. One plus is that who gathers and disseminates information is expanding far beyond full-time staff members, with virtually anyone now being able to become a citizen journalist. Also, decisions about what's being covered—and what's not—are no longer in the hands of a tiny number of publishers and corporate executives. That is, changes in how news organizations are financed means The Powers That Be now include entrepreneurs who create online startups, people who run nonprofit investigative reporting projects, and folks who put together community news sites composed of blogs and neighborhood reports.[2]

As a historian, I believe that looking back is essential to charting a course for the future. And as a *journalism* historian, I believe that these emerging citizens of the Fourth Estate should be guided by the case studies illuminated in this book, as well as by the news media traits listed in this concluding chapter. A number of those characteristics suggest principles of behavior that could help the American news media both survive and thrive in the future. Therefore, I say to anyone who practices the craft of journalism:

- Be willing to set the agenda.
- Be willing to break from the pack.
- Be willing to sacrifice financial gain for public good.
- Be willing to reach out to the politically or socially disenfranchised.
- Stay at the forefront of technological innovation.
- Don't be so arrogant as to think that journalism is the country's only institution of consequence.

Some wags and bean counters will criticize these suggestions, saying that such a call for news organizations to travel the journalistic high road ignores the economic realities facing the industry today. It's true that these suggestions are based on an idealistic premise that not everyone shares: journalism that's substantive in content and strong in backbone ultimately will succeed, prosper, and serve a democratic people well. This lofty principle is particularly important to keep in mind as journalism struggles to adapt to a media landscape that's changing at warp speed. That is, it's descriptors such as "substantive in content" and "strong in backbone" that are essential for journalism to remain vital and successful, whether in the form of words that are printed on paper, images that appear on the TV screen, or insightful interpretation that's sent through a wireless platform that's not yet been invented.

NOTES

INTRODUCTION

1. Thomas Jefferson, letter to Thomas Paine, 19 June 1792, in *The Works of Thomas Jefferson*, ed. Paul Leicester Ford (New York: Putnam, 1904), vol. 7, 122.

CHAPTER 1: SOWING THE SEEDS OF REVOLUTION

1. Samuel Adams, "Instructions of the Town of Boston to Its Representatives in the General Court," May 1764, in *The Writings of Samuel Adams*, ed. Harry A. Cushing (New York: Octagon, 1968), vol. 1, 5.

2. Samuel Adams, letter to James Warren, 9 December 1772, in *Collections of the Massachusetts Historical Society*, ed. W. C. Ford (Boston: Samuel Hall, 1795).

3. *New York Journal*, 13 October 1768, 2.

4. Oliver M. Dickerson, comp., *Boston Under Military Rule, 1768–1769* (Boston: Chapman & Grimes, 1936), ix.

5. *Boston Evening Post*, 1 May 1769, 1; *New York Journal*: 8 December 1768, 1; 29 December 1768, 1; 19 January 1769, 1; 13 April 1769, 1.

6. *New York Journal*: 10 November 1768, 1; 22 December 1768, 1.

7. *New York Journal* (*Supplement*): 29 June 1769, 1; 1 June 1769, 1.

8. *Boston Evening Post*, 26 June 1769, 1; *New York Journal* (*Supplement*): 29 June 1769, 1; 27 July 1769, 1.

9. *New York Journal*, 3 November 1768, 2; *New York Journal* (*Supplement*), 29 June 1769, 1; *Boston Evening Post*: 26 June 1769, 1; 24 July 1769, 1; 31 July 1769, 1.

10. Francis Bernard, letter to Lord Hillsborough, 25 February 1769, in Sir Francis Bernard Papers, New York Public Library, New York; Thomas Hutchinson, letter to Israel Williams, 26 January 1769, in Israel Williams Papers, Massachusetts Historical Society Library, Boston.

11. Thomas Hutchinson, letter to Israel Williams, 26 January 1769, in Israel Williams Papers, Massachusetts Historical Society Library, Boston.

12. *Boston Evening Post*, 26 June 1769, 1.

13. Samuel Adams, *Boston Gazette*: "Article," 31 December 1770, 1; "Article Signed Vindex," 28 January 1771, 1.

14. "A Monumental Inscription on the Fifth of March," 1772, reprinted in Philip Davidson, *Propaganda and the American Revolution* (Chapel Hill: University of North Carolina Press, 1941), 222.

15. David Ramsay, *The History of the American Revolution* (Philadelphia, 1789; reprinted New York: Russell & Russell, 1968), vol. 1, 91.

16. Benjamin Rush, letter to James Cheetham, in *The Letters of Benjamin Rush*, ed. Lyman H. Butterfield (Princeton, NJ: Princeton University Press, 1951), vol. 2, 1007.

17. Thomas Paine, *Common Sense*, in *The Writings of Thomas Paine*, ed. Moncure D. Conway (New York: AMS, 1967), 68, 84–85.

18. Ibid., 72, 84, 99.

19. Ibid., 118–119.

20. Philip S. Foner, ed., *The Complete Writings of Thomas Paine* (New York: Citadel, 1945), ix.

21. George Washington, letter to Joseph Reed, 1 April 1776, in *The Writings of George Washington from the Original Manuscript Sources, 1745–1799*, ed. John C. Fitzpatrick (Washington, DC: US Government Printing Office, 1931–1944), vol. 4, 455; Abigail Adams, letter to John Adams, 21 February 1776, in *Adams Family Correspondence*, ed. Lyman H. Butterfield (Cambridge, MA: Harvard University, 1909), vol. 1, 350; Thomas Jefferson, letter to Francis Eppes, 19 January 1821, in *The Works of Thomas Jefferson*, ed. Paul Leicester Ford (New York: Putnam, 1904), vol. 12, 195.

22. Eric Foner, *Tom Paine and Revolutionary America* (New York: Oxford University Press, 1976), 87.

23. Thomas Paine, *Crisis*, in *The Writings of Thomas Paine*, ed. Moncure D. Conway (New York: AMS, 1967), 170.

24. Ibid., 176.

25. Silas Bent, *Newspaper Crusaders: A Neglected Story* (Freeport, NY: Books for Libraries, 1939), 19.

CHAPTER 2: TURNING AMERICA AGAINST THE SINS OF SLAVERY

1. Elijah P. Lovejoy, *St. Louis Observer*, 11 February 1836.

2. *Missouri Republican*: 17 July 1837; 28 August 1837.

3. *Alton Observer*, 8 September 1836.

4. Elijah P. Lovejoy, speech delivered 30 October 1837 in Alton, IL, in Edward Beecher, *Narrative of Riots at Alton: In Connection with the Death of Rev. Elijah P. Lovejoy* (Alton, IL: George Holton, 1838; reprint Miami: Mnemosyne, 1969), 91.

5. William Lloyd Garrison, "A Martyr for Liberty," *Liberator*, 24 November 1837.

6. Minutes of the Executive Committee of the American Anti-Slavery Society, Boston Public Library, December 1837.

7. William Lloyd Garrison, "Black List," *Genius of Universal Emancipation*, 20 November 1829, 2.

8. William Lloyd Garrison, "To the Public," *Liberator*, 1 January 1831, 1.

9. William Lloyd Garrison, "Editors," *Liberator*, 29 January 1831, 2.

10. "Threats to Assassinate," *Liberator*, 10 September 1831, 1.

11. William Lloyd Garrison, "Address to the Friends of Freedom and Emancipation in the United States," *Liberator*, 31 May 1844, 2.

12. "The Meeting at Framingham," *Liberator*, 7 July 1854, 2.

13. "The 'Liberator' Released," *Nation*, 4 January 1866, 7.

14. Frederick Douglass, in John W. Blassingame and John R. McKivigan, eds., *The Frederick Douglass Papers* (New Haven, CT: Yale University Press, 1992), vol. 5, 369.

15. Samuel Cornish and John B. Russwurm, "To Our Patrons," *Freedom's Journal*, 16 March 1827, 1.

16. Maria Stewart, "An Address, Delivered at the African Masonic Hall, in Boston," *Liberator*, 4 May 1833, 4.

17. Frederick Douglass, "Prospectus," *North Star*, 5 November 1847, 4.

18. Frederick Douglass, "Colored People Must Command Respect," *North Star*, 24 March 1848, 2.

19. Frederick Douglass, *Life and Times of Frederick Douglass* (Hartford, CT: Park, 1881), 326; untitled article, *North Star*, 21 January 1848, 2.

CHAPTER 3: SLOWING THE MOMENTUM FOR WOMEN'S RIGHTS

1. Elizabeth Cady Stanton, Susan B. Anthony, and Matilda Joslyn Gage, eds., *History of Woman Suffrage* (New York: Fowler & Wells, 1881), 70.

2. "Thoughts on Women," *Ladies Magazine*, August 1792, 112; "To the Editors of the Ladies Magazine," *Ladies Magazine*, August 1792, 122; "On the Happy Influence of Female Society," *American Museum*, January 1787, 63.

3. "The Cultivation of the Mind Recommended," *Ladies Magazine*, April 1793, 220.

4. "On Fashionable Female Amusements," *Ladies Magazine*, February 1793, 125–126; "On Matrimonial Happiness," *Weekly Magazine*, 10 March 1798, 153; "On Conversation," *Weekly Magazine*, February 1798, 122–123.

5. "Woman's Rights Convention," *Seneca County Courier*, 14 July 1848, 1.

6. Stanton, Anthony, and Gage, *History*, 70; Aileen S. Kraditor, *Up from the Pedestal* (Chicago: Quadrangle, 1968), 186–188.

7. Kraditor, *Up*, 188.

8. Stanton, Anthony, and Gage, *History*, 71.

9. "The Woman's Rights Convention—The Last Act of the Drama," *New York Herald*, 12 September 1852, 2; "Insurrection Among the Women," *Worcester Telegraph*, reprinted in Stanton, Anthony, and Gage, *History*, 803; "The Women of Philadelphia," *Philadelphia Ledger and Daily Transcript*, reprinted in Stanton, Anthony, and Gage, *History*, 804.

10. *Syracuse Weekly Star*, 11 September 1852, reprinted in Stanton, Anthony, and Gage, *History*, 852–853; "Women's Rights in the Legislature," *Albany Daily State Register*, 6 March 1854, 1.

11. "Women Out of Their Latitude," *Mechanic's Advocate*, reprinted in Stanton, Anthony, and Gage, *History*, 802–803; "The Woman's Rights Convention—The Last Act of the Drama," *New York Herald*, 12 September 1852, 2.

12. "Female Follies and Fourrierism," *New York Herald*, 12 September 1852, 2.

13. *New York Sun*, reprinted in Ida Husted Harper, *The Life and Work of Susan B. Anthony* (Indianapolis: Hollenbeck, 1898), vol. 1, 90; "The Last Vagary of the Greeley Clique—The Women, Their Rights, and Their Champions," *New York Herald*, 7 September 1853, 4.

14. *Syracuse Weekly Star,* reprinted in Harper, *Anthony*, vol. 1, 267; "The Last Vagary of the Greeley Clique—The Women, Their Rights, and Their Champions," *New York Herald*, 7 September 1853, 4; "The Woman's Rights Convention—The Last Act of the Drama," *New York Herald*, 12 September 1852, 2; "Women's Rights in the Legislature," *Albany Daily State Register*, 7 March 1854, 1; "The Last Vagary of the Greeley Clique—The Women, Their Rights, and Their Champions," *New York Herald*, 7 September 1853, 2.

15. Miriam Gurko, *The Ladies of Seneca Falls: The Birth of the Woman's Rights Movement* (New York: Macmillan, 1974), 104.

16. Lucretia Mott, "National Convention at Cincinnati, Ohio," in Stanton, Anthony, and Gage, *History*, 164.

17. Laura Ballard, "What Flag Shall We Fly?" *The Revolution*, October 1870, 265.

18. Josephine St. Pierre Ruffin, "Editorial," *Woman's Era*, 24 March 1894, 8.

19. "A Cry from the Females," *New York Tribune*, reprinted in Harper, *Anthony*, vol. 1, 267; *New York World*, reprinted in Harper, *Anthony*, vol. 1, 264.

20. *New York World*, reprinted in Harper, *Anthony*, vol. 1, 264; *Utica Herald*, reprinted in Harper, *Anthony*, vol. 1, 367; *Richmond Herald*, 29 October 1879, reprinted in Harper, *Anthony*, vol. 1, 504.

21. "Manly Women," *Saturday Review*, 22 June 1889, 756–757; "Is Marriage a Failure?" *Cosmopolitan*, November 1888–April 1889, 196–203.

22. *Life*: "In Days to Come, Churches May Be Fuller," 23 July 1896, 588–589; "In a Twentieth Century Club," 13 June 1895, 395; William H. Walker, "The New Navy, About 1900 a.d.," 16 April 1896, 310–311.

23. "Her Ideal Journal; Miss Anthony Tells How She Would Make a Newspaper," *Chicago Tribune*, 28 May 1893, 33.

CHAPTER 4: ATTACKING MUNICIPAL CORRUPTION

1. Albert B. Paine, *Thomas Nast: His Period and His Pictures* (Gloucester, MA: Peter Smith, 1967), 179.

2. "Our Case Plainly Stated," *New York Times*, 27 July 1871, 4.

3. James Jackson Jarves, *The Art-Idea* (New York: Hurd and Houghton, 1864), 242.

4. Paine, *Thomas Nast*, 106; Morton Keller, *The Art and Politics of Thomas Nast* (New York: Oxford University Press, 1968), 13.

5. Thomas Nast, *Harper's Weekly*: "Robinson Crusoe," 4 December 1869, 777; "The Economical Council, Albany, New York," 25 December 1869, 825.

6. "The Democratic Millennium," *New York Times*, 20 September 1870, 4.

7. Thomas Nast, "The 'Brains,'" *Harper's Weekly*, 21 October 1871, 792.

8. Gustavus Myers, *The History of Tammany Hall* (New York: Burt Franklin, 1917), 239; Paine, *Thomas Nast*, 179.

9. Thomas Nast St. Hill, *Thomas Nast Cartoons and Illustrations* (New York: Dover, 1974), 18.

10. Untitled article, *New York Times*, 19 July 1871, 4.

11. "More Ring Villainy," *New York Times*, 8 July 1871, 4.

12. *New York Times*: "Will It 'Blow Over'?" 21 July 1871, 4; "The Tammany Frauds," 24 July 1871, 4; "Our Proofs of Fraud Against the City Government," 23 July 1871, 4; "The Secret Accounts," 22 July 1871, 4; "More Bills Which Are 'Perhaps Exorbitant,'" 26 July 1871, 4.

13. *New York Times*: "More Ring Villainy," 8 July 1871, 4; "Two Thieves," 19 July 1871, 4; "The Decoy-Ducks of the Ring," 11 July 1871, 4; "Stampede of the Ring," 29 July 1871, 1; "More Bills Which Are 'Perhaps Exorbitant,'" 26 July 1871, 4; "Proofs of Theft; How the Public Money Is Embezzled by the Tammany Rulers," 20 July 1871, 4; "The Betrayal of Public Liberties," 11 July 1871, 4.

14. "Democratic Economy," *Philadelphia Press*, 21 July 1871, 4; "Exposure of Tammany Corruption," *Boston Daily Advertiser*, 21 July 1871, 2; "Very Plain Talk," *Providence Daily Journal*, 24 July 1871, 2.

15. "The Times and Our City Administration—The Disease and the Remedy," *New York Herald*, 3 August 1871, 6; "The City Expenditures—Plumbing and Gas-Fitting," *New York Tribune*, 27 July 1871, 4.

16. "A Presbyterian View of Tammany," *New York World*, 10 July 1871, 4.

17. *New York Times*: "Our Case Plainly Stated," 27 July 1871, 4; "Two Thieves," 19 July 1871, 4; "Our Proofs of Fraud Against the City Government," 23 July 1871, 4.

18. A Taxpayer, "To the Editor of the *New York Times*," *New York Times*, 23 July 1871, 8. The supplement was published on 29 July 1871.

19. "The Tammany Leaders Still Admit Their Guilt," *New York Times*, 1 August 1871, 4; Thomas Nast, "Who Stole the People's Money?" *Harper's Weekly*, 19 August 1871, 764.

20. Thomas Nast, *Harper's Weekly*: "What Are You Going to Do About It?" 14 October 1871, 960; "The Only Thing They Respect or Fear," 21 October 1871, 977.

21. Thomas Nast, "The Tammany Tiger Loose—'What Are You Going to Do About It?'" *Harper's Weekly*, 11 November 1871, 1056–1057.

22. "Unto the Breach!" *Harper's Weekly*, 11 November 1871, 1050.

23. Thomas Nast, "What Are You Laughing At?" *Harper's Weekly*, 25 November 1871, 1097.

24. "The Capture of Tweed," *Harper's Weekly*, 7 October 1876, 821.

25. "Who Killed the Ring," *The Nation*, 23 November 1871, 334–335.

26. "The Victory of the People," *Harper's Weekly*, 25 November 1871, 1098.

CHAPTER 5: PUSHING AMERICA TOWARD AN INTERNATIONAL WAR

1. Untitled editorial, *New York Post*, 17 March 1898, 6.

2. Ireland Alleyne, *Joseph Pulitzer: Reminiscences of a Secretary* (New York: Mitchell Kennerley, 1914), 110.

3. *New York World*: "Baptized in Blood," 31 May 1883, 1; "A Brutal Negro Whips His Nephew to Death," 4 March 1884, 1.

4. Ishbel Ross, *Ladies of the Press* (New York: Harper, 1936), 61.

5. W. A. Swanberg, *Citizen Hearst: A Biography of William Randolph Hearst* (New York: Charles Scribner's Sons, 1961), 162.

6. W. R. Hearst, "The Appeal of Cuba," *New York Journal*, 11 October 1895, 4.

7. *New York Evening Journal*: "Spanish Brutality," 15 October 1896, 1; "Cuba," 23 October 1896, 1.

8. Willard G. Bleyer, *Main Currents in the History of American Journalism* (Boston: Houghton Mifflin, 1927), 342.

9. James Creelman, *On the Great Highway: The Wanderings and Adventures of a Special Correspondent* (Boston: Lothrop, 1901), 177–178.

10. Richard Harding Davis, "Does Our Flag Shield Women?" *New York Journal*, 12 February 1897, 1; George Bronson Rea, *Facts and Fakes About Cuba* (New York: G. Munro's Sons, 1897), 230; "Mr. Davis Explains; The Unclothed Woman Searched by Men Was an Invention of a New York Newspaper," *New York World*, 17 February 1897, 2.

11. *New York World*: "Cuba," 10 June 1896, 4; Sylvester Scovel, "Cuba," 29 May 1896, 1; James Creelman, "Cuba," 17 May 1896, 1.

12. *Congressional Record*, 26 January 1897, 1157.

13. *New York Journal*, 17 February 1898, 1: "Destruction of the War Ship *Maine* Was the Work of an Enemy"; "$50,000!"

14. *New York Journal*: "The War Ship *Maine* Was Split in Two by an Enemy's Secret Infernal Machine," 17 February 1898, 1; "War! Sure! *Maine* Destroyed by Spanish," 17 February 1898, 1; "The Whole Country Thrills with War Fever," 18 February 1898, 1.

15. "Game of War with Spain," *New York Journal*, 20 February 1898, 2; "The People's Letters," *New York Journal*, 26 February 1898, 12; Ferdinand Lundberg, *Imperial Hearst: A Social Biography* (New York: Modern Library, 1937), 81.

16. Swanberg, *Citizen Hearst*, 138.

17. *New York World*: "*Maine* Explosion Caused by Bomb or Torpedo?" 17 February 1898, 1; "Midnight Opinion from the President," 18 February 1898, 1; "*World's* Latest Discoveries Indicate *Maine* Was Blown Up by Submarine Mine," 20 February 1898, 1; "*World's* News of the Evidence of a Mine Under the *Maine* Changes the Feeling Throughout the Country," 20 February 1898, 1; "Free Cuba the Only Atonement," 26 February 1898, 6.

18. W. R. Hearst, "The Situation," *New York Evening Journal*, 24 February 1898, 10; "Peace—on a 'Cash Basis,'" *New York World*, 16 March 1898, 6.

19. "What the Court of Inquiry Has Found," *New York Evening Journal*, 11 March 1898, 1.

20. "Mob Burned M'Kinley in Effigy in Colorado," *New York Evening Journal*, 30 March 1898, 2; "M'Kinley Burned in Effigy, Jeered and Flouted," *New York Evening Journal*, 30 March 1898, 2; "M'Kinley and Hanna Burned in Effigy," *New York Evening Journal*, 31 March 1898, 2; "Patient Under the Loss of Her First Born," *New York Evening Journal*, 9 April 1898, 7; "A Chilly Message," *New York World*, 29 March 1898, 1.

21. "Now to Avenge the *Maine!*" *New York Journal*, 20 April 1898, 1.

22. "How Do You Like the *Journal's* War?" *New York Journal*, 9 May 1898, 1.

23. W. R. Hearst, "First American Newspaper Published in the Island," *New York Journal*, 11 July 1898, 1.

24. "Six Killed on the *Reina Mercedes*," *New York Journal*, 8 June 1898, 2; "Cervera Waits for the Blow That Will Crush Spain's Navy," *New York World*, 9 June 1898, 2.

25. Willis J. Abbot, *Watching the World Go By* (New York: Beekman, 1974), 141.

26. Creelman, *On the Great Highway*, 211–212; W. R. Hearst, "Journal's Editor Describes the Capture of El Caney," *New York Journal*, 4 July 1898, 1.

27. Creelman, *On the Great Highway*, 160, 187; John Winkler, *W. R. Hearst* (New York: Simon and Schuster, 1928), 146; Richard Harding Davis, "Cervera's Fleet Smashed," *New York Journal*, 4 July 1898, 1; Joseph Wisan, *The Cuban Crisis as Reflected in the New York Press* (New York, 1934), 458–459.

28. Abbot, *Watching*, 217; W. R. Hearst, "The Importance of Union Among Newspapers," *New York Journal*, 25 September 1898, editorial section 1.

CHAPTER 6: ACHIEVING REFORM BY MUCKRAKING

1. David M. Chalmers, *The Social and Political Ideas of the Muckrakers* (New York: Citadel, 1964), 11.

2. Theodore Roosevelt first used the term "muckraker" in April 1906, referring to a passage from John Bunyan's allegorical novel *Pilgrim's Progress*.

3. Lincoln Steffens, "Tweed Days in St. Louis," *McClure's*, October 1902, 577.

4. Arthur M. Schlesinger, *Political and Social History of the United States, 1829-1925* (New York: Macmillan, 1925), 442.

5. Lincoln Steffens, *McClure's*: "The Shame of Minneapolis," January 1903, 227–239; "Pittsburgh: A City Ashamed," May 1903, 24–39; "Philadelphia: Corrupt and Contented," July 1903, 249–264; "Chicago: Half Free and Fighting On," October 1903, 563–577; "New York: Good Government in Danger," November 1903, 84–92; "Enemies of the Republic," April 1904, 587–599; "Enemies of the Republic," August 1904, 395–408; "Rhode Island: A State for Sale," February 1905, 337–353; "New Jersey: A Traitor State," April 1905, 649–664.

6. *McClure's*: "On the Making of McClure's Magazine," November 1904, 108; William Allen White, "Editorial," June 1904, 221.

7. Lincoln Steffens, *The Shame of the Cities* (New York: Peter Smith, 1948).

8. Ida M. Tarbell, "The History of the Standard Oil Company," *McClure's*, November 1902, 3–16.

9. Ida M. Tarbell, *McClure's*: "The History of the Standard Oil Company," March 1903, 505–507; "The History of the Standard Oil Company: Part Two," March 1904, 497–498.

10. "On the Making of McClure's Magazine," *McClure's*, November 1904, 107–108.

11. Ida M. Tarbell, *The History of the Standard Oil Company* (New York: McClure, Phillips, 1904).

12. Ray Stannard Baker, *McClure's*: "The Railroad Rate," November 1905, 47–59; "Railroad Rebates," December 1905, 179–194; "Railroads on Trial," January 1906, 318–331; "Railroads on Trial," February 1906, 398–411; "Railroads on Trial," March 1906, 535–549; also, Daniel L. Cruice, "The Chicago Election," *Arena*, July 1904, 21–28; "Annual Net Earnings of State-Owned Railroads," *Arena*, July 1904, 87; Josiah Flynt, "Telegraph and Telephone Companies as Allies of the Criminal Pool Rooms," *Cosmopolitan*, May 1907, 50–57; Eugene P. Lyle, Jr., "The Guggenheims and the Smelter Trust," *Hampton's*, March 1910, 411–422; Judson C. Welliver, "The Mormon Church and the Sugar Trust," *Hampton's*, January 1910, 82–93; Judson C. Welliver, "The Annexation of Cuba by the Sugar Trust," *Hampton's*, March 1910, 375–388; Judson C. Welliver, "The Secret of the Sugar Trust's Power," *Hampton's*, May 1910, 717–722; Will Irwin, "Tainted New Methods of the Liquor Interests," *Collier's*, 13 March 1909, 27–31; Charles

Edward Russell, "The Greatest Trust in the World," *Everybody's*, February 1905, 147–156.

13. Upton Sinclair, "The Jungle," *Appeal to Reason*, 29 April 1905, 2.

14. Upton Sinclair, "What Life Means to Me," *Cosmopolitan*, October 1906, 593; Louis Filler, *Crusaders for American Liberalism* (Yellow Springs, OH: Antioch, 1939), 163.

15. George Brown Tindall, *America: A Narrative History* (New York: W. W. Norton, 1984), 918–919.

16. Edward Bok, *Ladies' Home Journal*, May 1904, 18: "The 'Patent-Medicine' Curse"; "The Alcohol in 'Patent Medicines.'"

17. "We Are Not So 'Holy,'" *Collier's*, 4 November 1905, 26; Edward Bok, "A Few Words to the W.C.T.U.," *Ladies' Home Journal*, September 1904, 16; "A Bold Paper," *Collier's*, 10 November 1906, 9.

18. E. W. Kemble, "Death's Laboratory," *Collier's*, 3 June 1905, 5.

19. "For the Safety of Yourself and Your Child," *Ladies' Home Journal*, February 1906, 1.

20. See, for example, "Samuel Hopkins Adams Is Dead," *New York Times*, 17 November 1958, 31; Arthur Weinberg and Lila Weinberg, *The Muckrakers* (New York: Simon and Schuster, 1961), 206.

21. Tindall, *America*, 907.

22. David Graham Phillips, "Treason of the Senate," *Cosmopolitan*, March 1906, 488.

23. Ibid., 489–490.

24. "Letters," *Cosmopolitan*, April 1906, 567.

25. Phillips, "Treason," *Cosmopolitan*: May 1906, 3–12; July 1906, 267–276; August 1906, 368–377.

26. *Cosmopolitan*, June 1906, cover.

27. David Graham Phillips, "The Treason of the Senate," *Cosmopolitan*, November 1906, 84.

28. Filler, *Crusaders*, 256–257.

29. Schlesinger, *Political and Social History*, 441.

30. Weinberg and Weinberg, *Muckrakers*, xx; C. C. Regier, *The Era of the Muckrakers* (Chapel Hill: University of North Carolina Press, 1932), 13; Vernon Parrington, *Main Currents in American Thought* (New York: Harcourt Brace, 1939), vol. 3, 406; Chalmers, *Social and Political Ideas*, 115.

31. Thomas W. Lawson, "Frenzied Finance: The Story of Amalgamated," *Everybody's*: July 1904, 1–10; August 1904, 154–164; September 1904, 289–301; October 1904, 455–468; November 1904, 599–613; December 1904, 747–760; Mark Sullivan, "The People's One Hour in Two Years," *Collier's*, 13 March 1909, 10–11; Ray Stannard Baker, "Following the Color Line," *American Magazine*, April 1907, 563–579.

32. Schlesinger, *Political and Social History*, 442.

CHAPTER 7: DEFYING THE KU KLUX KLAN

1. "Congressional Committee Told of Outrages by Ku Klux Klan," *New York World*, 12 October 1921, 2; Kenneth T. Jackson, *The Ku Klux Klan in the City: 1915–1930* (New York: Oxford University Press, 1967), 254.

2. "Ku Klux Klan Exposed!" *New York World*, 5 September 1921, 12.

3. Rowland Thomas, "Secrets of the Ku Klux Klan Exposed by the *World*," *New York World*, 6 September 1921, 1.

4. *New York World*: Rowland Thomas, "Holds Simmons Has Avowed Klan Aims to Restore Slavery," 13 October 1921, 2; Rowland Thomas, "The *World* Exposes Klan's Oath-Bound Secret Ritual and Ku Klux Tests of Racial and Religious Hate," 10 September 1921, 1; "Kleagles Peddle Membership; Grand Goblin Their District Boss," 9 September 1921, 1–2.

5. *New York World*: Rowland Thomas, "Ku Klux Questionnaire," 10 September 1921, 1; "Received by the *World* Yesterday," 6 September 1921, 1.

6. Rowland Thomas, "Clarke and Mrs. Tyler Arrested While in House of Ill Repute," *New York World*, 19 September 1921, 1.

7. *New York World*: "U.S. Must Get Rid of Ku Klux Klan, Leaders in Nation's Life Insist," 9 September 1921, 2; "Enright Says Klan Won't Be Permitted to Operate in City," 9 September 1921, 1; "Aldermen Call Klan 'Masked Band of Criminal Lawbreakers,'" 12 October 1921, 2.

8. *New York World*: Rowland Thomas, "Ku Klux's Record of Atrocities Grows," 19 September 1921, 1; "152 Valid Objections," 19 September 1921, 1.

9. Jackson, *Ku Klux Klan*, 12; David M. Chalmers, *Hooded Americanism: The History of the Ku Klux Klan* (Durham, NC: Duke University Press, 1987), 38.

10. Chalmers, *Hooded Americanism*, 198–199; Jackson, *Ku Klux Klan*, 11; John Hohenberg, ed., *The Pulitzer Prize Story* (New York: Columbia University Press, 1959), 336.

11. C. P. J. Mooney, "The Affair at Mer Rouge," *Commercial Appeal*, 17 March 1923, 4.

12. J. P. Alley, *Commercial Appeal*: "His 'Noble Work,' Done in the Dark!" 21 August 1923, 1; "No Wonder He Puts a Sack over That Mug!" 18 September 1923, 1; "I'm Unworthy—My Religion Ain't Right!" 28 August 1923, 1.

13. "Election," *Tri-State American*, 7 November 1923, 1.

14. *Commercial Appeal*: "Eyes of Nation Turn to Memphis Election," 5 November 1923, 1; "Charge Klan Balked Mer Rouge Inquiry," 31 October 1923, 1; "Klan's Press Agent Kills Chief Lawyer of Simmons Faction; Bloody Climax in Klan Feud; 'I'm Glad He's Dead,'" 6 November 1923, 1; "Warrants for Arrest of Klan Wizard Evans and Advisors Issued," 7 November 1923, 1; "Victim and Slayer in Klan Blood-Feud," 8 November 1923, 1.

15. J. P. Alley, "The Sinister Hand," *Commercial Appeal*, 8 November 1923, 1.

16. "Paine Wins Victory in Race for Mayor: Kluck Runs Second," *Commercial Appeal*, 9 November 1923, 1.

17. "100,000 Klansmen Go to Fort Wayne," *New York Times*, 10 November 1923, 15; Hohenberg, *Pulitzer Prize*, 336.

18. Grover Cleveland Hall, "Imperial Jefferson Flogs a Helpless Negro," *Montgomery Advertiser*, 14 July 1927, 4.

19. Grover Cleveland Hall, "Unmask!" *Montgomery Advertiser*, 14 July 1927, 4.

20. Reprinted from *Alabama Christian Advocate* in Grover Cleveland Hall, "The Comic Gyrations of 'Fraid Cat Editors," *Montgomery Advertiser*, 31 July 1927, 4; reprinted from *Monroe Journal* as "The Advertiser and the Weekly Press," *Montgomery Advertiser*, 23 July 1927, 4; reprinted from *Monroe Journal* as "Lawlessness and the Press," *Montgomery Advertiser*, 16 July 1927, 4; reprinted from *Evergreen Courant* in Hall, "Comic Gyrations," *Montgomery Advertiser*, 31 July 1927, 4.

21. Reprinted from *New York Herald Tribune* as "As Ye Sow," *Montgomery Advertiser*, 21 July 1927, 4; reprinted from *Milwaukee Journal* as "'Chivalry' in the South," *Montgomery Advertiser*, 22 July 1927, 4; reprinted from *New York Times* as "Alabama Law Enforcement," *Montgomery Advertiser*, 15 July 1927, 4.

22. Grover Cleveland Hall, "A Shameless Speech for a Sinister Measure," *Montgomery Advertiser*, 21 July 1927, 4.

23. Grover Cleveland Hall, *Montgomery Advertiser*: "The State of Silent Treads Threatened with a Silent Press," 21 August 1927, 4; "The Klan Would Strike Down a Free and Untrammeled Press in Alabama!" 20 August 1927, 4.

24. "Press Muzzling Bill Defeated in House," *Montgomery Advertiser*, 24 August 1927, 1.

25. Hohenberg, *Pulitzer Prize*, 348.

26. Henry P. Fry, *The Modern Ku Klux Klan* (New York: Negro Universities Press, 1922), 247; "100,000 Klansmen Go to Fort Wayne," *New York Times*, 10 November 1923, 15; Chalmers, *Hooded Americanism*, 78–82.

27. Chalmers, *Hooded Americanism*, 38; Jackson, *Ku Klux Klan*, 12.

28. Hohenberg, *Pulitzer Prize*, 71; Silas Bent, *Newspaper Crusaders: A Neglected Story* (Freeport, NY: Books for Libraries, 1939), 138.

CHAPTER 8: SPREADING ANTI-SEMITISM VIA THE RADIO

1. Martin Ostrow, producer, *America and the Holocaust: Deceit and Indifference* (Alexandria, VA: Public Broadcasting Service, 1994).

2. "Communism Is Jewish," *American-Ranger*, August 1938, 1; "Jews Defile Our Christmas!" *National American*, 31 October 1935, 1.

3. Charles E. Coughlin, radio broadcast delivered 14 February 1932, excerpts of which were reprinted in David H. Bennett, *Demagogues in the Depression:*

American Radicals and the Union Party, 1932–1936 (New Brunswick, NJ: Rutgers University Press, 1969), 34.

4. Sheldon Marcus, *Father Coughlin: The Tumultuous Life of the Priest of the Little Flower* (Boston: Little, Brown, 1973), 34.

5. Alan Brinkley, *Voices of Protest: Huey Long, Father Coughlin, and the Great Depression* (New York: Knopf, 1982), 97; Wallace Stegner, "The Radio Priest and His Flock," in *The Aspirin Age: 1919–1941,* ed. Isabel Leighton (New York: Simon and Schuster), 234; Marcus, *Tumultuous Life,* 37, 222.

6. "Smith Denounces Coughlin's Charge of Link to Morgan," *New York Times,* 29 November 1933, 1.

7. "Coughlin Asserts America 'Retains Her Sovereignty,'" *New York Times,* 30 January 1935, 2; "Senate Beats World Court, 52–36, 7 Less Than 2/3 Vote; Defeat for the President," *New York Times,* 30 January 1935, 1; Arthur Krock, "Defeat for Court a Roosevelt Upset," *New York Times,* 30 January 1935, 1; Elliott Roosevelt, ed., *F.D.R.: His Personal Letters, 1928–1945* (New York: Duell, Sloan and Pearce, 1950), vol. 1, 45.

8. The first issue of *Social Justice* was published in March 1936.

9. T. R. B., "Coughlin Calls the Tune," *New Republic,* 3 June 1936, 100–101.

10. "Coughlin: Thousands Salute Their Leader and Swear Fealty," *Newsweek,* 22 August 1936, 12.

11. "Spellman Warned on Christian Front," *New York Times,* 26 September 1939, 24.

12. Charles E. Coughlin, "From the Tower: 'The Protocols of Zion,'" *Social Justice,* 18 July 1938, 5.

13. Charles E. Coughlin, *Social Justice,* "From the Tower: 'The Protocols of Zion'": 18 July 1938, 5; 8 August 1938, 5.

14. Coughlin, *Social Justice:* "From the Tower: 'Protocols of the Wise Men of Zion,'" 8 August 1938, 5; "The Fifth Protocol," 29 August 1938, 5.

15. *Detroit Free Press:* "Dr. Wise Scores Coughlin Charges," 5 December 1938, 2; "Ford Statement Was Authorized," 5 December 1938, 1.

16. Charles E. Coughlin, "Persecution—Jewish and Christian," radio broadcast delivered 20 November 1938 and reprinted in *Am I an Anti-Semite?* (Royal Oak, MI: Radio League of the Little Flower, 1939), 37, 39.

17. *New York Times:* "WMCA Contradicts Coughlin on Jews," 21 November 1938, 7; "Priest Won't Meet WMCA Conditions," 27 November 1938, 42.

18. "Coughlin Answered by Catholic Layman," *Detroit News,* 12 December 1938, 1.

19. "Catholic 'Worker' in Smear Campaign," *Social Justice,* 22 May 1939, 15; "Anti-Semitism Is Part of the Coughlin Campaign," *Christian Century,* 24 May 1939, 661.

20. Charles E. Coughlin, "I Know Three Germanies," *Social Justice,* 7 December 1936, 5; "Coughlin Denounces 'Mongerers of War,'" *New York Times,* 27 March 1939, 7.

21. Charles E. Coughlin, radio broadcast delivered 30 July 1939, excerpts of which were reprinted in Donald S. Strong, *Organized Anti-Semitism in America: The Rise of Group Prejudice During the Decade 1930–40* (Washington, DC: American Council on Public Affairs, 1941), 66.

22. Marcus, *Tumultuous Life*, 176.

23. "New Radio Code Hits Coughlin," *Detroit News*, 4 October 1939, 1.

24. "Federal Officials Prepare 'Front' Case," *New York Times*, 18 January 1940, 3; Charles E. Coughlin, "I Take My Stand," *Social Justice*, 29 January 1940, 4. The seventeen men ultimately were not convicted.

25. "Comment: No Coughlin Broadcast," *Social Justice*, 23 September 1940, 4.

26. "Comment: Who Started the 'Sacred' War?—and When? Mr. Untermeyer Answers the Question," *Social Justice*, 16 March 1942, 3.

27. "Text of the Dep't of Justice Coughlin Document," *In Fact*, 11 February 1946, 2.

28. "Coughlin Weekly Ends Publication," *New York Times*, 5 May 1942, 23.

29. Ibid.

30. "Calm for a Stormy Priest," *Life*, 14 November 1955, 119.

31. "Father Coughlin," *Fortune*, February 1934, 34; "Catholic 'Worker' in Smear Campaign," *Social Justice*, 22 May 1939, 15.

32. Marcus, *Tumultuous Life*, 37.

CHAPTER 9: USING "ROSIE THE RIVETER" TO PROPEL WOMEN INTO THE WORKFORCE

1. *Saturday Evening Post*, 29 May 1943, cover; US Department of Labor, Bureau of Labor Statistics, *Handbook of Labor Statistics*, bulletin 916 (Washington, DC: Government Printing Office, 1947).

2. Among the works arguing that World War II did not have a permanent impact on women's rate of employment is Leila J. Rupp, *Mobilizing Women for War: German and American Propaganda, 1939–1945* (Princeton, NJ: Princeton University Press, 1978), especially 176; Dorothy Thompson, "Women and the Coming World," *Ladies' Home Journal*, October 1943, 6.

3. "Women Urged to Get Jobs," *Baltimore Sun*, 2 March 1943, 20.

4. "Recruiting by Air," *Business Week*, 10 July 1943, 115.

5. Elizabeth Gordon, "Needed: 50,000 Nurses," *New York Times Magazine*, 12 April 1942, 10; "Nightingales Needed," *Time*, 28 December 1942, 55; "More Women Must Go to Work as 3,200,000 New Jobs Beckon," *Newsweek*, 6 September 1943, 74.

6. Adelaide Kerr, "Should the United States Draft Its Womanpower?" *Washington Post*, 3 September 1943, B4.

7. Frank S. Adams, "Women in Democracy's Arsenal," *New York Times Magazine*, 19 October 1941, 10.

8. Elizabeth Gordon, "Needed: 50,000 Nurses," *New York Times Magazine*, 12 April 1942, 10.

9. Mary Hornaday, "From French Heels to Slacks," *Christian Science Monitor Weekly Magazine*, 27 June 1942, 5; Joseph Ripley, "It's Woman's Day Right Now," *Christian Science Monitor*, 23 October 1943, 7.

10. Elinore M. Herrick, "With Women at Work, the Factory Changes," *New York Times Magazine*, 24 January 1943, 4; Frank S. Adams, "Women in Democracy's Arsenal," *New York Times Magazine*, 19 October 1941, 29; Sally Reston, "Girls' Town—Washington," *New York Times Magazine*, 23 November 1941, 8–9.

11. "Civilian Defense," *Time*, 26 January 1942, 61; "Girls in Uniform," *Life*, 6 July 1942, 41; "Glory Girls," *American Magazine*, March 1942, 83.

12. "Ladies of Washington's Working Press," *Newsweek*, 1 March 1943, 64.

13. "Output: Ladies Welcome," *Newsweek*, 30 November 1942, 56; "Females in Factories," *Time*, 17 July 1944, 60; Elizabeth Hawes, "Do Women Workers Get an Even Break?" *New York Times Magazine*, 19 November 1944, 13.

14. Elinore M. Herrick, "With Women at Work, the Factory Changes," *New York Times Magazine*, 24 January 1943, 34.

15. William H. Chafe, *The American Woman: Her Changing Social, Economic, and Political Roles, 1920–1970* (New York: Oxford University Press, 1972), 146–147.

16. "Women Help Build Planes," *Los Angeles Times*, 2 June 1941, 18.

17. Elizabeth Hawes, "Woman War Worker: A Case History," *New York Times Magazine*, 21 December 1943, 9.

18. Ibid.

19. Ibid.

20. "Nursery Cares for Children of War Workers," *Chicago Tribune*, 29 November 1943, 17.

21. *American Magazine*: Steve King, "Danger! Women at Work," September 1942, 117; "Amazons of Aberdeen," January 1943, 98–99.

22. "Women in Forestry," *New York Times Magazine*, 4 October 1942, 31; "Daughters for Harvard," *Time*, 9 October 1944, 90.

23. "Output: Ladies Welcome," *Newsweek*, 30 November 1942, 54.

24. Margaret Bourke-White, "Women in Lifeboats," *Life*, 22 February 1943, 49.

25. Ibid., 48.

26. Margaret Bourke-White, "Women in Steel," *Life*, 9 August 1943, 76, 79.

27. "Girls in Uniform," *Life*, 6 July 1942, 41–43.

28. "Females in Factories," *Time*, 17 July 1944, 60; "Women at Work," *Newsweek*, 5 January 1942, 36; Amy Lyon Schaeffer, "She Works in an Arms Plant," *New York Times Magazine*, 12 April 1942, 9; Nona Baldwin, "Woman Mans the Machine," *New York Times Magazine*, 23 August 1942, 8; Elinore M. Herrick, "With Women at Work, the Factory Changes," *New York Times Magazine*, 24 January 1943, 4.

29. US Department of Labor, Bureau of Labor Statistics, *Handbook of Labor Statistics*, bulletin 916.

30. On scholars seeing the American media's influence as central to changing women's role in society, see, for example, Karen Anderson, *Wartime Women: Sex Roles, Family Relations, and the Status of Women During World War II* (Westport, CT: Greenwood, 1981), especially 27–28, 60–61; Chafe, *American Woman*, 146–147; Sherna Berger Gluck, *Rosie the Riveter Revisited: Women, the War and Social Change* (Boston: Twayne, 1987), especially 15–16; Susan M. Hartmann, *The Home Front and Beyond: American Women in the 1940s* (Boston: Twayne, 1982), especially 189, 210–211; Maureen Honey, *Creating Rosie the Riveter: Class, Gender, and Propaganda During World War II* (Amherst: University of Massachusetts Press, 1984), especially 12–14; Rupp, *Mobilizing Women*, especially 137–165; Mary Martha Thomas, *Riveting and Rationing in Dixie: Alabama Women and the Second World War* (Tuscaloosa: University of Alabama Press, 1987), 23–24. For the specific quotations, see Chafe, *American Woman*, 146–147; Rupp, *Mobilizing Women*, 165; Hartmann, *Home Front*, 189.

CHAPTER 10: STANDING TALL AGAINST JOSEPH MCCARTHY

1. Frank Desmond, "M'Carthy Charges Reds Hold U.S. Jobs," *Wheeling Intelligencer*, 10 February 1950, 1. McCarthy based the 205 figure on a letter that Secretary of State James Byrnes had written to a congressman in 1946. In the letter Byrnes stated that after the war, 3,000 workers had been transferred to the State Department. After being subjected to preliminary examination, 284 of them were recommended for dismissal for various reasons, such as frequent absences from work and lack of dependability. Of this number, 79 were fired, although no comment was made about them being Communists or even security risks. Nevertheless, McCarthy subtracted the 79 fired workers from the 284 identified and came up with the idea that 205 communists were still working in the State Department.

2. Edwin R. Bayley, *Joe McCarthy and the Press* (New York: Pantheon, 1981), 69–70.

3. Ibid., 70.

4. Ibid., 71.

5. Ibid., 67, 68.

6. Ibid., 68–69.

7. Hugh Greene in *Good Night and Good Luck* (1975 British Broadcasting Corporation production), distributed by Instructional Media Services, Washington State University; Gary Paul Gates, *Air Time: The Inside Story of CBS News* (New York: Harper & Row, 1978), 13.

8. Alexander Kendrick, *Prime Time: The Life of Edward R. Murrow* (Boston: Little, Brown, 1969), 4; A. William Bluem, *Documentary in American Television*

(New York: Hastings House, 1970), 99–100; Christopher H. Sterling and John M. Kitross, *Stay Tuned: A Concise History of American Broadcasting*, 2nd ed. (Belmont, CA: Wadsworth, 1990), 657–658.

9. "The Case of Milo Radulovich, A0589839," *See It Now*, 20 October 1953. Transcripts of the *See It Now* programs are held in the Edward R. Murrow Papers, Edwin Ginn Library, Fletcher School of Law and Diplomacy, Tufts University, Medford, Massachusetts.

10. "Radulovich," *See It Now*, 20 October 1953.

11. Ibid.

12. "Eyes of Conscience: 'See It Now,'" *Newsweek*, 7 December 1953, 65–66; Jack Gould, "Video Journalism: Treatment of Radulovich Case History by 'See It Now' Is Fine Reporting," *New York Times*, 25 October 1953, B-13.

13. Fred W. Friendly, *Due to Circumstances Beyond Our Control . . .* (New York: Random House, 1967), 18.

14. Laurence Bergreen, *Look Now, Pay Later: The Rise of Network Broadcasting* (Garden City, NY: Doubleday, 1980), 186.

15. "A Report on Senator Joseph R. McCarthy," *See It Now*, 9 March 1954.

16. Ibid.

17. Bergreen, *Look Now*, 187; Gilbert Seldes, "Murrow, McCarthy and the Empty Formula," *Saturday Review*, 24 April 1954, 26; "Salute to a Brave Man," *New York Herald Tribune*, 12 March 1954, 19.

18. Val Adams, "Praise Pours in on Murrow Show," *New York Times*, 11 March 1954, A-12.

19. Philip Hamburger, "Man from Wisconsin," *New Yorker*, 20 March 1954, 71; "TV in Controversy," *Newsweek*, 22 March 1954, 50; Jack Gould, "Murrow versus McCarthy," *New York Times*, 11 March 1954, B-38.

20. On scholars identifying the broadcast as the most important news program in history, see, for example, Fred J. Cook, *The Nightmare Decade: The Life and Times of Senator Joe McCarthy* (New York: Random House, 1971), 497; Kendrick, *Prime Time*, 4; Daniel J. Leab, "'See It Now': A Legend Reassessed," in *American History/American Television: Interpreting the Video Past* (New York: Frederick Ungar, 1983), 26; Thomas Rosteck, *See It Now Confronts McCarthyism*, ed. John E. O'Connor (Tuscaloosa: University of Alabama Press, 1994), 113; Gilbert Seldes, *The Public Arts* (New York: Simon and Schuster, 1956), 226. On historians extolling the program's impact on McCarthy, see, for example, George N. Gordon, *The Communications Revolution: A History of Mass Media in the United States* (New York: Hastings House, 1977), 270–271; Kendrick, *Prime Time*, 53–54; Michael D. Murray, "The Persuasive Dimensions of See It Now's 'Report on Senator Joseph R. McCarthy,'" *Today's Speech* 22 (1975), 18; Rosteck, *See It Now*, 134–135; Seldes, *Public Arts*, 226. For the specific quotations, see Rosteck, *See It Now*, 134–135; Seldes, *Public Arts*, 226; Gordon, *Communications Revolution*, 270–271.

21. Jack Gould, "Public Service," *New York Times*, 13 June 1954, X-11.

22. Michael Straight, *Trial by Television* (Boston: Beacon, 1954), 249.

23. Ibid., 251.

24. Ibid.

25. Ibid., 252.

26. James Reston, "On McCarthy," *New York Times*, 30 May 1954, X-9.

27. Bayley, *McCarthy and the Press*, 209; Erik Barnouw, *Tube of Plenty: The Evolution of American Television* (New York: Oxford University Press, 1975), 182; Richard M. Fried, *Nightmare in Red: The McCarthy Era in Perspective* (New York: Oxford University Press, 1990), 138; Roy L. Cohn, *McCarthy* (New York: New American Library, 1968), 204.

28. Fried, *Nightmare in Red*, 138.

29. Barnouw, *Tube of Plenty*, 183; Bayley, *McCarthy and the Press*, 209.

CHAPTER 11: PUSHING CIVIL RIGHTS
ONTO THE NATIONAL AGENDA

1. The Supreme Court announced its *Brown v. Board of Education of Topeka* decision on 17 May 1963.

2. On journalists discussing the vital role that television played in the Civil Rights Movement, see, for example, Joseph L. Brechner, "Were Broadcasters Color Blind?" in *Race and the News Media*, ed. Paul L. Fisher and Ralph L. Lowenstein (New York: Praeger, 1967), 100–101; William J. Drummond, "About Face: Blacks and the News Media," *American Enterprise*, July/August 1990, 24–26; Robert MacNeil, *The People Machine: The Influence of Television on American Politics* (New York: Harper & Row, 1968), 71; William B. Monroe, Jr., "Television: The Chosen Instrument of Revolution," in Fisher and Lowenstein, *Race and the News Media*, 84, 89; William Peters, "The Visible and Invisible Images," in Fisher and Lowenstein, *Race and the News Media*, 81–82, 89, 97; William Small, *To Kill a Messenger* (New York: Hastings House, 1970), 3, 43–44; *Television*, PBS, aired on Washington, DC, station WETA, 15 February 1988; Mary Ann Watson, *The Expanding Vista: American Television in the Kennedy Years* (New York: Oxford University Press, 1990), 94; William A. Wood, *Electronic Journalism* (New York: Columbia University Press, 1967), 106. On scholars praising the role that broadcast journalism played in the Civil Rights Movement, see, for example, David J. Garrow, *Protest at Selma* (New Haven, CT: Yale University Press, 1978), 163; Benjamin Muse, *The American Negro Revolution* (Bloomington: Indiana University Press, 1968), 102; *Television*, PBS; Wood, *Electronic Journalism*, 89, 101–106. For specific quotations, see Wood, *Electronic Journalism*, 105, 106; Peters, "Visible and Invisible," 81.

3. Because the television networks did not record the film shown on their newscasts during the late 1950s and early 1960s, it is impossible to identify the specific date or network on which particular images were shown. All footage

referred to in this chapter appeared on ABC, CBS, or NBC between 1957 and 1965. That footage can be viewed on one or more of three sources: *Dateline Freedom: Civil Rights and the Press*, PBS, aired on Washington, DC, station WETA, 18 January 1989; *Television*, PBS; *A Time for Justice* (video) (Washington, DC: Guggenheim Productions, 1992).

4. Monroe, "Television," 84.

5. Watson, *Expanding Vista*, 95.

6. *Dateline Freedom*, PBS.

7. Ibid.

8. The first day of classes was 4 September 1957. On Little Rock coverage, see Brechner, "Were Broadcasters Color Blind?" 99; Garrow, *Protest at Selma*, 166; MacNeil, *People Machine*, 8; Watson, *Expanding Vista*, 90–91; Wood, *Electronic Journalism*, 18.

9. *A Time for Justice*, Guggenheim.

10. *Dateline Freedom*, PBS. The black students entered the school for the first time on 25 September 1957.

11. *A Time for Justice*, Guggenheim.

12. On television coverage of university desegregation crises, see Garrow, *Protest at Selma*, 144; Gary Paul Gates, *Air Time: The Inside Story of CBS News* (New York: Harper & Row, 1978), 292; MacNeil, *People Machine*, 306; Muse, *Negro Revolution*, 6–7; Watson, *Expanding Vista*, 57, 95–98, 103, 145; Wood, *Electronic Journalism*, 99.

13. Charlayne Hunter-Gault, "We Overcame Too," *TV Guide*, 17 January 1987, 34.

14. On coverage of the Freedom Riders, see Small, *To Kill*, 43; Arthur I. Waskow, *From Race Riot to Sit-In* (Garden City, NY: Doubleday, 1966), 231–232; Watson, *Expanding Vista*, 92–93; Wood, *Electronic Journalism*, 99.

15. *A Time for Justice*, Guggenheim. The first two buses left Washington, DC, on 4 May 1961.

16. Ibid.

17. On television coverage of the Birmingham crisis, see Michael Dorman, *We Shall Overcome* (New York: Delacorte, 1964), 150; Garrow, *Protest at Selma*, 2–3, 136–144, 167; MacNeil, *People Machine*, 70–71; Muse, *Negro Revolution*, 5–6, 26–27; Small, *To Kill*, 45; Waskow, *From Race Riot*, 233–236, 238; Watson, *Expanding Vista*, 101–102.

18. The pickets and sit-ins began on 3 April 1963.

19. The protest began to include children on 2 May 1963.

20. Garrow, *Protest at Selma*, 139.

21. Ibid., 141; *A Time for Justice*, Guggenheim.

22. Garrow, *Protest at Selma*, 167–168; Waskow, *From Race Riot*, 234.

23. "Outrage in Alabama," *New York Times*, 5 May 1963, E-10.

24. The agreement was announced on 10 May 1963.

25. Watson, *Expanding Vista*, 105.

26. On television coverage of the March on Washington, see Erik Barnouw, *Tube of Plenty: The Evolution of American Television* (New York: Oxford University Press, 1990), 324–325; Fisher and Lowenstein, *Race and the News Media*, 157; Small, *To Kill*, 45; Watson, *Expanding Vista*, 106–109.

27. Bill Gold, "March Provided Unequaled TV Show," *Washington Post*, 29 August 1963, D-16.

28. Muse, *Negro Revolution*, 16.

29. Wood, *Electronic Journalism*, 100; Jack Gould, "N.B.C. Devotes Three Hours to Civil Rights," *New York Times*, 3 September 1963, 67. *The American Revolution of '63* aired on 2 September 1963.

30. Wood, *Electronic Journalism*, 100.

31. Watson, *Expanding Vista*, 110.

32. Ibid., 110.

33. Val Adams, "Reaction to a Cancellation," *New York Times*, 14 November 1963, 71; "Stanton Raps House Probe into Web Coverage of Civil Rights Issue," *Variety*, 3 July 1963, 20.

34. On television coverage of the voter registration campaign, see Brechner, "Were Broadcasters Color Blind?" 99; Garrow, *Protest at Selma*, 163; MacNeil, *People Machine*, 70–71; Muse, *Negro Revolution*, 163–173; Edwin Newman, *Television*, PBS.

35. *Television*, PBS.

36. Muse, *Negro Revolution*, 166.

37. *Television*, PBS.

38. Ibid.

39. Ibid.

40. Muse, *Negro Revolution*, 168.

41. Ibid., 169.

42. *Television*, PBS.

43. Gary Orfield, The *Reconstruction of Southern Education* (New York: Wiley Interscience, 1969), 33; *Television*, PBS.

CHAPTER 12: BRINGING THE VIETNAM WAR
INTO THE AMERICAN LIVING ROOM

1. See, for example, Edward Jay Epstein, *News from Nowhere: Television and the News* (New York: Random House, 1973), 9; George N. Gordon, *The Communications Revolution: A History of Mass Media in the United States* (New York: Hastings House, 1977), 226, 315–316; David Halberstam, *The Powers That Be* (New York: Knopf, 1979), 429; Daniel C. Hallin, *The "Uncensored War": The Media and Vietnam* (New York: Oxford University Press, 1986), 147; Guenter Lewy, *America in Vietnam* (New York: Oxford University Press, 1978), 433;

Timothy P. Meyer, "Some Effects of Real Newsfilm Violence on the Behavior of Viewers," *Journal of Broadcasting* 15 (Summer 1971), 275–285; Don Oberdorfer, *Tet!* (Garden City, NY: Doubleday, 1971), 239, 241; Austin Ranney, *Channels of Power: The Impact of Television on American Politics* (New York: Basic, 1983), 4–5, 133–134; Edward Shils, "American Society and the War in Indochina," in *The Vietnam Legacy: The War, American Society and the Future of American Foreign Policy*, ed. Anthony Lake (New York: New York University Press, 1976), 49; William Small, *To Kill a Messenger: Television News and the Real World* (New York: Hastings House, 1970), 3; *Television*, PBS, aired on Washington, DC, station WETA, 15 February 1988; Kathleen J. Turner, *Lyndon Johnson's Dual War: Vietnam and the Press* (Chicago: University of Chicago Press, 1985), 4. For specific quotations, see Shils, "American Society," 49; *Television*, PBS.

2. Ranney, *Channels of Power*, 13–14; US Senate, Committee on Governmental Operations, *Confidence and Concern: Citizens View American Government* (Washington, DC: Government Printing Office, 1973), 79. In the Roper survey, which allowed multiple responses, 58 percent of the respondents said television was their major news source, 56 percent said newspapers were, 26 percent radio, and 8 percent magazines. According to the Louis Harris poll commissioned by the US Senate, 64 percent of respondents said they relied on television as their major news source.

3. *NBC Huntley-Brinkley Report*, 27 October 1967.

4. Ibid., 11 January 1966.

5. Epstein, *News from Nowhere*, 250.

6. *NBC Huntley-Brinkley Report*, 11 August 1967.

7. *CBS Evening News with Walter Cronkite*, 5 August 1965.

8. Halberstam, *Powers That Be*, 490.

9. *CBS Evening News with Walter Cronkite*, 2 February 1968; *ABC Evening News*, 1 February 1968.

10. Edward Jay Epstein, *Between Fact and Fiction* (New York: Vintage, 1975), 225.

11. George A. Bailey and Lawrence W. Lichty, "Rough Justice on a Saigon Street: A Gatekeeper Study of NBC's Tet Execution Film," *Journalism Quarterly* 49, no. 2 (Summer 1972), 222–223.

12. Ibid., 224.

13. Epstein, *Between Fact*, 221.

14. Bailey and Lichty, "Rough Justice," 227.

15. Ibid., 229, 238.

16. "By Book and Bullet," *Time*, 23 February 1968, 32; *Television*, PBS.

17. Oberdorfer, *Tet!* 158.

18. *Report from Vietnam by Walter Cronkite*, 27 February 1968.

19. Ibid.

20. For the Johnson quotation, see presidential aide Tom Johnson on *Cronkite Remembered*, CBS, 23 May 1996; Hallin, *Uncensored War*, 170; Ranney, *Channels of Power*, 5; Small, *To Kill*, 123; Turner, *Johnson's Dual War*, 232. On the shift in

public opinion, see John E. Mueller, *War, Presidents, and Public Opinion* (New York: Wiley, 1973), 201.

21. Halberstam, *Powers That Be*, 514.

22. Hallin, *Uncensored War*, 161.

23. Bob Greene, "How Do You Fight a War with TV Looking On?" *Los Angeles Times*, 13 April 1982, B-5; *Television*, PBS.

CHAPTER 13: EXPOSING CRIMINAL ACTIVITY
IN RICHARD NIXON'S WHITE HOUSE

1. Alfred E. Lewis, "5 Held in Plot to Bug Democrats' Office Here," *Washington Post*, 18 June 1972, A-1.

2. *Washington Post*, Bob Woodward and E. J. Bachinski: "White House Consultant Tied to Bugging Figure," 20 June 1972, A-1; "Mission Incredible," 21 June 1972, A-22.

3. Carl Bernstein, "Watergate: Tracking It Down," *Quill*, June 1973, 46; James McCartney, "The Washington 'Post' and Watergate: How Two Davids Slew Goliath," *Columbia Journalism Review*, July/August 1973, 14.

4. Bob Woodward and E. J. Bachinski, "White House Consultant Tied to Bugging Figure," *Washington Post*, 20 June 1972, A-1.

5. Carl Bernstein and Bob Woodward, "Bug Suspect Got Campaign Funds," *Washington Post*, 1 August 1972, A-1.

6. Carl Bernstein and Bob Woodward, "Spy Funds Linked to GOP Aides," *Washington Post*, 17 September 1972, A-1.

7. Carl Bernstein and Bob Woodward, "FBI Finds Nixon Aides Sabotaged Democrats," *Washington Post*, 10 October 1972, A-1.

8. Carl Bernstein and Bob Woodward, "Key Nixon Aide Named as 'Sabotage' Contact," *Washington Post*, 15 October 1972, A-1.

9. Carl Bernstein and Bob Woodward, "Testimony Ties Top Nixon Aide to Secret Fund," *Washington Post*, 25 October 1972, A-1.

10. Carl Bernstein, "Watergate: Tracking It Down," *Quill*, June 1973, 45; Dave Griffiths, "The Watergate Pair: Bernstein & Woodward," *Editor & Publisher*, 28 April 1973, 12; McCartney, "'Post' and Watergate," 14.

11. "'All the President's Men'—And Two of Journalism's Finest," *Senior Scholastic*, 13 January 1976, 14; McCartney, "'Post' and Watergate," 14.

12. John J. Sirica, *To Set the Record Straight* (New York: W. W. Norton, 1979), 54.

13. David Von Drehle, "FBI's No. 2 Was 'Deep Throat,'" *Washington Post*, 1 June 2005, A6.

14. McCartney, "'Post' and Watergate," 9.

15. Charles Peters, "Why the Press Didn't Get the Watergate Story," *Washington Monthly*, July/August 1973, 8.

16. "Dynamic Duo," *Newsweek*, 30 October 1972, 77.

17. McCartney, "'Post' and Watergate," 11, 19.

18. Ibid., 18; *Watergate: The Secret Story*, CBS, 17 June 1992.

19. Carl Bernstein and Bob Woodward, "Magazine Says Nixon Aide Admits Disruption Effort," *Washington Post*, 30 October 1972, A-6.

20. Carl Bernstein and Bob Woodward, "Testimony Ties Top Nixon Aide to Secret Fund," *Washington Post*, 25 October 1972, A-1.

21. McCartney, "'Post' and Watergate," 21; Carl Bernstein and Bob Woodward, "Magazine Says Nixon Aide Admits Disruption Effort," *Washington Post*, 30 October 1972, A-1.

22. Walter Rugaber, "House Report Raises Questions on Nixon Campaign Financing; The Watergate Mystery," *New York Times*, 1 November 1972, A-28.

23. "'Woodstein' Meets 'Deep Throat,'" *Time*, 22 April 1974, 56.

24. "An 'Awfully Rough' Game," *Newsweek*, 27 May 1974, 29. The taped conversation took place 15 September 1972.

25. Ibid., 29.

26. Ibid.; "'Woodstein' Meets Deep Throat," *Time*, 22 April 1974, 56; Robert Parry, "The Rise of the Right-Wing Media Machine," *Extra!* March/April 1995, 6. Haldeman's diary entry was dated 29 May 1971.

27. McCartney, "'Post' and Watergate," 19.

28. "Dynamic Duo," *Newsweek*, 30 October 1972, 76–77; McCartney, "'Post' and Watergate," 8–22.

29. "'Woodstein' Meets Deep Throat," *Time*, 22 April 1974, 56; Carl Bernstein and Bob Woodward, *All the President's Men* (New York: Simon and Schuster, 1974); Margaret Ronan, "A Rap With . . . ," *Senior Scholastic*, 13 January 1976, 12.

30. William B. Dickinson, *Watergate: Chronology of a Crisis* (Washington, DC: Congressional Quarterly, 1973), 6.

CHAPTER 14: FAILING THE AMERICAN PUBLIC WITH 9/11 COVERAGE

1. On news organizations beginning to discuss bin Laden's grievances, see, for example, Fareed Zakaria, "The Politics of Rage: Why Do They Hate Us?" *Newsweek*, 15 October 2001, 22.

2. Serge Schmemann, "U.S. Attacked; President Vows to Exact Punishment for 'Evil,'" *New York Times*, 12 September 2001, A-1.

3. Ibid.

4. N. R. Kleinfield, "U.S. Attacked; Hijacked Jets Destroy Twin Towers and Hit Pentagon in Day of Terror," *New York Times*, 12 September 2001, A-1.

5. Michael Grunwald, "Terrorists Hijack 4 Airliners, Destroy World Trade Center, Hit Pentagon," *Washington Post*, 12 September 2001, A-1.

6. Serge Schmemann, "U.S. Attacked; President Vows to Exact Punishment for 'Evil,'" *New York Times*, 12 September 2001, A-1.

7. Felicity Barringer, "A Day of Terror: The Media," *New York Times*, 12 September 2001, A-25; Lisa De Moraes, "Putting Rivalries Aside, TV Networks Share All Footage of Tragedies," *Washington Post*, 12 September 2001, C-7; Howard Kurtz, "Wall Street Journal Picks Up and Publishes," *Washington Post*, 14 September 2001, C-1; Peter Johnson, "Journalists Under Pressure," *USA Today*, 12 September 2001, D-2; Lucia Moses, Dave Astor, Joe Strupp, and Wayne Robins, "With the World Crashing Down All Around Them, New York–Based Daily Newspapers Provided Praiseworthy Public Service After Worst-Ever Terrorist Attack on U.S.," *Editor & Publisher*, 17 September 2001, 4; Sherry Ricchiardi, "The Biggest Story," *American Journalism Review*, October 2001; Alina Tugend, "'The Simple Act of Getting to Work Was an Ordeal,'" *American Journalism Review*, October 2001.

8. Lori Robertson, "'We Have a Breaking Story . . . ,'" *American Journalism Review*, October 2001.

9. On news organizations failing to report the motivations of the hijackers, see, for example, Alina Tugend, "Explaining the Rage," *American Journalism Review*, December 2001, 24; Fareed Zakaria, "The Politics of Rage: Why Do They Hate Us?" *Newsweek*, 15 October 2001, 22.

10. For a particularly thorough summary of Bush's strategy, see Douglas Kellner, *From 9/11 to Terror War: The Dangers of the Bush Legacy* (New York: Rowman & Littlefield, 2003).

11. Elisabeth Bumiller with David E. Sanger, "A Day of Terror: The President," *New York Times*, 12 September 2001, A-1.

12. Ibid.

13. "Address to a Joint Session of Congress and the American People," US Capitol, Washington, DC, 20 September 2001, 9 p.m. EDT.

14. Ibid.

15. Serge Schmemann, "War Zone: What Would 'Victory' Mean?" *New York Times*, 16 September 2001, D-1; "Dan Rather on David Letterman Show One Week After 9–11," LiveLeak, www.liveleak.com/view?i=2cc_1339992689.

16. Matt Welch, Mallory Jensen, and Jacqueline Reeves, "Blogsworld and Its Gravity," *Columbia Journalism Review*, September/October 2003, 20.

17. Among the websites that reproduced the jihad are those operated by the Library of Cornell University at http://www.library.cornell.edu/colldev/mideast /wif.htm; the South Asia Terrorism Portal at http://www.satp.org/satporgtp/usa /IIFstatement.htm; the Global Information Society Project at http://information -retrieval.info/docs/1998_statement.html; IslamistWatch at http://www.islamist watch.org/texts/fatwas/killamis.html; Metareligion.com at http://www.meta -religion.com/Extremism/Islamic_extremism/al-qaida/jihad_against_americans .htm; Hartford Web Publishing at http://www.hartford-hwp.com/archives/27c /072.html; Columbia International Affairs Online at http://www.ciaonet.org /cbr/cbr00/video/cbr_ctd/cbr_ctd_28.html; the Centre for Policy Modelling at

http://cfpm.org/~majordom/memetics/2000/8653.html; MidEastWeb at http://www.mideastweb.org/osamabinladen1.htm.

18. See, for example, "Jihad Against Jews and Crusaders," www.library.cornell.edu/colldev/mideast/wif.htm.

19. Ibid.

20. Ibid.

21. On the reason for the United States invading Iraq, see, for example, Kelly Patterson, "Anatomy of a Terrorist," *Ottawa Citizen*, 16 September 2001, C-4.

22. The site was located at http://akajanedoe.us/islamicjihad.html.

23. Alina Tugend, "Explaining the Rage," *American Journalism Review*, December 2001, 24. On criticism of the news media for failing to identify the terrorists' grievances against the United States, see also Kellner, *From 9/11 to Terror War*, especially 63–69.

24. Susan Sontag, "The Talk of the Town," *New Yorker*, 24 September 2001, 32.

25. Peter Carlson, "Still Pictures That Are Far More Moving," *Washington Post*, 25 September 2001, C-1; Charles Krauthammmer, "Voices of Moral Obtuseness," *Jewish World Review*, 24 September 2001, 1.

26. Bradley Graham, "U.S., Coalition Kill Hundreds of Opposition, Officials Say," *Washington Post*, 13 March 2002, A-21.

27. Amy Goldstein and Mike Allen, "Bush Vows to Defeat Terror, Recession," *Washington Post*, 30 January 2003, A-1.

28. Elisabeth Bumiller and James Dao, "Cheney Says Peril of a Nuclear Iraq Justifies Attack," *New York Times*, 27 August 2002, A-1.

29. Todd S. Purdum, "Bush Officials Say the Time Has Come for Action on Iraq," *New York Times*, 9 September 2002, A-1.

30. "Congressional Joint Resolution to Authorize Use of Force Against Iraq," *Washington Post*, 11 October 2002, A-12.

31. Dana Milbank and Mike Allen, "President Tells Hussein to Leave Iraq Within 48 Hours or Face Invasion," *Washington Post*, 18 March 2003, A-1; Ian MacLeod, "Saddam Gets 48 Hours to Leave," *Ottawa Citizen*, 18 March 2003, A-1.

32. Fred Kaplan, "Billy Bush: The President Is Botching the Iraq Crisis with His Clumsy, Naïve Unilateralism," *Slate*, 5 March 2003.

33. David E. Sanger, "Bush Declares 'One Victory in a War on Terror," *New York Times*, 2 May 2003, A-1.

34. E. J. Dionne, Jr., "9/11 Credibility Gap," *Washington Post*, 22 June 2004, A-17; R. Jeffrey Smith, "'Operational Relationship' with al-Qaeda Discounted," *Washington Post*, 23 July 2004, A-1; Susan Page, "Poll Finds Bush Suffering from 'Second-Term-Itis,'" *USA Today*, 6 April 2005, 4-A. The Abu Ghraib scandal was first reported on the CBS news magazine *60 Minutes II* on 28 April 2004. For one of the earliest comparisons between Iraq and Vietnam, see Walter Pincus, "A Quagmire?" *Washington Post*, 31 August 2003, B-5.

35. Ron Suskind, *The Price of Loyalty: George W. Bush, the White House, and the Education of Paul O'Neill* (New York: Simon and Schuster, 2004), 86.

36. Michael Grunwald, "Opposition to the War Buoys Democrats," *Washington Post*, 8 November 2006, A-31.

37. Susan D. Moeller, "Follow the Leader," *American Journalism Review*, May 2004; John R. MacArthur, "Voices: The Lies We Bought," *Columbia Journalism Review*, May 2003. For more criticism of the news media for allowing the White House to gain support for the Iraq War, see Byron Calame, "Approaching Iran Intelligence with Intelligent Skepticism," *New York Times*, 25 February 2007, D-14; "From the Editors," *New York Times*, 26 May 2004, A-2; Nicholas D. Kristof, "The Cowards Turned Out to Be Right," *New York Times*, 28 November 2006, A-23; Paul Krugman, "To Tell the Truth," *New York Times*, 28 May 2004, A-21; Howard Kurtz, "N.Y. Times Cites Defects in Its Reports on Iraq," *Washington Post*, 26 May 2004, C-1; Daniel Okrent, "Weapons of Mass Destruction? Or Mass Distraction?" *New York Times*, 30 May 2004, D-2; Jim Rutenberg and Robin Toner, "A Nation at War: The News Media," *New York Times*, 22 March 2003, B-10; Jacques Steinberg, "Washington Post Rethinks Its Coverage of War Debate," *New York Times*, 13 August 2004, A-14; Paul Waldman, "Why the Media Don't Call It as They See It," *Washington Post*, 28 September 2003, B-4.

38. Fred Kaplan, "Billy Bush: The President Is Botching the Iraq Crisis with His Clumsy, Naïve Unilateralism," *Slate*, 5 March 2003; Rachel Smolkin, "Are the News Media Soft on Bush?" *American Journalism Review*, November 2003.

39. Barbie Zelizer, "Which Words Is a War Photo Worth?" *Online Journalism Review*, 28 April 2004; Al Gore, "A Coalition of Fear," *Salon*, 11 February 2004.

40. Frank Rich, *The Greatest Story Ever Sold: The Decline and Fall of Truth* (New York: Penguin, 2006), 209. For the Cheney video, see http://www.youtube .com/watch?v=IjiNtpIpD6k.

41. Robert D. McFadden, "Bin Laden's Journey from Rich, Pious Boy to the Mask of Evil," *New York Times*, 30 September 2001, B-5; Michael Dobbs, "Inside the Mind of Osama bin Laden," *Washington Post*, 20 September 2001, A-1, A-20.

42. Bush first made his good-versus-evil statement on September 11, 2001, and then repeated it during his address to a joint session of Congress on September 20.

43. On Bush wanting to bring freedom to the people of Iraq, see "Leader: The End of the Line," *The Economist*, 17 October 2002, 2; Dana Milbank and Mike Allen, "President Tells Hussein to Leave Iraq Within 48 Hours or Face Invasion," *Washington Post*, 18 March 2003, A-1. On Bush wanting to control the world's oil supply, see John Berry, "Pipeline Brigade," *Newsweek*, 8 April 2002, 41; Nicholas Lemann, "After Iraq: The Plan to Remake the Middle East," *New Yorker*, 17 February 2003, 70; "A Postwar Plan," *Washington Post*, 17 October 2002, A-20; Howard Schneider and Thomas E. Ricks, "Iraqis See Escalation by Bush," *Washington Post*, 19 February 2001, A-1. On Bush wanting to protect Israel, see Peter Baker,

"An Iraq Success Story's Sad New Chapter," *Washington Post*, 21 March 2006, A-1; Nicholas D. Kristof, "Talking About Israel," *New York Times*, 18 March 2007, D-13. On Bush wanting to finish the war his father began, see Peter Baker, "Conflicts Shaped Two Presidencies," *Washington Post*, 31 December 2006, A-21; Elisabeth Bumiller, David E. Sanger, and Richard W. Stevenson, "A Nation at War: The President," *New York Times*, 14 April 2003, A-1; Arlene Getz, "Targeting Saddam," *Newsweek* (online), 2 August 2002. On Bush wanting to flex American military muscle, see Roger Cohen, "Strange Bedfellows: 'Imperial America' Retreats from Iraq," *New York Times*, 4 July 2004, D-1; Christopher Dickey, "The Great Divide," *Newsweek*, 24 February 2003, 12; Rich, *The Greatest Story Ever Sold*, 211.

CHAPTER 15: ELECTING AN AFRICAN-AMERICAN PRESIDENT

1. Alexander Burns, "Halperin at Politico/USC Conf.: 'Extreme Pro-Obama' Press Bias," *Politico*, 22 November 2008, www.politico.com/news/stories/1108 /15885.html (the analyst was Mark Halperin); "President Obama's First Two Years in Office," *The Diane Rehm Show*, NPR, 21 April 2011 (the editor was Ron Elving); Michael S. Malone, "Media's Presidential Bias and Decline," http://abcnews .go.com/print?id=6099188; Project for Excellence in Journalism, "Winning the Media Campaign: How the Press Reported the 2008 Election," Pew Research Center, 22 October 2008, http://www.journalism.org/analysis_report/winning _media_campaign. On the news media favoring Obama, see also James W. Ceaser, Andrew E. Busch, and John J. Pitney Jr., *Epic Journey: The 2008 Elections and American Politics* (New York: Rowman & Littlefield, 2009), 30–31; David Freddoso, *The Case Against Barack Obama: The Unlikely Rise and Unexpected Agenda of the Media's Favorite Candidate* (Washington, DC: Regnery, 2008), especially ix–x, 62–63, 103; Bernard Goldberg, *A Slobbering Love Affair: The True (and Pathetic) Story of the Torrid Romance Between Barack Obama and the Mainstream Media* (Washington, DC: Regnery, 2009), especially 15–19, 30–32, 117–125; John F. Harris and Jim VandeHei, "Why McCain Is Getting Hosed in the Press," *Politico*, 28 October 2008; John Heilemann and Mark Halperin, *Game Change: Obama and the Clintons, McCain and Palin, and the Race of a Lifetime* (New York: HarperCollins, 2010), especially 265, 329–330; Rich Noyes, "Obama's Margin of Victory: The Media," special report of the Media Research Center, 20 August 2008, http://www.mrc.org/SpecialReports/2008/obama/obama.asp; Douglas E. Schoen, *The Political Fix: Changing the Game of American Democracy, from the Grass Roots to the White House* (New York: Henry Holt, 2010), 182–184.

2. Mark Leibovich, "The Other Man of the Hour; Barack Obama Is the Party's New Phenom," *Washington Post*, 27 July 2004, C1.

3. *MSNBC Special Report*, MSNBC, 28 August 2008.

4. Oprah Winfrey gave the speech on 8 December 2007; *NBC Nightly News*, NBC, 9 December 2008.

5. John Harris made the comments on the CNN program *Reliable Sources* on 13 January 2008, http://transcripts.cnn.com/TRANSCRIPTS/0801/13/rs.01.html.

6. On the news media being biased toward Obama because he is a man of color, see Ceaser, Busch, and Pitney, *Epic Journey*, 31; Ron Elving during "President Obama's First Two Years"; and Goldberg, *Slobbering Love Affair*, 4–5, 51–52, 140.

7. Cook and Rothenberg made the statements during a postelection forum sponsored by the US Chamber of Commerce on 7 November 2008. The forum was titled "Election and Presidential Transition" and aired on C-SPAN, http://www.c-spanvideo.org/program/PostElectionAna.

8. Michael Weiss, "History!" *Slate*, 4 June 2008; Scott Helman, "Obama Clinches Nomination; Clinton Not Conceding Defeat," *Boston Globe*, 4 June 2008, A-1.

9. *Election Coverage*, NBC, 3 June 2008; *CBS Evening News*, CBS, 4 June 2008.

10. Arianna Huffington, "Obama Wins Iowa: Why Everyone Has a Reason to Celebrate," *Huffington Post*, 3 January 2008, http://www.huffingtonpost.com/ariana-huffington/obama-wins-iowa-why-every_b_79663.html.

11. Charisse Jones, "Blacks Optimistic, Anxious About Obama," *USA Today*, 6 June 2008.

12. Goldberg, *Slobbering Love Affair*, 4–5.

13. Computer Geeks Obama Hats, Trucker Hats, and Baseball Caps, Café Press, http://www.cafepress.com/+computer_geeks_for_obama_cap.

14. Adam Nagourney and Jeff Zeleny, "Obama Chooses Biden as Running Mate," *New York Times*, 23 August 2008, A1.

15. Eric Boehlert, *Bloggers on the Bus: How the Internet Changed Politics and the Press* (New York: Free Press, 2009), 256.

16. "McCain Admits He Doesn't Know How to Use a Computer," *Daily Voice*, 12 June 2008; "McCain Admits He Doesn't Know How to Use a Computer," *Huffington Post*, 11 June 2008; Jonathan Stein, "John McCain Doesn't Know How to Use a Computer" (video), *Mother Jones*, 24 March 2008.

17. Jose Antonio Vargas, "Obama Raised Half a Billion Online," *Washington Post*, 20 November 2008; Brian Stelter, "Finding Political News Online, the Young Pass It On," *New York Times*, 27 March 2008. On Obama having six times as many Facebook friends as McCain had, see Michael Learmonth, "McCain Advisor: We Don't Need Facebook," *Business Insider*, 24 June 2008.

18. Jeff Jarvis, "Obama, the Internet Victor?" Buzz Machine, 8 January 2008, http://www.buzzmachine.com/2008/01/08/obama-the-internet-victor/; Sarah Lai Stirland, "Obama's Secret Weapon: Internet, Databases and Psychology," *Wired*, 29 October 2008; Michael Learmonth, "Social Media Paves Obama's Way to White House," *Advertising Age*, 30 March 2008.

19. On the news media downplaying the Jeremiah Wright story, see "Barack's Un-Righteous Rev," *New York Post*, 18 January 2008; Goldberg, *Slobbering Love Affair*, 8, 40–41, 59, 63–81; Charles Krauthammer, "Obama the Healer?" *National Review*, 17 October 2008; and Noyes, "Obama's Margin of Victory."

20. Ben Wallace-Wells, "The Radical Roots of Barack Obama," *Rolling Stone*, 22 February 2007. (*Rolling Stone* later changed the title of the article to "Destiny's Child.")

21. Goldberg, *Slobbering Love Affair*, 70.

22. Ibid., 63–64; "The Wright Message," *ABC News*, 13 March 2008; Kate Kenski, Bruce W. Hardy, and Kathleen Hall Jamieson, *The Obama Victory: How Media, Money, and Message Shaped the 2008 Election* (New York: Oxford University Press, 2010), 88.

23. The Brian Ross segment aired on ABC's *Good Morning America* on 13 March 2008, http://abcnews.go.com/Blotter/DemocraticDebate/story?id =4443788&page=1.

24. "Barack Obama's Speech on Race," *New York Times*, provided by Obama Campaign, 18 March 2008, http://www.nytimes.com/2008/03/18/us/politics /18text-obama.html.

25. "Mr. Obama's Profile in Courage," *New York Times*, 19 March 2008.

26. Kenski, Hardy, and Jamieson, *Obama Victory*, 71–72.

27. McCain television advertisement, "Joe Biden on Barack Obama," 25 August 2008; Republican National Committee television advertisement, "Chair," 16 October 2008.

28. "Barack Obama for President," *New York Times*, 24 October 2008; "Barack Obama for President," *Los Angeles Times*, 19 October 2008; "The Newsday Editorial Board Endorses: For President," *Newsday*, 1 November 2008.

29. "Obama for President, Biden for Vice President," *Houston Chronicle*, 1–9 October 2008.

30. Seth Colter and Nico Pitney, "Colin Powell Endorses Obama," *Huffington Post*, 19 October 2008. See also Marcus Baram, "Powell's Obama Endorsement Sparks Reaction," *Huffington Post*, 19 October 2008; and Sam Stein, "Some Conservatives See Race in Powell's Obama Endorsement," 19 October 2008, *Huffington Post*.

31. On the news media emphasizing John McCain's weaknesses, see Jay Carney and Michael Scherer, "McCain's Bias Claim: Truth or Tactic?" *Time*, 8 September 2008; Goldberg, *Slobbering Love Affair*, especially 14–19, 30–31, 89–90, 110–115, 129–130; Kenski, Hardy, and Jamieson, *Obama Victory*, especially 39–43, 57–61, 63–65, 180–181; and Schoen, *Political Fix*, 182–183.

32. "Obama Is the Choice"; "Barack Obama for President," *New York Times*; "Obama for President," *Boston Globe*, 13 October 2008.

33. Evan Thomas, "What These Eyes Have Seen," *Newsweek*, 11 February 2008, 27; Anna Quindlen, "How Old Is Too Old?" *Newsweek*, 4 February 2008, 64, 84; James Carney, "The Phoenix," *Time*, 4 February 2008, 37.

34. *The Daily Show with Jon Stewart*, Comedy Central, 8 October 2008.

35. Audio replayed on *CNN Election Center*, CNN, 21 August 2008; Kenski, Hardy, and Jamieson, *Obama Victory*, 63, 182; *CBS Evening News*, CBS, 15 September 2008.

36. Harris and VandeHei, "Why McCain Is Getting Hosed."

37. On the news media being biased in their coverage of Joe Biden compared to Sarah Palin, see Goldberg, *Slobbering Love Affair*, especially 32, 45–50; Heilemann and Halperin, *Game Change*, especially 367–368, 397–400; and Kenski, Hardy, and Jamieson, *Obama Victory*, 5, 123–148.

38. Nagourney and Zeleny, "Obama Chooses Biden"; Carrie Budoff Brown and Bill Nichols, "Obama on Biden: 'He Gets It,'" *Politico*, 23 August 2008; "A Look at Biden's Net Worth," *RealClearPolitics*, 23 August 2008.

39. Michael Cooper and Elisabeth Bumiller, "Alaskan Is McCain's Choice," *New York Times*, 30 August 2008, A-1; Cintra Wilson, "Pissed About Palin," *Salon*, 10 September 2008.

40. Jeanne Cummings, "RNC Shells Out $150K for Palin Fashion," *Politico*, 21 October 2008; Goldberg, *Slobbering Love Affair*, 59; "Palin's Wild Shopping Spree," *Daily Beast*, 22 October 2008; Sam Stein, "Palin Clothes Spending Has Dems Salivating, Republicans Disgusted," *Huffington Post*, 22 October 2008.

41. Howard Kurtz, "A Giddy Sense of Boosterism," *Washington Post*, 17 November 2008.

42. Rachel Weiner, "Bill Maher Takes on Obama," *Huffington Post*, 14 June 2009; MSNBC, 15 June 2010.

43. Elizabeth Titus and John F. Harris, "Management Experts Knock Obama," *Politico*, 31 December 2013; Jodi Kantor, "The Competitor in Chief," *New York Times*, 2 September 2012, A-1.

44. "Romney for President," *Houston Chronicle*, 21 October 2012; "Mitt Romney Offers a Fresh Economic Vision," *Des Moines Register*, October 27, 2012; "Editorial: Elect Mitt Romney President of the United States," *Newsday*, 3 November 2012.

45. "Romney for President," *Houston Chronicle*, 21 October 2012; "Mitt Romney Offers a Fresh Economic Vision," *Des Moines Register*, October 27, 2012; "Editorial: Elect Mitt Romney president of the United States," *Newsday*, 3 November 2012.

46. Diana Owen, "Voters to the Sidelines: Old and New Media in the 2012 Election," in *Barack Obama and the New America: The 2012 Election and the Changing Face of Politics*, ed. Larry J. Sabato (New York: Rowman & Littlefield, 2013), 107; John Sides and Lynn Vavreck, *The Gamble: Choice and Chance in the 2012 Presidential Election* (Princeton, NJ: Princeton University Press, 2013), 99, 139. On the news media not treating Obama favorably in 2012, see also "The Master Character Narratives in Campaign 2012," Pew Research Center's Journalism Project Staff, 22 August 2012, http://www.journalism.org/2012/08/23/2012-campaign-character-narratives.

CHAPTER 16: SUPPORTING GAY AND LESBIAN RIGHTS

1. "Perverts Called Government Peril," *New York Times*, 10 April 1950, A25; "Sex Perverts Called Risks to Security," *San Francisco Chronicle*, 16 December,

1950, A9; "A Battle for the Military's Soul," *Chicago Tribune*, 2 January, 1993, A21. On gay men being no more likely to be pedophiles than straight men, see, for example, Kurt Freund, Robin Watson, and Douglas Rienzo, "Heterosexuality, Homosexuality, and Erotic Age Preference," *Journal of Sex Research* 26, no. 1 (February 1989): 107–117; Kurt Freund and Robin Watson, "The Proportion of Heterosexual and Homosexual Pedophiles Among Sex Offenders Against Children: An Exploratory Study," *Journal of Sex & Marital Therapy* 18, no. 1 (1992): 34–43; A. Nicholas Groth and H. Jean Birnbaum, "Adult Sexual Orientation and Attraction to Underage Persons," *Archives of Sexual Behavior* 7, no. 3 (1978); 175–181; Carole Jenny, Tom Roesler, and Kimberly Poyer, "Are Children at Risk for Sexual Abuse by Homosexuals?" *Pediatrics* 94, no. 1 (July 1994): 41–44.

2. On the news media treating gay people favorably in the 2000s, see, for example, Kevin G. Barnhurst, ed., *Media Queered: Visibility and Its Discontents* (New York: Peter Lang, 2007), xi, 152–153, 181–195, 221; Christine Chinlund, "A Bias in Favor of Gay Marriage?," *Boston Globe*, 15 December, 2003, A-19; David Folkenflik, "Is There Bias in Media's Coverage of Gay Marriage Fight?" *All Things Considered*, NPR, 27 June 2013; Larry Gross, *Up from Invisibility: Lesbians, Gay Men, and the Media in America* (New York: Columbia University Press, 2001), especially 110–130; Lisa Henderson, *Love and Money: Queers, Class, and Cultural Production* (New York: New York University Press, 2013), especially 41–43; Deborah T. Meem, Michelle A. Gibson, and Jonathan F. Alexander, *Finding Out: An Introduction to LGBT Studies* (Thousand Oaks, CA: Sage, 2010), 43–44; Leigh Moscowitz, *The Battle over Marriage: Gay Rights Activism Through the Media* (Urbana: University of Illinois Press, 2013), especially 102–105; Brian Stelter, "Study Finds Supportive Tilt to Gay Marriage Coverage," *New York Times*, 17 June 2013, B-4; Rodger Streitmatter, *From "Perverts" to "Fab Five": The Media's Changing Depiction of Gay Men and Lesbians* (New York: Routledge, 2009), especially 1–5, 159–168, 179–188; Suzanna Danuta Walters, *All the Rage: The Story of Gay Visibility in America* (Chicago: University of Chicago Press, 2001), especially 3–29.

3. Charles Lane, "High Court to Hear Texas Gay Rights Case," *Washington Post*, 24 March 2003, A2.

4. Edward Walsh, "Justices Hear Challenge to Texas Sodomy Law," *Washington Post*, 27 March 2003, A-9. Of the thirteen states with sodomy laws, nine banned anal and oral sex between opposite-sex couples as well as same-sex couples, whereas four banned sodomy between same-sex couples only. The nine states banning sodomy without regard to the sex of those involved were Alabama, Florida, Idaho, Louisiana, Mississippi, North Carolina, South Carolina, Utah, and Virginia. The four states banning sodomy between members of the same sex were Kansas, Missouri, Oklahoma, and Texas.

5. Laurence R. Helfer, "Not Leading the World but Following It," *New York Times*, 18 June 2003, 25.

6. "Breakthrough," *Washington Post*, June 27, 2003, A-28; Nancy Gibbs, Perry Bacon Jr., Mark Thompson, Jeffrey Ressner, Andrea Sachs, and Jyoti Thottan, "The Supreme Court Scraps Sodomy Laws, Setting Off a Hot Debate," *Time*, 7 July 2003, 38. On the significance of news coverage of *Lawrence v. Texas*, see Barnhurst, *Media Queered*, 220; Moscowitz, *Battle over Marriage*, 7, 33, 55.

7. *ABC News: Nightline*, 2 July 2003.

8. Pam Belluck, *New York Times*, "Marriage by Gays Gains Big Victory in Massachusetts," 19 November 2003, A1; "Hundreds of Same-Sex Couples Wed in Massachusetts," 18 May 2004, A1.

9. Michael Kinsley, "Abolish Marriage," *Slate*, 2 July 2003, http://www.unz.org/Pub/Slate-2003jul-00010; "Same-Sex Semantics," *Boston Globe*, 25 November 2003, A-14.

10. Charisse Jones and Fred Bayles, "First Weddings Intensify Gay-Marriage Debate," *USA Today*, 18 May 2004, A2; Jonathan Finer, "Gay Couples Line Up for Mass. Marriages," *Washington Post*, 17 May 2004, A2; Rona Marech, "Gay Couples Can Be as Stable as Straights, Evidence Suggests," *San Francisco Chronicle*, 27 February 2004, A19.

11. Laurie Goodstein, "Gay Couples Seek Unions in God's Eyes," *New York Times*, 30 January 2004, A1; Katharine Mieszkowski, "I Now Pronounce You Wife and Wife," *Salon*, 10 June 2008, http://www.salon.com/2008/06/10/marriage_equality/.

12. Eun-Kyung Kim, "Gay Marriage Would Make Their Families Official, Kids Say," *St. Louis Post-Dispatch*, 7 April 2004, A1 (the sociology professor quoted in the story was Tim Biblarz of the University of Southern California); *60 Minutes II*, 10 March 2004 (the segment was titled "Marry Me!" and was reported by Bob Simon).

13. James Brooks, "Gay Man Dies from Attack," *New York Times*, 13 October 1998, A1; Tom Kenworthy, "Gay Wyoming Student Succumbs to Injuries," *Washington Post*, 13 October 1998, A7; *ABC World News*, 12 October 1998; *CBS Evening News*, 12 October 1998; *NBC Nightly News*, 12 October 1998.

14. *NBC Nightly News*, 5 February 1999; Katharine Q. Seelye, "Citing 'Primitive' Hatreds, Clinton Asks Congress to Expand Hate-Crime Law," *New York Times*, 7 April 1999, A18; "Two Tests of Fairness for Congress," *New York Times*, 22 October 2000, WK14.

15. Carl Hulse, "Congressional Maneuvering Dooms Hate Crime Measure," *New York Times*, 7 December 2007, A26; David Stout, "House Votes to Expand Hate-Crime Protection," *New York Times*, 4 May 2007, A19.

16. Carl Hulse, "Senate Votes to Add Sexual Orientation to Hate Crime Protections," *New York Times*, 18 July 2009, A11.

17. "Hate-Crimes Bill Is a Human-Rights Issue," *Minneapolis Star Tribune*, 13 October 2009, A6; "Matthew Shepard Act," *Politico*, 6 May 2009, www.politico.com/2009/05/matthew-shepard-act; "The Consequences of Same-Sex Marriage,"

Huffington Post, 28 May 2009, http://www.huffingtonpost.com/2009/05/28/the -consequences-of-same-sex-marriage.

18. Carl Hulse, *New York Times*, "House, 281–146, Votes to Define Antigay Attacks as Hate Crimes," 9 October 2009, A1; "Senate Votes to Add Sexual Orientation to Hate Crime Protections," 18 July 2009, A11. The House vote was 281 to 146; the Senate vote was 63 to 28.

19. "Obama Signs Hate Crimes Bill into Law," CNN.com, 28 October 2009, http://www.cnn.com/2009/POLITICS/10/28/hate.crimes/index.html?_s=PM :POLITICS.

20. David W. Dunlap, "Congressional Bills Withhold Sanction of Same-Sex Unions," *New York Times*, 9 May 1996, B15. The Defense of Marriage Act was introduced in response to three same-sex couples in Hawaii filing a lawsuit claiming that the state violated the Hawaii constitution by denying them the right to marry.

21. "Sexuality Discrimination," *Boston Globe*, 10 September 1996, A22; "Constitution-Bashing," *New York Times*, 20 July 1996, A18; "Gay Marriage Bill Denies Rights," *Slate*, 15 June 1996, http://www.slate.com/articles/news_and _politics/gay_marriage_bill_denies_rights/1996/06/html.

22. Jerry Gray, "House Passes Bar to U.S. Sanction of Gay Marriage," *New York Times*, 13 July 1996, A1; John F. Yang, "Senate Passes Bill Against Same-Sex Marriage," *Washington Post*, 11 September 1996, A1; Peter Baker, "President Quietly Signs Law Aimed at Gay Marriages," *Washington Post*, 22 September 1996, A21.

23. "Same-Sex Marriage and the Missouri Constitution," *St. Louis Post-Dispatch*, 24 May 2004, B7; "Voters Should Reject Gay Marriage Ban," *Detroit News*, 26 September 2004, A18. "Our Opinion," *Atlanta Journal-Constitution*, 31 October 2004, D10.

24. Jesse McKinley, "With Same-Sex Marriage, a Court Takes on the People's Voice," *New York Times*, 21 November 2008, A18.

25. *All Things Considered*, NPR, 18 October 2007.

26. Ibid. Religious-based businesses, such as Christian bookstores, were excluded in the proposed ENDA legislation.

27. "The Right to Work: Congress Must Protect Gay Men and Lesbians from Workplace Discrimination," *Washington Post*, 29 April 2007, B6; "Smokescreen for Antigay Bias," *Huffington Post*, 26 November 2007; "Act of Tolerance," *Pittsburgh Post-Gazette*, 12 November 2007, B6.

28. David Herszenhorn, "Party's Liberal Base Proves Trying to Democrats Back in Power," *New York Times*, 12 October 2007, A23.

29. Ibid.

30. David Herszenhorn, "House Backs Broad Protections for Gay Workers," *New York Times*, 8 November 2007, A1; Chris Johnson, "Senate Panel Hears ENDA Testimony, *Washington Blade*, 13 November 2009, 12. The vote in the House was 235 to 184.

31. Jesse McKinley and Kirk Johnson, "Mormons Tipped Scale in Ban on Gay Marriages," *New York Times*, 15 November 2008, A1.

32. "Reneging on a Right," *Los Angeles Times*, 8 August 2008; "Gay Marriage Right Should Not Be Repealed," *San Diego Union-Tribune*, 18 September 2008; "California Prop. 8," *Orange County Register*, 1 October 2008.

33. McKinley and Johnson, "Mormons Tipped," A1.

34. *CNN: State of the Union with John King*, 5 July 2009.

35. "Editorial: Walking Point for an Open Military," *Philadelphia Inquirer*, 13 July 2009, A10; "After 16 Years, 'Don't Ask, Don't Tell' Deserves to Die," *USA Today*, 8 July 2009, A8; "The Victims of Don't Ask, Don't Tell," *Daily Beast*, 3 February 2010, http://www.thedailybeast.com/articles/2010/02/03/the-victims-of-dont-ask-dont-tell.html.

36. Sheryl Gay Stolberg, "Obama to Party: 'Don't Run for the Hills,'" *New York Times*, 28 January 2010, A1.

37. *NBC Nightly News*, 30 November 2010; *ABC World News*, 30 November 2010.

38. Ibid.; Ibid.

39. Steve Kornacki, "Who (and What) Could Still Trip Up DADT Repeal," *Salon*, 16 December 2010; "A GOP Roadblock?" *Politico*, 22 November 2010, www.politico.com/2010/11/a-GOP-roadblock.

40. Danny Hernandez, "Don't Ask, Don't Tell: Obama Signs Repeal of Military's Long-Standing Policy," *Washington Post*, 23 December 2010, A1.

41. After same-sex marriage began in Massachusetts in 2004, the next states to follow were California and Connecticut in 2008, Iowa and Vermont in 2009, New Hampshire (as well as the District of Columbia) in 2010, New York in 2011, and Washington and Maine in 2012. Maryland approved same-sex marriage in 2012, and marriages began on January 1, 2013.

42. Jim Dwyer, "She Waited 40 Years to Marry, Then When Her Wife Died, the Tax Bill Came," *New York Times*, 8 June 2012, A21.

43. Dwyer, "She Waited 40 Years," A21.

44. "Proposition 8 Battle Heading to Federal Arena," *Los Angeles Daily News*, 28 May 2009, A1. The gay male couple was Paul Katami and Jeff Zarrillo, and the lesbian couple was Kris Perry and Sandy Stier.

45. Tom Keane, "Act on Marriage," *Boston Globe*, 16 December 2012, K10; "A Stand for Equality," *Washington Post*, 24 February 2011, A18; Suze Orman, "Gay Americans Pay More Taxes for Fewer Rights," *CNN.com*, 25 February 2013, http://www.cnn.com/2013/02/25/opinion/orman-marriage-equality/index.html.

46. "Editorial: Waiting til 2012 on Gay Marriage? Wise Move," *San Jose Mercury News*, 13 August 2009, A10; "In Defense of Marriage," *New York Times*, 14 August 2010, A18; "SCOTUS Takes It Slow on Gay Marriage," *Daily Beast*, 26 March 2013, www.thedailybeast.com/articles/2013/03/26/SCOTUS-takes-it-slow-on-gay-marriage.html.

47. *ABC World News*, 27 March 2013.

48. Adam Liptak and Peter Baker, "Justices Cast Doubt on U.S. Law Defining Marriage," *New York Times*, 28 March 2013, A1.

49. "Victory for Equal Rights," *New York Times*, 27 June 2013, A30; "Equality Triumphs," *Washington Post*, 27 June 2013, A20; William Saletan, "Anti-Gay Is Yesterday," *Slate*, 26 June 2013, http://www.slate.com/articles/news_and_politics /frame_game/2013/06/gay_marriage_polls_and_public_opinion_the_supreme _court_s_rulings_upheld.html.

50. Sam Stein and Amanda Terkel, "60 Percent of Americans Soon Will Live in States with Marriage Equality," *Huffington Post*, 6 October 2014, http:// www.huffingtonpost.com/2014/10/06/gay-marriage-states_n_5939440.html. On *Huffington Post* being the country's most popular political online publication, see "Top 15 Most Popular Political Websites," http://www.ebizmba.com /articles/political-websites.

51. Nate Silver and Allison McCann, "Same-Sex Marriage Is Now Legal for a Majority of the U.S.," *FiveThirtyEight*, 6 October 2014, http://fivethirtyeight.com /datalab/same-sex-marriage-is-now-legal-for-a-majority-of-the-u-s/; Jack Healy, Michael D. Shear, and Erik Eckholm, "Scenes of Exultation in Five States as Gay Couples Rush to Marry," *RealClearPolitics*, 6 October 2014, http://www.nytimes .com/2014/10/07/us/same-sex-marriage-ruling.html.

52. "Editorial: Time to Vote on the Future of Marriage," *Chicago Tribune*, 23 October 2013; "Inquirer Editorial: Say Yes to Equality," *Philadelphia Inquirer*, 22 May 2014.

CHAPTER 17: FOCUSING ON HOW

1. On the challenges facing journalism, see, for example, Paul Farhi, "Don't Blame the Journalism: The Economic and Technological Forces Behind the Collapse of Newspapers," *American Journalism Review*, October/November 2008, 14–15.

2. On some of the changes taking place in journalism, see, for example, Leonard Downie Jr. and Michael Schudson, "The Reconstruction of American Journalism," *American Journalism Review*, November/December 2009, 28–51.

BIBLIOGRAPHY

This brief listing contains some of the principal writings that may be of interest to readers of this book, arranged by chapter.

CHAPTER 1: SOWING THE SEEDS OF REVOLUTION

Bailyn, Bernard. *The Ideological Origins of the American Revolution*. Cambridge, MA: Harvard University Press, 1967.

Conway, Moncure D. *The Writings of Thomas Paine*. New York: AMS, 1967.

Davidson, Philip. *Propaganda and the American Revolution*. Chapel Hill: University of North Carolina Press, 1941.

Foner, Eric. *Tom Paine and Revolutionary America*. New York: Oxford University Press, 1976.

Miller, John C. *Sam Adams: Pioneer in Propaganda*. Stanford, CA: Stanford University Press, 1936.

CHAPTER 2: TURNING AMERICA AGAINST THE SINS OF SLAVERY

Dillon, Merton L., *Elijah P. Lovejoy, Abolitionist Editor*. Urbana: University of Illinois Press, 1961.

Garrison, W. P., and F. J. Garrison. *William Lloyd Garrison: The Story of His Life as Told by His Children*, 4 vols. New York, 1885–1889.

Merrill, Walter M. *Against Wind and Tide: A Biography of Wm. Lloyd Garrison*. Cambridge, MA: Harvard University Press, 1963.

Tripp, Bernell E. *Origins of the Black Press: New York, 1827–1847*. Northport, AL: Vision, 1992.

CHAPTER 3: SLOWING THE MOMENTUM FOR WOMEN'S RIGHTS

Harper, Ida Husted. *The Life and Work of Susan B. Anthony*. Indianapolis, IN: Hollenbeck, 1898.

List, Karen K. "The Post-Revolutionary Woman Idealized: Philadelphia Media's 'Republican Mother.'" *Journalism Quarterly* 66 (Spring 1989): 65–75.

Solomon, Martha M., ed. *A Voice of Their Own: The Woman Suffrage Press, 1840–1910*. Tuscaloosa: University of Alabama Press, 1991.

Stanton, Elizabeth Cady, Susan B. Anthony, and Matilda Joslyn Gage, eds. *History of Woman Suffrage*. New York: Fowler & Wells, 1881.

CHAPTER 4: ATTACKING MUNICIPAL CORRUPTION

Keller, Morton. *The Art and Politics of Thomas Nast*. New York: Oxford University Press, 1968.

Paine, Albert B. *Thomas Nast: His Period and His Pictures*. Gloucester, MA: Peter Smith, 1967.

CHAPTER 5: PUSHING AMERICA
TOWARD AN INTERNATIONAL WAR

Milton, Joyce. *The Yellow Kids: Foreign Correspondents in the Heyday of Yellow Journalism*. New York: Harper & Row, 1989.

Swanberg, W. A. *Citizen Hearst: A Biography of William Randolph Hearst*. New York: Charles Scribner's Sons, 1961.

Wisan, Joseph E. *The Cuban Crisis as Reflected in the New York Press (1895–1898)*. New York: Columbia University Press, 1934.

CHAPTER 6: ACHIEVING REFORM BY MUCKRAKING

Filler, Louis. *Crusaders for American Liberalism*. Yellow Springs, OH: Antioch, 1939.

McGlashan, Zena Beth. "Club 'Ladies' and Working 'Girls': Rheta Childe Dorr and the *New York Evening Post*." *Journalism History* 8 (1981): 7–13.

Weinberg, Arthur, and Lila Weinberg. *The Muckrakers*. New York: Simon and Schuster, 1961.

CHAPTER 7: DEFYING THE KU KLUX KLAN

Bent, Silas. *Newspaper Crusaders: A Neglected Story*. Freeport, NY: Books for Libraries, 1939.

Chalmers, David M. *Hooded Americanism: The History of the Ku Klux Klan*. Durham, NC: Duke University Press, 1987.

Hohenberg, John, ed. *The Pulitzer Prize Story*. New York: Columbia University Press, 1959.

Jackson, Kenneth T. *The Ku Klux Klan in the City: 1915–1930*. New York: Oxford University Press, 1967.

CHAPTER 8: SPREADING ANTI-SEMITISM VIA THE RADIO

Brinkley, Alan. *Voices of Protest: Huey Long, Father Coughlin, and the Great Depression*. New York: Knopf, 1982.

Marcus, Sheldon. *Father Coughlin: The Tumultuous Life of the Priest of the Little Flower*. Boston: Little, Brown, 1973.

Strong, Donald S. *Organized Anti-Semitism in America: The Rise of Group Prejudice During the Decade 1930–40*. Washington, DC: American Council on Public Affairs, 1941.

CHAPTER 9: USING "ROSIE THE RIVETER" TO PROPEL WOMEN INTO THE WORKFORCE

Chafe, William H. *The American Woman: Her Changing Social, Economic, and Political Roles, 1920–1970*. New York: Oxford University Press, 1972.

Honey, Maureen. *Creating Rosie the Riveter: Class, Gender, and Propaganda During World War II*. Amherst: University of Massachusetts Press, 1984.

Rupp, Leila J. *Mobilizing Women for War: German and American Propaganda, 1939–1945*. Princeton, NJ: Princeton University Press, 1978.

Weatherford, Doris. *American Women and World War II*. New York: Facts on File, 1990.

CHAPTER 10: STANDING TALL AGAINST JOSEPH MCCARTHY

Barnouw, Erik. *The Image Empire: A History of Broadcasting in the United States from 1953*. New York: Oxford University Press, 1970.

Bayley, Edwin R. *Joe McCarthy and the Press*. New York: Pantheon, 1981.

Leab, Daniel J. "'See It Now': A Legend Reassessed." In *American History/American Television: Interpreting the Video Past*, edited by John E. O'Connor, 1–32. New York: Frederick Ungar, 1983.

Rosteck, Thomas. *See It Now Confronts McCarthyism*. Tuscaloosa: University of Alabama Press, 1994.

Straight, Michael. *Trial by Television*. Boston: Beacon, 1954.

CHAPTER 11: PUSHING CIVIL RIGHTS
ONTO THE NATIONAL AGENDA

Fisher, Paul L., and Ralph L. Lowenstein, eds. *Race and the News Media*. New York: Praeger, 1967.

MacNeil, Robert. *The People Machine: The Influence of Television on American Politics*. New York: Harper & Row, 1968.

Muse, Benjamin. *The American Negro Revolution*. Bloomington: Indiana University Press, 1968.

Watson, Mary Ann. *The Expanding Vista: American Television in the Kennedy Years*. New York: Oxford University Press, 1990.

Wood, William A. *Electronic Journalism*. New York: Columbia University Press, 1967.

CHAPTER 12: BRINGING THE VIETNAM WAR
INTO THE AMERICAN LIVING ROOM

Braestrup, Peter. *Big Story: How the American Press and Television Reported and Interpreted the Crisis of Tet 1968 in Vietnam and Washington*. Boulder, CO: Westview, 1977.

Hallin, Daniel C. *The "Uncensored War": The Media and Vietnam*. New York: Oxford University Press, 1986.

Oberdorfer, Don. *Tet!* Garden City, NY: Doubleday, 1971.

CHAPTER 13: EXPOSING CRIMINAL ACTIVITY
IN RICHARD NIXON'S WHITE HOUSE

Genovese, Michael A. *The Watergate Crisis*. Westport, CT: Greenwood, 1999.

Marshall, Jon. *Watergate's Legacy and the Press: The Investigative Impulse*. Evanston, IL: Northwestern University Press, 2011.

McCartney, James. "The Washington 'Post' and Watergate: How Two Davids Slew Goliath." *Columbia Journalism Review* (July/August 1973): 8–22.

Olson, Keith W. *Watergate: The Presidential Scandal That Shook America*. Lawrence: University Press of Kansas, 2003.

CHAPTER 14: FAILING THE AMERICAN
PUBLIC WITH 9/11 COVERAGE

Rich, Frank. *The Greatest Story Ever Sold: The Decline and Fall of Truth*. New York: Penguin, 2006.

Tugend, Alina. "Explaining the Rage." *American Journalism Review* (December 2001): 24–27.

Zakaria, Fareed. "The Politics of Rage: Why Do They Hate Us?" *Newsweek*, 15 October 2001.

CHAPTER 15: ELECTING AN AFRICAN-AMERICAN PRESIDENT

Goldberg, Bernard. *A Slobbering Love Affair: The True (and Pathetic) Story of the Torrid Romance Between Barack Obama and the Mainstream Media.* Washington, DC: Regnery, 2009.

Heileman, John, and Mark Halperin. *Game Change: Obama and the Clintons, McCain and Palin, and the Race of a Lifetime.* New York: HarperCollins, 2010.

Kenski, Kate, Bruce W. Hardy, and Kathleen Hall Jamieson. *The Obama Victory: How Media, Money, and Message Shaped the 2008 Election.* New York: Oxford University Press, 2010.

Schoen, Douglas E. *The Political Fix: Changing the Game of American Democracy, from the Grass Roots to the White House.* New York: Henry Holt, 2010.

CHAPTER 16: SUPPORTING GAY AND LESBIAN RIGHTS

Barnhurst, Kevin G., ed. *Media Queered: Visibility and Its Discontents.* New York: Peter Lang, 2007.

Henderson, Lisa. *Love and Money: Queers, Class, and Cultural Production.* New York: New York University Press, 2013.

Moscowitz, Leigh. *The Battle Over Marriage: Gay Rights Activism Through the Media.* Urbana: University of Illinois Press, 2013.

Streitmatter, Rodger. *From "Perverts" to "Fab Five": The Media's Changing Depiction of Gay Men and Lesbians.* New York: Routledge, 2009.

INDEX